R   I   V   E   R

G   R   E   A   T

R   I   V   E   R   S

G   R   E   A   T

R   I   V   E   R   S

G   R   E   A   T

R   I   V   E   R   S

G   R   E   A   T

GREAT

RIVERS

GREAT

RIVERS

GREAT

RIVERS

GREAT

RIVERS

GREAT RIVERS OF THE WORLD

GREAT RIVERS

NATIONAL GEOG

OF THE WORLD

GREAT RIVERS
of the World

Published by
The National Geographic
Society

Gilbert M. Grosvenor
President

Melvin M. Payne
Chairman of the Board

Owen R. Anderson
Executive Vice President

Robert L. Breeden
*Vice President,
Publications and
Educational Media*

Prepared by
National Geographic
Book Service

Charles O. Hyman
Director

Ross S. Bennett
Associate Director

Staff for this book

Margaret Sedeen
Editor

David M. Seager
Art Director

Linda B. Meyerriecks
Illustrations Editor

Suzanne P. Kane
Chief Researcher

William P. Beaman
Ross S. Bennett
Mary B. Dickinson
Richard Kovar
Edward Lanouette
Carol Bittig Lutyk
Anne H. Meadows
Elizabeth L. Newhouse
Robert M. Poole
David F. Robinson
Shirley L. Scott
Robert D. Selim
Jonathan B. Tourtellot
Editor-Writers

LaVerle Berry
Catherine Herbert Howell
Judy A. Reardon
Lise Swinson Sajewski
Susan Eckert Sidman
Jean Kaplan Teichroew
Marilyn Murphy Terrell
Penelope A. Timbers
Jayne Wise
Editorial Researchers

Lise Swinson Sajewski
Style

Greta Arnold
Illustrations Research

Diana E. McFadden
Illustrations Assistant

Charlotte Golin
Design Assistant

Karen F. Edwards
Traffic Manager

John F. C. Frith
Production Manager

Richard S. Wain
Assistant Production Manager

Andrea Crosman
Production Assistant

Georgina L. McCormack
Teresita Cóquia Sison
Editorial Assistants

Natalia Bourso-Leland
Todd Carrel
Zbigniew Jan Lutyk
Field Interpreters

John T. Dunn
Ronald E. Williamson
Engraving and Printing

Continent Maps by
William E. Carmel, Jr.
Charles F. Case
Mary C. Latham
Tibor G. Toth
John G. Weber
Cartographic Division

Chapter Maps by
John D. Garst, Jr.
Virginia L. Baza
Judith Bell
Patricia K. Cantlay
Mark Carlson
Gary M. Johnson
Robert W. Northrop
Hildegard Schantz
Publications Art

*Cover logo and
chapter titles by*
Gerard Huerta

*Page borders
computer generated by*
John R. Reap

George I. Burneston, III
Jeffrey A. Brown
Index

Janet M. Drake
Deborah L. Slorach
Stephen Young
Geography Interns

Patricia Bangs
Paul Mathless
Editorial Contributions

Contributions by
Caroline Hottenstein
Stuart J. McCutchan
Deborah L. Robertson

First edition
230,000 copies

339 illustrations, 22 maps

Copyright © 1984
National Geographic Society,
Washington, D. C.
All rights reserved.
Reproduction of the whole
or any part of the contents
without written permission
is prohibited.

Library of Congress
CIP data page 448

"RIVER, RUN DOWN TO THE SEA" *John M. Kauffmann* 6

THE RIVERS OF AFRICA 22
& other continental essays
Ronald Reed Boyce & Book Service Editors

THE NILE *Geoffrey Moorhouse & Robert Caputo* 33
THE ZAIRE *Georg Gerster* 69

THE RIVERS OF EUROPE 84

THE DANUBE *Ross S. Bennett & Adam Woolfitt* 95
THE VOLGA *Margaret Sedeen & Cary Wolinsky* 131
THE THAMES *Cameron Thomas* 153
THE RHÔNE *Mary B. Dickinson & Farrell Grehan* 167

THE RIVERS OF ASIA 182

THE GANGES *George F. Mobley* 195
SIBERIA *Ernest B. Furgurson* 231
THE YANGTZE *Robert M. Poole & Thomas Nebbia* 243

THE RIVERS OF AUSTRALIA 276

THE RIVERS OF SOUTH AMERICA 288

THE AMAZON *Jonathan B. Tourtellot & David Louis Olson* 299
THE PARANÁ-LA PLATA *Carol Bittig Lutyk & David Louis Olson* 333

THE RIVERS OF NORTH AMERICA 350

THE MISSISSIPPI-MISSOURI *Amanda Parsons & Nathan Benn* 361
THE YUKON *Bill Thomas & George F. Mobley* 401
THE ST. LAWRENCE *William Howarth & Nathan Benn* 415
THE RIO GRANDE *Edward Abbey* 429

Earth's Longest Rivers 444
Acknowledgments 444
Authors & Photographers 445
Index 446

"RIVER, RUN DOWN TO THE SEA"

S U S Q U E H A N N A   T O   T H E   B A Y

By John M. Kauffmann

"When I had asked the name of a river . . . and heard that it was called the Susquehanna, the beauty of the name seemed to be part and parcel of the beauty of the land. . . . That was the name, as no other could be, for that shining river and desirable valley."

So wrote Robert Louis Stevenson, the Scottish novelist, in 1879 as a railroad train bore him along the longest river of the largest river system in the eastern United States. By whatever name, rivers have been part and parcel of human destiny since Eden. Desirable valleys have cradled civilization, and shining rivers have ever beckoned men and women to adventurous new life. The significance of many a nation has been gauged by its rivers. Many an individual as well has been measured in fluvial terms: the pure, strong flow of his goodness; the purposefulness of her life's channel.

Few rivers have welcomed humanity with wider arms than the Susquehanna. Its lower half, drowned by a rising sea, forms the largest estuary in North America and one of the most productive areas on earth. We, like the Algonquin Indians, call this bay Chesapeake—"great shellfish bay." The native culture rested lightly there. Colonists who braved the Atlantic crossing from a jaded old world to a new one were amazed and thrilled at the freshness, the fragrance, the fecundity of an environment almost untouched by human exploitation. According to Captain John Smith, who charted the bay in 1608, "Heaven and earth never agreed better to frame a place for man's habitation."

Missionary Andrew White sailed up another of the bay's rivers, the Potomac, in 1634. "This is the sweetest and greatest river I have seen," he wrote, "so that the Thames is but a little finger to it. . . . It abounds with delicate springs which are our best drinke. Birds, diversely feathered here are infinite. . . . The place abounds not alone with profit, but also with pleasure."

The Potomac is but one of the 150 or so rivers and streams that spill into the Chesapeake Bay. The major rivers include the James, York, Rappahannock,

Potomac, Patuxent, and Patapsco to the west, the Chester, Choptank, and Pocomoke to the east. All were once direct tributaries to the sovereign Susquehanna until, 10,000 years ago, the last great ice age ended and glacier melt raised the level of the sea, gradually drowning the Susquehanna's lower 200 miles. The bay and its rivers form a many-fingered hand stretching 400 miles long and 300 miles wide, spanning 64,000 square miles and including all of mid-eastern America's varied environments.

The Susquehanna begins at New York's Otsego Lake, a basin scooped and dammed by glaciers. There trout swim in the cold waters; balsam and spruce give the surrounding forests a northern cast. But subtropical swamps also feed the system. Cypress knees thrust up in Maryland's Nassowango Creek and in Virginia's Dragon Run. Other headwaters bubble from springs or seep from grottoes in the hardwood ridges of Appalachia.

The watershed is a historical sampler of the region as well. Like the pelagic bluefish that swim in to feast in Chesapeake Bay, the early colonists who sailed into the "faire bay" found bounty in that great palm of the Susquehanna's hand. With fortunes made from tobacco, they built stately homes beside the rivers. Ports and mills thrived along the fall line, where the rivers make their cascading descent to the coastal plain. One man who lived beside the Potomac and had explored its headwaters saw it as politically central to a new nation: halfway between New England and the South, with valleys reaching west to link seaboard with frontier. There, where the Potomac's flow merges with the tides of Chesapeake Bay, George Washington chose the site for the nation's capital.

Like shad seeking to spawn in Chesapeake inlets, many of our ancestors schooled up the rivers to their own new life. They threaded the great gaps through the ridges of the Appalachians. They settled in broad timber-filled valleys that would become breadbaskets for America. In feats of engineering they cut canals along rivers too shallow and unpredictable for more than flatboat travel. Railroads followed the canal routes. Highways, too, were faithful to the valleys until technology cut through the mountains. Discovery of coal fueled America's young industries, and rivers seemed less important.

The Susquehanna River has run red with Indian massacres. The York River watched British colors dip in surrender. The Patapsco saw a star-spangled banner still waving. "All quiet along the Potomac tonight," says a song of the Civil War. "No sound save the rush of the river. . . ."

The tragic gore of the nation's conflicts has washed away, but the water of the rivers remains, as always, the lifeblood of the land. Evaporated from an oceanic heart, blown inland on arteries of wind, condensed again as rain, the water trickles down the surface of the earth or sinks into subterranean capillaries to seep forth as the first rills of a river.

These rills splash down in an almost predictable sequence of riffles and pools. Indeed, geologists find a uniform pattern in the drainages of rivers—rules of the flow. Drainage patterns vary with rock types and structures, but streams of similar widths tend to have similar lengths, proportionate to the area drained. As the water descends from high land, taking the most efficient, least resistant course, it soon begins to swing in a rhythmic sinuosity of energy dispersion. In bends proportionate to the stream's size, it winds like a twitched rope, working its way down the valley. As the land begins to flatten, the river's loops tighten into meanders, ranging back and forth across the valley—and helping to broaden it. Rivers in spate sometimes bypass these tight bends, cutting off old channels and isolating them as oxbow lakes. But a river's nature is to wind, and some have wound deeply into the landscape.

Water is a mighty carver of the land. Ranges are pierced and continents brought low. Waterborne gravel, sand, and silt are the tools with which rivers rout gorges such as the Susquehanna's West Branch and the "Grand Canyon" of tributary Pine Creek. Thus the worn land wears the land away.

As a watercourse seeks to establish a smooth, slightly concave profile from source to mouth, its rate of flow powers the cutting, with much of it done during floods. This rate often remains surprisingly constant, even across the lower valleys. As slopes become gentler, increased volume from tributary streams maintains the flow rate. But downward cutting slows as the river nears its base level at a lake or the sea. When heavy rains or snowmelt swell the flow, it spills over the valley. This floodplain is nature's holding basin for excess water. The payment that a river often makes for this temporary accommodation is a rich layer of fertile silt, deposited from the slackened flow.

T he final deposits are made in the sea. Rivers that meet the sea directly, such as the Nile and the Mississippi, are almost halted by the ocean. Remaining sediments drop, piling up into a muddy landmass—a delta. These deltas usually form in the center of the river's mouth, since the faster central flow carries the largest load of sediments. As a delta grows, it splits the river into two branches. This same river-splitting process occurs again within each branch, and again, until the river becomes a tangle of many streams reaching to the sea.

But other rivers, like the Susquehanna, meet the sea in an estuary, a sheltered bay where the river's silt-laden fresh water mixes with the salt tides. Each year the Chesapeake's rivers bring more than three million tons of sediment down to the bay. Tides slosh this sediment back and forth for a time, but eventually it settles into marshland or vast shallow flats. In 15,000 years or so, the bay will be filled and the geologic cycle will be complete.

But the bay's tributaries will run on, no doubt, in the changed conditions of a new chapter of earth history. After all, the Susquehanna has been flowing in

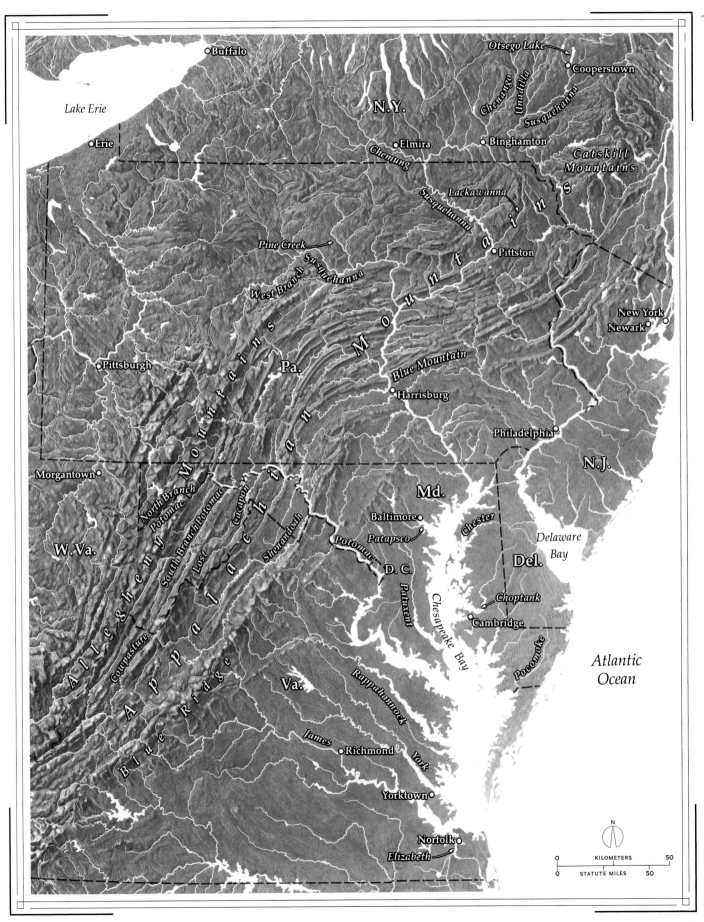

one form or another for some 250 million years. In a sense, it has flowed from the sea as well as toward it; its headwaters region was once a seabed. As the Susquehanna formed, it slowly cut through the rising mountains. This geologic history can be read in the high walls of the gorge: layers of sediment and fossil sea life. Black seams of coal attest to the lush vegetation of a bygone era.

As the Susquehanna cut its way across the Appalachians, so did the Potomac and the James. The water gaps the rivers made are major scenic features. Indeed, when Thomas Jefferson first saw the Potomac's gorge at Harper's Ferry, West Virginia, he declared the view worth a voyage across the Atlantic.

Smaller streams once crossed the Appalachians, but their headwaters were gradually stolen by larger, stronger rivers. Their ancient gorges are now only wind gaps, nicks in the Appalachian ridge lines, convenient crossings for the early pioneers—and for modern road builders.

The Chesapeake's rivers once flowed far more torrentially than they do today. The Susquehanna drained the continental ice sheet of the last glacial age. The Potomac and James, though untouched by glaciers, were also abrim in that wet time. Today their valleys seem oversize for a comparatively meager flow, though periodic floods can rage them full again.

Down from the Allegheny Plateau, across the foothills to the coastal plain, the Chesapeake's rivers drain much of what is now New York, Pennsylvania, West Virginia, Virginia, Maryland, and a bit of Delaware, sculpting the varied landscapes that are the special beauty of the American East. In some parts of the world, terrain, climate, and culture have established broad landscape themes. Scenes change gradually. The eastern United States, however, is wild and awesome at one turn in a river or, at another turn, smiling with pastoral charm. Around each bend a different scene presents itself. From sylvan seclusion, the rivers swing past proper towns, stately cities, pulsing industry, yet return again and again to forest, field, and marsh.

At Otsego Lake the forested hills still whisper Leatherstocking tales of Indians and scouts. But farmsteads and white silos now dot sunny fields along the tributary Chenango and Unadilla. Above Elmira, New York, shopping centers and an airport occupy what was once the bottom of a lake, formed when a glacier dammed the original course of the Chemung River.

The Susquehanna loops into Pennsylvania, back into New York, then again back into Pennsylvania, writhing under beetling crags and around bends lush with crops. On one serene stretch, French aristocrats prepared a refuge for Marie Antoinette, their fugitive queen. The guillotine detained her.

The Susquehanna slips on toward its confluence with the Lackawanna, then into Pittston and the world of coal and industry. From coal country also comes the West Branch, threading its gorge for some 50 miles. The combined rivers breach the main Appalachian ridges above Harrisburg and sweep past the

Pennsylvania state capitol with a majesty that cannot be gainsaid by the bordering expressways and railways.

In similar stateliness the Potomac and James descend upon their respective capital cities and rumble into final falls. The Susquehanna's energetic exit, however, has been stilled—dammed and piped for hydroelectric power. The once bountiful fish runs have been blocked. But in their long constancy, rivers know change. Dams are for the decades; rivers for the ages.

Rivers can be central presences in their valleys. They can also be hidden, secretive. Cross a field, climb a hill, and we make a shining discovery. The Susquehanna has inlaid itself so deeply among the mountains of Pennsylvania that it seems to dodge the river seeker. So does the James, playing hide-and-seek as it flows behind field and woodland in an almost imperceptible valley.

But when we travel a river, it becomes our whole world. The swallows diving in the air, the turtle on the log, the huge bankside sycamore, most of all the pooled or purling water itself, the tug of current . . . we savor all the components of that river world. Perhaps that is why we identify our own lives with the life of a river. "River, take me along," sings folksinger Bill Staines as he ripples the guitar notes of his moving "River" song. "Let's you and me, River, run down to the sea."

There is a mysterious element to the ever changing changelessness of flowing water. Rivers prompt us to ask *wherefrom, whereto, how deep, what is around the bend?* Much of the mystery is geological. Lost River, a Potomac tributary, disappears underground to emerge as the beautiful Cacapon. There is biological mystery as well. It heightens in spring when warblers swarm through the tall valley poplars and the wetlands pulse with an unseen amphibian chorus. Insects appear as if by magic on the water's surface. In summer, mallows nod in the sun. There are strange slitherings through the marshlands. A heron stands motionless in bankside shadow. Fireflies wink along the shore as darkness falls. Autumn comes, and the river is afloat with leaves. Waterfowl squadrons follow it south; ducks burst up from river restings. The coves congeal, sealing the beavers snug in winter houses, safe from the prowling predators of the river's wintertime.

What a reasonable and graceful design for living the river accords us. Timberlands in upper valleys help regulate the runoff of the rain. Valley flanks and uplands offer logical sites for habitation and industry. The rich bottomlands bespeak agriculture and provide safety space for the periodic floods. So do the wetlands, which hold and process excess nutrients that otherwise would overload a river's biotic regime. The miles of river margin, where land is brushed by water, support a wealth of wildlife and provide two living lanes of green natural beauty through the world of human enterprise. *(Continued on page 20)*

W herefrom? Whereto? *Many a great river begins in quietness and obscurity, welling up from the earth, trickling from hidden springs. The South Branch of the Potomac makes its first appearance as a soggy path across remote highland pastures of Virginia (opposite). Rain, snowmelt, and lesser rivulets swell the flow as the Potomac begins its 382-mile journey to Chesapeake Bay and the Atlantic. Plunging downhill, the sparkling young river carves a channel for itself (above) and a home for wetland creatures like the newt (right).*

Rivers also begin as runnels of glacier melt or as lake outlets. The Susquehanna flows from Otsego Lake, a glacier-carved basin in the Appalachian Mountains of New York State.

14

The rushing West Branch of the Susquehanna (left) scours a narrow valley through Pennsylvania mountains. This panorama from Hyner View offers adventure and a bird's-eye look at the river 1,340 feet below. Tributary Pine Creek (above) races through its 1,100-foot-deep "Grand Canyon." Around the world, erosion by rivers averages 12 inches in nine thousand years. Were it not for earth's land-raising processes, all existing relief on our globe would be washed away in 25 million years.

B ridges cross the broad and shallow Susquehanna River at Harrisburg, Pennsylvania (above), where trader John Harris's flatboats once ferried pioneers to the Cumberland Valley. Throughout history, the world's great cities have risen beside its great rivers, vital sources for food, water, power, and transport. Rivers sustain and enhance human life, and we are learning to treat them with respect. But sewage and industrial waste still poison our rivers. Fertilizer runoff changes the water's chemical composition. Fish and other aquatic life struggle to survive. The pollution of the Potomac River's Tidal Basin in Washington, D. C. (left), is still typical of a river's lower reaches, far distant and far different from the clear, sparkling cascades (right) of its headwaters.

*W*inding down, the Potomac River broadens as it nears the end of its long journey *(above).* Waters spread over the coastal lowlands, depositing rich sediment brought hundreds of miles by the river's flow. Marshes and mud flats formed by Chesapeake Bay's tributary rivers total nearly half a million acres of prime habitat for waterfowl. A third of the continent's swans spend the winter here, as do hundreds of thousands of Canada geese and at least 24 species of ducks. Some of this habitat, such as Blackwater National Wildlife Refuge *(right)* on Maryland's Eastern Shore, is protected and managed by federal, state, or private agencies as havens for wildlife and for the weary human spirit.

The river itself is, of course, the central element, a nourishing, beautifying aquaskein of life. Though rivers seem ever changing, flowing water is one of earth's most enduring habitats. From springhead to tidewater, rivers abound with an astonishing variety of creatures, unexcelled in vigor and adaptability. Be they microscopic diatoms, aquatic insects, or the fish we try to catch, they are each exquisitely attuned to their fluvial environment. A biologist can lift a rock from a riffle and know exactly who will be living where upon it.

ll the life channels that are the Chesapeake's rivers feed into what is, both in shape and in productivity, a great cornucopia.

The Chesapeake Bay seems to present a timeless scene. Yet change is its only constant. Estuaries like the Chesapeake are perhaps the most dynamic environments on earth, frontiers between the push of fresh water and the shove of salt. The salt tide slides under the freshwater discharge; they mix in zones ranging up-bay or down with the relative strengths of river flow and tidal surge. The temperature, chemistry, turbidity, and current of an estuary may alter as much in one hour as oceans change in months, years, or even centuries.

So stressful is the Chesapeake that relatively few species have been able to adapt there in the short time since ice caps melted and seas flooded in. But for the creatures that can thrive there, the bay is a bonanza. An average of 73,000 cubic feet of nutrient-rich water flows down in every second from the Chesapeake's huge watershed, fertilizing subaquatic gardens that feed and shelter a wide range of life. Sediments from the rivers have created nearly half a million acres of marshland, rich as the finest of grainfields. These marshes help store and regulate the fertility of Chesapeake water, offering it, recycled through decay, in a movable feast as tides breathe in, breathe out. The mixing currents cradle the spawn and nurse the young of many a creature directly important to humans as well as to the chain of life itself. The Chesapeake produces the world's largest harvest of blue crabs, half the United States' catch of softshell clams, more than a third of the oysters.

The bay provides not only a nursery but also a rich broth of anchovies, menhaden, and silversides for bluefish and other pelagic fishes that crowd in to feast. The Chesapeake ranks third among U. S. fishing waters (the others being oceanic), quite a feat for a mere 4,300 square miles of water averaging only 30 feet deep. The bay is also the principal focal point for wildfowl in the East.

"Incredible" is the adjective most often used to describe what has been called the queen of America's bays, an immense protein factory, a national treasure. But the bay is in trouble, dying before its time.

We are catching one-sixth the number of oysters and clams we harvested a century ago. Catches of striped bass are down almost as far in a bay where up to 90 percent of East Coast stripers are born. In 1983 only a few thousand shad were counted in the entire upper bay; a century ago that was just one good haul of the nets. Waterfowl find less to eat now, for the bay's bottom, once covered with delectable aquatic grasses, has become bald in many areas.

The cause of the trouble? People, of course. We ask the rivers to wash away our sins of waste and carelessness, but we have become too numerous and our cumulative sins too great for the rivers to bear. So much sewage, so much fertilizer runoff washes into the rivers that algae in the bay overbloom, blocking out sunlight and killing the grasses. Decay absorbs the dissolved oxygen on which aquatic life depends. The bay does not flush itself, as one might suppose. The sediments and pollutants that flow into the bay remain there.

Much of the trouble comes from afar, the Susquehanna watershed providing more than half. Wetlands that could detain excess nutrients are now built up with homes and industries. Fertilizers and animal wastes drain from countless Susquehanna farms. Urban woes beset the bay area itself, where the population continues to grow, and more and more of the drainage area becomes classified as urban and residential, to replace forests and pastures.

The entire watershed bleeds with poisons: acids from abandoned coal mines, industrial excretions, all manner of loathsome, noxious materials dumped into gullies or down old mine shafts in the dead of night. Eventually they ooze into the rivers. So polluted is the water of the lower Patapsco and Elizabeth Rivers, at the great industrial ports of Baltimore and Norfolk, that researchers wear rubber gloves when working there. In 1975, an insecticide dumped into the lower James necessitated a temporary ban on all fishing.

But we are beginning to remember our rivers again, to stop taking them for granted. As a change from backyard abuse, we are commencing to accord them frontyard pride. The federal government, in cooperation with the states and the District of Columbia, has spent a billion dollars trying to make the Potomac swimmable again. Rural landowners have banded together to protect the winsome little Cowpasture River that feeds the James. The Tri-State Association is promoting river education throughout the Susquehanna basin. The Chesapeake Bay Foundation is doing the same for the bay region. "This is not the time for handwringing," says William Baker, the foundation's president. "This is a time for rolling up our sleeves and getting to work."

Now three state governments and that of the District of Columbia are pledged to save and cherish the bay. There is no nobler cause, Maryland's governor declared at a major conference on bay problems. "We must recognize that our place is in nature, not above it."

So we have not quite forgotten that flowing waters are fountains of life, designs for wholesome living. We are realizing now that they can be teachers, and that we have much to learn before we can make our rivers again sweet, our bays again fair.

THE RIVERS OF AFRICA

Ferry plies Ethiopia's Lake T'ana, source of the Blue Nile. By Robert Caputo.

ivers have often been Africa's sorrow. Geological processes that placed the continent squarely within the tropics and thrust much of its bedrock above sea level left most of the land overheated and poorly drained. Eight river basins hold nearly 75 percent of Africa's water. The large northern and southern deserts have almost none, while the remaining areas vary.

From the breakup of the huge landmass called Gondwanaland some 180 million years ago emerged the African Continent—a sloping plateau, higher on the east and south, rimmed by steep escarpments. More recent tectonic movements pocked the plateau with large basins. This landscape explains the peculiar courses of many of Africa's rivers, which flow into these basins. During the rainy season the basins brim with water and flood, turning vast areas into lakes, marshes, and swamps. But in the dry season the rivers trickle and the basins become dusty pans.

Only a few rivers break through the steep escarpments near the coast to tear through the uplifted bedrock and tumble down valleys to the sea where they end in deltas or sandbars. Their passage has created some of the most spectacular cataracts and waterfalls in the world and given Africa the largest hydroelectric power potential of any continent—between 25 and 40 percent of the world's total—but at the cost of good anchorages and natural harbors.

For centuries these spectacular and treacherous landforms helped to deter Europeans from penetrating the interior. Rivers served as barriers instead of roads. Less than 200 years ago not much more than the continent's outline existed on European charts. The few mapped rivers were disappointingly short or turned out to be imaginary, their courses based on legend. The major portions of the interior were marked "unknown" or "unexplored."

Today, thanks to some intrepid 19th-century explorers, ruler-straight borders crisscross modern maps of Africa, and well-charted rivers and their tributaries web them. We know the Nile to be earth's longest river—4,160 miles from its delta to its source in Burundi. The Zaire, formerly the Congo, is far greater than the Nile in the breadth of its sources. The Zaire arches over the Equator, the only river system in the world to flow in both the Southern and the Northern Hemispheres. In West Africa the Volta drops abruptly to the sea and is not navigable; the Sénégal and the Gambia admit oceanborne commerce.

. Not far from the sources of these western rivers, rising less than 200 miles from the Atlantic Ocean, the far-flung Niger flows in the opposite direction, toward the Sahara, and then swings southward to join the Benue coming from the east. From their confluence the broadened river courses south through mangrove swamps and humid tropical forests to form a delta under the continent's huge hump. Along the middle course of the Niger, spring rains normally flood a 250-mile-long inland delta, turning it into an island-studded lake. Paddies, millet and sorghum fields, and breeding grounds for fish provide a

harvest for the Bozos, Fulani, Bambara, Songhais, and other groups that live along the river. But when drought hits, as it did once again in the early 1980s, the rivers dry up and tens of thousands of people die of starvation and disease.

On Africa's southwestern flank, the Zaire and the Cunene, another short plunging river, partly bound the former Portuguese colony of Angola. Three other rivers—the Orange, the Vaal, and the Limpopo—create green valleys in the high, dry veld of the continent's southern tip. The Zambezi draws on a fan of southward-draining tributaries and runs eastward to dash itself in a pillar of rainbow spray over Victoria Falls as it begins its long descent to the Indian Ocean. In the 1850s the Scottish missionary-explorer Dr. David Livingstone traced the course of the Zambezi. Yet Europeans had been trying since Roman times to penetrate Africa's secrets, particularly the origin of the gold traded out of West Africa by close-mouthed Moors of the Mediterranean coast. European dreams of wealth were fed after 1324 by stories from Cairo about a visit there of Mansa, or King, Musa of Mali—"lord of the negroes of Guinea." The monarch was supposed to have ferried down the Niger a hundred camel loads of gold which he spent liberally while on his journey.

nother century passed before anyone mounted a full-fledged expedition to find a water route to the gold-bearing interior of Africa. Prince Henry of Portugal sent ship after ship around the curving coast, searching for rivers to follow inland. In the Portuguese wake adventurers and merchants from most of the other seafaring nations of Europe found that beyond the river mouths the short continental shelf invariably led to impassable cataracts.

Africans along the lower rivers traded gold, ivory, animal skins, and pepper for cloth, beads, tobacco, and iron bars, and a few Dutch and Portuguese traders brought gold dust and nuggets down the Sénégal and Gambia. But slaves were what kept the white traders coming, and by the 18th century the slave trade had swamped all other African commercial pursuits. The willingness of captors to deliver slaves at seaside landings meant that European traders did not venture upriver, so for another hundred years the map of Africa remained pretty much as Prince Henry's navigators had charted it.

It was finally a mixture of scientific curiosity, Christian missionary zeal, and the desire to discover other marketable commodities in the interior—including the still elusive gold of Timbuktu—that brought together a group of London merchants and philanthropists in June 1788 to found the African Association.

The association's first objective was to learn the source, direction, and navigability of the Niger, and its relationship to Timbuktu. Mungo Park, a red-bearded young Scottish physician, set out from the falls of the Gambia River in December 1795. Though harassed by robbers, Park found the Niger seven months later, "as broad as the Thames at Westminster, and flowing slowly to the eastward." Park had to abandon his attempt to paddle to Timbuktu when clouds of mosquitoes attacked, leaving him swollen and raging with fever.

Park returned to Africa in 1805 to finish charting the Niger's course. Most of his group died of fever before reaching the river at Bamako. The few who struggled on—including Park himself—were killed in an ambush near Busa in Nigeria. Two English brothers, John and Richard Landers, completed Park's mission in 1830. They canoed the last 500 miles to the Niger's mouth and proved that waterways penetrated the interior of West Africa.

We now know that for more than a thousand years, until the late 16th century, successive empires based on gold mining did flourish along the Niger. They raised armies, administered their lands, and traded extensively. From the Sahara and North Africa they imported copper, cloth, beads, shells, perfumes, horses, and especially the salt so vital to life in the hot, humid climate—at times traded pound for pound for gold. These empires faded away because of

A hippopotamus with "a malignant pleasure in upsetting canoes" adds a perilous note (below) to the journals of David Livingstone in 1865. For 32 years Livingstone probed Africa and helped awaken his world to its potential.

Pages 28-29: Liquid thunder booms over the ledges of mile-wide Victoria Falls, named by Livingstone for the British queen. Here the Zambezi plunges 350 feet.

T. Baines, Royal Geographical Society. Opposite: National Museum, Lagos, Nigeria: Dirk Bakker

"The Mosi-o-a-Funya (Smoke Resounding)," wrote English adventurer Thomas Baines in notes on his painting of Victoria Falls in 1874. Though his accounts and sketches fascinated Europeans, few of them glimpsed the awesome falls until the 20th century.

invasions, struggles over the gold trade, perhaps the exhaustion of their mines. Cyclical droughts may also have depleted and scattered the peoples of ancient Ghana, Mali, and Songhai, leaving Timbuktu no more than a dusty caravan stop. Today vestiges of these great states are scattered across West Africa from the present state of Mali to the Songhai tribal lands on the Niger. Ghana's Ashanti chiefs and their retinues still wear centuries-old gold regalia, an echo of the fabled adornments of the vanished court of Mansa Musa. The Niger River still binds these scattered peoples, though tenuously. During the high water season from August to March, barges pushed by diesel tugs carry salt, dried fish, grain, and rice among the some 40 million people living in the great arc between Bamako and the Benue. Benin, Chad, Guinea, Ivory Coast, Mali, Niger, Nigeria, Cameroon, and Upper Volta—the nine countries watered by the Niger and Benue—jointly approved construction of the Kainji dam and lake, which now flood Busa, where Mungo Park died.

Many other African countries, hungry to industrialize, find the temptation to develop their water resources for electricity hard to resist, even though they have neither the financial nor the technical means to do it themselves—nor the capacity to use much of the power once it's generated. But projects built by outsiders are often difficult to operate and control. In 1975 the world's sixth largest dam was completed at the Cabora Bassa gorge, Mozambique, 300 miles upriver from the mouth of the Zambezi. The Portuguese, Mozambique's former colonial rulers, built it with South African encouragement—mostly to benefit South Africa. For the past several years, however, the supply of electricity to South Africa has been unreliable. The South Africans blame Mozambique for lacking the skilled technicians to maintain the system. Guerrilla bands opposing the Mozambican regime have interfered with the massive transmission lines to Pretoria. Finally, in May 1984, the countries signed an agreement that should get the power moving again. Similarly, politics in Angola and Namibia have hindered South African-backed projects on the Cunene, a river vital to the development of both countries.

Throughout Africa water projects that work are often plagued by environmental problems. Malarial mosquitoes breed in irrigation ditches; the pesticides that only partially control them poison the environment. Especially worrisome is the skyrocketing incidence of bilharzia, or schistosomiasis. Some 68 percent of the workers on South Africa's irrigated farms come down with this debilitating affliction, in which tiny waterborne wrigglers called blood flukes invade the human bloodstream and liver. Epidemiologists predict that when the fluke-ridden waters of the Cunene River are diverted into Namibia, a bilharzia explosion will occur in its densely populated province, Ovamboland. Unfortunately, what is needed for this and all large-scale African water projects is what they usually get too late: a thorough evaluation of the repercussions.

"Remoteness . . . difference of custom . . . luxuriance of nature, savage life, personal danger"—thus the explorer Richard Burton explained the attraction of Africa for those who filled out its map. But the fruits of these adventures have yet to be exploited for the benefit of Africans. The turmoil of independence struggles and post-independence politics have held the pace of river development to a slow crawl.

For centuries beside the Niger this 21-inch-high copper image endured ritual scrubbings with river gravel to ensure the fertility of fish and local river people. Master metalworkers of the 14th century crafted it.

THE NILE

By Geoffrey Moorhouse / Photographs by Robert Caputo

The longest river in the world begins in one of the tiniest nations on earth. On a hilltop in Burundi, which is scarcely bigger than the state of Maryland, stands the symbolic but locally incongruous shape of a pyramid. It overlooks a setting no pharaoh ever knew, a landscape of bush-covered hills where the air is warm and always moist. The Equator is but four degrees to the north. This is the Africa of tropical growth, of thatched homes corralled against predatory beasts, of a wildness to make the stranger tingle with excitement. The Ruwenzori, the legendary Mountains of the Moon, are not so far away, and near there the gorilla abides in forest that is still inimical to man. Here, on the hill crowned by that pyramid, naught but cattle browse on grasses that soften the rocky outcrops. A bronze plaque has been hammered into the monument at the riverhead, bearing the words *"Caput Nili."* From a spring in a gully just below, there do indeed flow the first traceable headwaters of the almighty River Nile.

It says much about the eternal magnetism of the Nile that this infant gusher, which the local Tutsi know as Kasumo, or "cascade," was not identified by Westerners until 1937. We had, after all, been obsessed with its origins from the time of our own ancient past. The Greek historian Herodotus had inquisitively made his way from the Mediterranean as far south as Egypt's First Cataract some 460 years before Christ was born. The Romans had investigated even farther, Nero extending his imperial ambitions briefly into southern Sudan before retreating from an impenetrable swamp. Western explorers left the uttermost parts of the Nile alone until the 19th century, when African history becomes littered with the names of those who doggedly sought the river's source. Livingstone and Stanley, Baker, Burton and Speke, all spent much of themselves in hazardous travel to establish the beginning of the mythical river.

That two mighty torrents, not one, contributed to the Egyptian Nile was already understood. In the 1770s the Scotsman James Bruce had demonstrated that the so-called Blue Nile reached the confluence at Khartoum after running a thousand miles from the east, where Lake T'ana pours out of the Ethiopian

Feluccas ferry passengers and cargo on the Nile. For thousands of years, sailboats have ridden the current north and let dependable winds push them south.

highlands. The White Nile fixated explorers for much longer, even after the Englishman John Speke established in 1862 that its great volume issued from the inland sea of Lake Victoria. But there was still the compelling matter of tracing Lake Victoria's principal feeder. We weren't to find this ultimate source until 1937, when an obscure German explorer, Dr. Burkhart Waldecker, climbed the gully in what is now Burundi, tasted its streaming water, and caused the memorial pyramid to be built.

From that scrubby hilltop in central Africa, the Nile flirts under more than one name with several countries before settling into its measured pace to the north across vast Sudan. It rushes youthfully from Burundi into neighboring Tanzania and Rwanda. It turns east to the inland sea named after the imperial British queen and thereafter crosses central Uganda as the Victoria Nile until it reaches Lake Albert. Translated by this brief contact into the Albert Nile, it rolls on for another hundred miles to the frontier between Uganda and Sudan, where they know it as Bahr el Jebel, "sea of the mountain." The rest of us call that stream the White Nile until it merges with the Blue.

Thus far the Nile has traversed country where rainfall is high and vegetation lush, where big game is prolific along the river's banks, where tribesmen herd their cattle and grow maize and beans, sorghum and cassava for subsistence more than income. For a while after the river passes into Sudan, a thousand miles from its source, nothing of this is changed.

The biggest menace to river commerce in southern Sudan is the swamp that the Arabs well named the Sudd, or "obstacle." It is a bog as big as England, compounded of towering papyrus and tentacular water hyacinth, growing out of and rotting into yet more ooze, a wilderness of vegetation in which human beings can hopelessly lose themselves and the boats by which they entered. In this fashion the Sudd trapped the Italian adventurer Romolo Gessi and 600 men who were going by steamer to Khartoum in 1880. Even after resorting to cannibalism, only a handful of them made their way to safety again.

In the early 20th century the British and Egyptians, jointly responsible for governing Sudan, began talking of a canal that might bypass the Sudd. By diverting water before it entered the swamp, where the Nile loses half of itself to evaporation, the canal would improve the vigor of the river on which Egypt's economy depended. Sudan, it was argued, would also benefit. Seasonal flooding would be reduced. More land would be available for cultivation and grazing. Diseases that thrive on moisture, like malaria, would diminish. Though the reasons for cutting a canal in this remote place were impressive, not until 1978 did work on the Jonglei Canal begin, and it is still incomplete.

This monstrous ditch, 213 feet wide and 16 feet deep, will run from one kink in the Nile to another one 224 miles away, helping to regulate the rise and fall of water in the seasons of dryness and torrential rain, the natural cycle that has

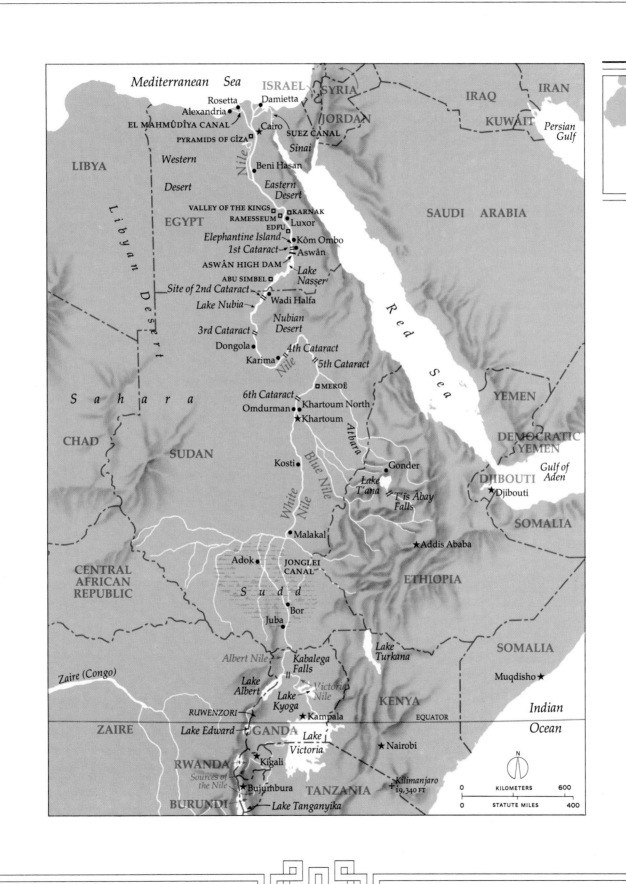

Mediterranean Sea

ISRAEL
SYRIA
Rosetta   Damietta
Alexandria
EL MAHMÛDÎYA CANAL
Cairo   SUEZ CANAL
PYRAMIDS OF GÎZA
Sinai
JORDAN
IRAQ
IRAN
KUWAIT
Persian
Gulf

LIBYA

Western

Desert

Beni Hasan

Eastern
Desert

VALLEY OF THE KINGS   KARNAK
EGYPT   RAMESSEUM   Luxor
EDFU
Elephantine Island   Kôm Ombo
1st Cataract   Aswân
ASWÂN HIGH DAM
ABU SIMBEL
Lake
Nasser
Site of 2nd Cataract
Lake Nubia   Wadi Halfa

SAUDI ARABIA

Nubian
Desert

3rd Cataract

Dongola
Karima   4th Cataract
5th Cataract

Red Sea

Sahara

MEROË
6th Cataract
Omdurman   Khartoum North
Khartoum

YEMEN

DEMOCRATIC
YEMEN

CHAD

SUDAN

Atbara

Kosti   Gonder
Lake
T'ana
T'is Âbay
Falls

Gulf of
Aden

DJIBOUTI
Djibouti

SOMALIA

White Nile   Blue Nile

Malakal

Addis Ababa

CENTRAL
AFRICAN
REPUBLIC

Adok   JONGLEI
CANAL

S u d d

Bor

Juba

ETHIOPIA

Lake
Turkana

SOMALIA

Albert Nile   Kabalega
Falls

Muqdisho

Zaire (Congo)

Lake
Albert   Lake
Kyoga   Victoria
Nile
RUWENZORI   Kampala

KENYA

EQUATOR

Indian
Ocean

ZAIRE   Lake Edward   UGANDA   Lake

Nairobi

Victoria

RWANDA   Kigali

Sources of
the Nile   Bujumbura   TANZANIA

Kilimanjaro
19,340 FT

BURUNDI   Lake Tanganyika

N

0   KILOMETERS   600
0   STATUTE MILES   400

meant plenty or famine for the millions who dwell lower down the river. A German contraption—a goliath that can excavate 9,000 tons of earth an hour—has been shuffling from Malakal toward a destination just above Juba for six years now, with a third of the total distance still to be cut. When finished, the waterway will be half again as long as the Suez and Panama Canals combined.

In the rainy season, when the Sudd becomes a morass, goliath often breaks down, and the local work force takes time to mend it. Political troubles, too, have hampered the excavation. The degree of autonomy that President Gaafar Nimeiri granted the Christian and animist south of his country from the Muslim north in 1972 seemed to have ended the civil war that had raged in Sudan for 17 years. But toward the end of 1983, insurrection was again disturbing the southern tranquility. It has brought work on the canal to a standstill.

I found traveling down the Nile here a depressing experience. Sudan, the largest country in Africa, is also one of the most sadly impoverished places on the continent. Yet the river, properly handled, could transform much of the surrounding wastes into a green and fruitful land. The Nile could also provide a thoroughfare between the equatorial south and the bleak desert that begins just north of Khartoum. Now a solitary steamboat, an antique survivor from the turn of the century, occasionally makes its way from Juba to Kosti, 900 miles to the north, laden with passengers who overflow onto barges lashed to the hull. The voyage downstream takes a week, 12 days or more the other way, the crew sometimes having to saw through the thick tangle of papyrus and water hyacinth that impedes the boat's passage across the Sudd. Shilluk fishermen, spearing mudfish from their dugouts, probably have a more congenial ride.

Nor are things much better by the time the White Nile reaches Khartoum and its junction with the Blue. An odd three-decker takes a pathetic handful of tourists for brief cruises, its half-empty accommodation fairy lit. A number of similar craft lie like stranded hippos on the slipways in Khartoum North. A clutch of sailing dinghies, manned by the capital's international set, tack back and forth across the Blue Nile. Apart from these vessels, I saw very little move across these tremendous waters except the small boats of fishermen hunting the massive Nile perch, a thumping creature that looks as if it would merit the attentions of deep-sea fishermen in mid-Atlantic. Even the country cargo boat, rigged like the characteristic felucca of Egypt, seldom appears any more.

Yet the sense of arriving at a place pregnant with history and latent with a mighty natural power dominates Khartoum and its twin city, Omdurman, so long as the stranger does not stray too far from the riverside. Elsewhere, I discovered, one can easily be discouraged by the dusty drabness of the capital city, where too much has broken down and been left unrepaired, where there is little to lighten the spirits in the stifling heat. When I strolled by the two rivers, though, I always found a cooling breeze coming off the waters as they roll toward their meeting place around the thick half-moon of Tuti Island. After the rainy season the two Niles here are neither blue nor white, but an indistinguishable brown. As the waters subside, the eponymous colors are restored, the one a shade on the earthly side of azure, the other with a touch of milkiness lightening the gray. Whatever the season, both rivers flow wide and majestically. It takes a bridge with seven spans to carry the dilapidated railway trains safely across the Blue Nile from Khartoum to Khartoum North.

As for history, inside the presidential palace are the steps on which English Gen. Charles Gordon met his end in 1885 at the hands of his great foe, the Muslim prophet called the Mahdi. A mile down the road an unexpectedly magnificent museum, arranged with United Nations help, displays murals, carvings, and bric-a-brac dating back to 1500 B.C. Most come from Sudanese Nubia to the north, reminders that this now largely empty land once had a civilization modeled on that of the Egyptians. At Omdurman the past is much closer. A triumphant crescent and spearpoint cap the Mahdi's silver-domed tomb. Across the sandy street is the house where the Mahdi's successor, Khalifa Abdullahi, lived before English Gen. Herbert Kitchener exacted his terrible revenge at the Battle of Omdurman—which was hardly a battle at all, with 11,000 dead on one side and only 49 on the other. Kitchener's machine guns, now displayed in the Khalifa's house with other imperial detritus, massacred zealots armed only with ancient muskets and swords—like World War I infantry facing a nuclear strike.

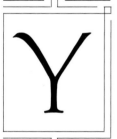

et even that appalling day in 1898 did not extinguish those dervishes. Just before sunset each Friday in Omdurman, scores of them gather on wasteland outside the mosque containing the tomb of their saint, Hamed El Nil. A circle forms. Within it a file of men begin to shuffle round under the leadership of an old fellow in spectacles, who is said to be the Mahdi's grandson, while drummers beat the time. At first the performance is casual, almost absentminded, but gradually the beat quickens and the dancers bob with each step. Men forming the circle imitate this bobbing with enthusiasm. Excitement slowly mounts, and voices in the crowd ululate weirdly to spur it on. A strange youth, a holy fool perhaps, leaps into the ring and races round and round with a lost expression on his face, while half the crowd roars with laughter at his stumbling rush. Then another figure peels away from the file to gyrate on one leg like a spinning top, flourishing a whip to maintain his balance in a swirl of green-and-orange cloak. Another man follows him, and soon the area inside the circle is full of spinning figures. As the drumming becomes frenetic, men fall with dizziness and lie prostrate in the dust (but carefully roll out of the way if it seems they will be trodden on). From time to time the dancers pause to gather their wits, and the crowd roars its applause until a cry of "*Allahu Akbar*" rouses the performers again. This goes on for an hour or more, until the sun has disappeared behind

Hamed El Nil's mosque. Then, quite suddenly, the performance stops. The dervishes have danced their way into another week.

How powerfully Omdurman speaks of Islam can be seen on the foreshore where the two Niles have at last united into one. Smashed beer cans and liquor bottles litter the mud where flop-eared goats forage and boatbuilders hew timber for fishing boats. Here, in September 1983, President Nimeiri himself led a ceremonial disposal of all the alcohol in Khartoum. Now Westerners in the hotel bars of the city savor bottles of soft drink with all the mannerisms usually reserved for Scotch and gin. In the same fit of Islamic zeal, which did not bode well for relations with his troublesome and non-Islamic south, the president ordained that the full repercussions of Muslim law must henceforth be visited on the land. Before the end of 1983 two hapless thieves had been judicially deprived of their right hands at a public amputation in Khartoum. There was a riot outside the prison that day—of people unable to get in to watch.

Khartoum is the last place along the Nile where the hodgepodge of Sudanese races mingle in any quantity. A good sprinkling of folk represent black Africa to the south—among them the Dinka, Shilluk, and Nuer, marked with elaborate cicatrices on the forehead. They stand out from the generally stockier peoples of northern Sudan, whose color has paled from generations of fusing with Arab strains: the Beja from the Egyptian border, who were the Fuzzy-Wuzzies of Kipling's disparaging imagination, and the Nubians, who served Egypt's pharaohs as soldiers, laborers, and middlemen in black Africa. Seeing them all in a haphazard mixture with a quorum of Arabs at the city's big marketplace, I realized in one bewildered glance what a gigantic and intricate continent Africa is.

T he full and now grander Nile, its volume more than doubled by the waters from Ethiopia, rolls north toward the ancient kingdom of Kush, with desert spreading on either side. For some distance downriver from Khartoum, and sporadically wherever there is a town or settlement, I saw cultivation along the riverbanks. Ribbons of green no more than a few hundred yards wide stretch from the water to the endless wastes of sand and rock. By river, Egypt is still almost a thousand miles away, with five of the six historic cataracts barring the way. The Sixth Cataract is 60 miles outside Khartoum. "Cataract" suggests a great tumult almost as thunderous as a waterfall, but the reality is less intimidating. The Nile swoops between high rock walls for eight miles, where boulders are tumbled about its bed often enough to make things too boisterous for any vessel. And so, again, the river is neglected as a thoroughfare except between Karima and Dongola, where a steamer plies from June to March before the Nile has lowered itself too much to be of any use for the next three months. From Khartoum people making for Egypt or northern Sudan do so by truck or train. If they choose the latter, theirs is a memorably uncomfortable journey of

30 hours or more across the Nubian Desert to Wadi Halfa.

Only reputation had prepared me for what I met at the end of the long railway line—nothing but a sprawl of low buildings hastily thrown together in the midst of a dried-up wilderness. The Nile is out of sight, a couple of miles from the railway buffers. When I reached it, I found no longer a river but a great sheet of water stretching to the northern horizon. I had come to Lake Nasser, formed by the Aswân High Dam that Egypt built between 1960 and 1970. Somewhere just beyond the water's edge, several fathoms deep now, lies the old village of Wadi Halfa, submerged like much else as the lake began to fill.

Lake Nasser is a little more than 300 miles long, and two waterborne days and nights pass between stepping off Sudanese soil and setting foot in Egypt. Unlike Lake Victoria, where it is possible to sail clean out of sight of land, the shores are always visible here—low desert coming to the western water's edge, ranges of sandy hills stretching toward the Red Sea in the east. Gulls trail our steamer by day but go ashore at night, after the passengers have spared them bits of orange peel and other garbage. The passengers are a motley collection: Sudanese students heading for Cairo University; Egyptians and Sudanese bent on small-time trading in the bazaars at either end of the lake; a tiny clique of Westerners thrilled to be seeing Africa the rough-and-ready way. Only the Westerners travel light. The Sudanese travels with his entire family, ten big cardboard boxes, and three dozen storm lanterns (made in China). Half a day is laboriously spent in the vigorous processes of embarkation; another half day goes by after arrival before the Egyptians allow anyone to go ashore.

In between these two robust events, the steamer sails over history. From the moment Lake Nasser began to fill in 1963, much of ancient Nubia gradually vanished beneath its waves. The world was well aware of this process because it was subscribing to the cost (42 million dollars) of the greatest archaeological salvage operation of all time: the dismembering of the Abu Simbel temples, built by the edge of the Nile 3,200 years earlier to the glory of Ramses II and his queen Nofretari, and the restoration of the temples 212 feet higher up the cliff.

In the lee of this monumental enterprise, many other losses to the lake went unnoticed—except by those whose lives were altered. Many villages disappeared; some 90,000 Nubians were obliged to pack all their worldly goods and resettle in other parts of Sudan and Egypt. The Sudanese mostly fetched up beside the Atbara River, a Nile tributary far to the east of Khartoum. The Egyptians were placed farther down the valley of the Nile itself, near Kôm Ombo, but at a much greater distance from their blessed river than they and their ancestors had been accustomed. The steamer across Lake Nasser sails over the drowned folk memories of an entire race, as well as the submerged ruins of their former prosperity. In the slow cruise to the north, I saw a few desolate dwellings, abandoned in the migration but not engulfed by the inundation. We passed Abu Simbel in the night, a twinkle of lights to port revealing nothing but black shadows and the outline of two hillocks.

The cause of this unnatural redistribution of the Nile comes out of the morning heat haze like a gigantic harbor wall, though the gray projection at one end turns out not to be a lighthouse but a strange piece of sculpture commemorating the brief Soviet-Egyptian amity that went into the making of the Aswân High Dam. The ambition behind it was colossal. At last the Egyptian Nile would be properly regulated, no longer having a nation at its mercy. Gone would be the years when too much water came down, with the force of 3,500 miles behind it, to flood the landscape all the way to the Mediterranean. Gone would be those other equally disastrous years when the Nile waywardly gave too little of itself and Egypt suffered famine from drought. Henceforth, a steady flow would bring mounting prosperity to the fellahin, peasant farmers who from the beginning of recorded history have made their living from the soil bordering the Nile. And, in truth, much of the ambition has been realized. Some 2.5 million acres of Egypt have been steadily irrigated, giving two or three crops every year instead of only one at the best of times. Some 500,000 acres of desert have been reclaimed, to add to the common wealth. Hydroelectricity has come in quantities unknown before the dam, and industry has developed in Upper Egypt on a scale that could not have been contemplated earlier.

But now the scientists (as is their wont) nod sagely and argue an alternative case. I read some of the dense volumes they have produced in the past 20 years and wondered whether the High Dam should have been built at all. The land below Aswân, they say, has lost much of its old fertility because silt that started its journey in Ethiopia or deeper inside Africa no longer reaches Egypt, and chemical fertilizers are an expensive luxury for the fellahin. The annual floods once washed salts from soil that now retains them and becomes sterile. The incidence of bilharzia, a wasting disease that has long afflicted Egyptian peasants (perhaps as many as 40 per cent), is rising because the slower flow of the Nile below Aswân promotes the growth of the dangerous parasite that causes anemia, dysentery, and tissue damage. The multitude of scientific doubts about the benefits of Aswân range from unexpected seepage out of the dam to a drastic reduction of fish stocks along the coast of the delta, almost 600 miles downstream. Sardines have vanished, deprived of nutrients from silt-laden water.

As a distinctly unscientific observer of this river, I can only remark on the transformation I saw on reaching Egypt from Sudan. I had come from a benighted land where people appear to be hanging onto existence by their fingernails, and I suddenly found myself in a country where life is at the very least modestly flourishing—and often opulent. The town of Aswân, eight miles below the dam, is a revelation of industry and growth, style and glamour after the ramshackle improvisations of Wadi Halfa. Aswân has phosphate and iron mines, a huge fertilizer factory, and a bazaar where traders do business with strolling crowds far into the evening under glaring electric light. It has floating hotels that have come upriver from Luxor or even Cairo, packed with foreigners eager to indulge in the primitive, pharaonic past, so long as they are not deprived of their international cuisine, flamboyant cocktails, and well-sprung sleeping arrangements every inch of the way. At Aswân these luxurious steamships tie up where the Nile's east bank has a whiff of the south of France, with palm trees, idling visitors, clopping horse-drawn carriages that only tourists use, and even a Riviera Bazaar. The road hugging the riverside is known as the corniche, the French reminding us that Napoleon came to Egypt, too.

H ere, at last, the Nile becomes the thoroughfare that it ought to have been far upriver. The First Cataract, just above Aswân, is no longer "bristling with rocks and boiling with foam," as Egyptologist Amelia Edwards found it in 1874. The dam has turned it into nothing more treacherous than a succession of eddies in which boatmen must take a bit of care as they pick their way round the islets. It is a place for soothing dalliance in a pseudo-felucca, which will probably be named *Ananas, Mango,* or *Cleopatra* to beguile the tourists who have hired it in all its freshly painted and artificial charm. The boats sail in their dozens up and down this stretch of the Nile, where the pied kingfisher hovers like a hummingbird before plunging down for its catch, and where, on the edge of Elephantine Island, stands the stone nilometer engraved with lines by which the river's seasonal rise was measured to gauge the annual taxations.

But the Nile now also becomes a working river in the grand manner. Genuine feluccas, wide-beamed craft with two masts, head downriver with stone from the Aswân quarry. Occasionally they go as far as Cairo itself, in which case they will be on the way for 45 days. To travel down this almighty river by one of these country boats is to feel the pulse of Egypt as it has throbbed in both ancient and modern times. In my ears were the squeak of tackle and the slatter of lateens as the boatmen altered course to catch the wind. Every puff—chiefly from the north in winter, from the south in summer—has carried these sounds since the days of the pharaohs and before. So, too, the plash and plop of oars, long beams of timber without blades at the end, which the boatmen use when they become tired of waiting for a breeze and decide to make way themselves.

Cultivation starts between Aswân and Kôm Ombo. Green strips on both banks of the Nile persevere and slowly widen until, by the time Luxor comes round the bend, the fields stretch for miles on either hand. Irrigation channels furrow the plots where men cut sugarcane, sickle fodder, or ponder patches of damp earth where rice is beginning to sprout. Donkeys heavily laden with vegetation trot along dike tops. Egrets tiptoe in the fields, almost treading on the laboring fellahin, avid to share in the bounty. For a mile or more the landscape beyond the east bank hides behind a thick wall of banana trees bowed with fruit nearly ready to yellow. Most farmers still toil with bent backs and hand implements. But the primitive shadoof, an earthenware pot roped to a beam and used to transfer Nile water from the river to the land, is giving way to waterwheels of galvanized iron. Blindfolded water buffaloes, urged on by children, drive the waterwheels endlessly round and round.

Between Aswân and Luxor the river flows by some of the greatest monuments of Egyptian antiquity. At Kôm Ombo, just above the water's edge, stands a tumbledown temple dedicated to the falcon-headed Horus and to Sobek, the crocodile god. An old man with a toothless leer points to a crypt where mummified crocodiles are piled like bundles of discarded linoleum. At Edfu the best preserved temple in all Egypt still stands almost as perfectly as when it was built in the name of Horus a few hundred years before Christ. The interior is gloomy—except the innermost wall, where the god's image was artfully situated to catch the sun's rays through a doorway several hundred yards away.

As for Luxor, it is antiquity run riot. Foreigners obsessively pursue it all, and a resident population has calculated to the last piaster how much can be squeezed from strangers with more money than common sense. It is the temples at Karnak on the east bank, where a Midwestern voice says to its spouse: "You remember that James Bond movie they made in here?" It is the Ramesseum across the river, where relatively recent graffiti have been added to ancient hieroglyphs—Leonardo 1820, R.H.A. Appleyard 1889, and the like. It is the Valley of the Kings, where Howard Carter found the tomb of Tutankhamun. It is the child who, with cool blackmail, demands an extortionate price for a soapstone scarab: "I do not have any work, and I want to go to school."

The antiquities diminish somewhat as the Nile rolls on to Cairo. The religious rivalries of Sudan are missing here. A Coptic church stands companionably next to almost every mosque. The heavy feluccas now carry bricks and cement as well as stone. At a wharf one craft loads hundreds of earthenware pots, which are stacked along its grimy deck like row upon row of sandy cannonballs. Near Cairo the traditional craft of the Nile are augmented by diesel-engined barges. They butt up and down the river in tandem, one pushing the other to save fuel and blaring horns to warn that they are on their way.

As a fanfare for the Egyptian capital and the biggest city in Africa, this will suffice. Cairo is not the loveliest metropolis in the world, though it makes Khartoum seem like a grubby provincial town. Cairo is full of demented traffic and whispering citizens who deal surreptitiously in all currencies at illegal rates of exchange. The famous pyramids of Gîza lie not out in the open desert, as the picture postcards would have us believe, but near the end of the municipal tram tracks. More than 50,000 Cairenes live in shanties spread across a sprawling cemetery—and appropriately call their home the City of the Dead. Another

50,000 dwell in a hideous rubbish dump for which no one has yet produced a brave title. On the other hand, the neon signs of wealth flicker from skyscrapers that increasingly rear up beside the Nile. You may eat, at considerable cost, some of the best food in the Middle East, served in surroundings that would not be thought out of place in Las Vegas. A belly dancer, an attractively chubby girl whose charms are not quite concealed by an expensive caftan, walks hand in hand with her boyfriend across the El Tahrir Bridge one afternoon. Unlike some other Cairene females in similar circumstances, she does not hesitate to look strange Western men in the eye as they pass, hoping maybe to see a recognition of her performance in the Sheraton or the Hilton the night before.

T hese are the flavors of Cairo as the Nile passes through before its great dissipation in the delta. What wealth Cairo enjoys has come because of the river. And here, because of the winter breeze off the Mediterranean, the Nile seems to be flowing the wrong way, rippling toward the south. Down in the delta it can be as smooth as a millpond. After the staggering distance the Nile has come, it seems to hesitate before surrendering to the sea. Canals and small watercourses by the hundred, if not by the thousand, network the farmlands below Cairo. On an immense plain as flat and intensively cultivated as Holland, orange groves stretch out of sight. Cabbages and cauliflowers grow so big here that people carry them by the stalk over their shoulders, one at a time, instead of under their arms. Tractors rumble up and down, reworking the land as soon as it has been harvested. The fertility, the abundance of it all, made me blink. A Sudanese peasant simply would not believe it possible.

Some of the earth's mighty rivers rush into the oceans open-mouthed, but that is not the Nile's way, though it is one of the mightiest rivers of them all. It divides into two natural branches again not long after Cairo, and down them meets the Mediterranean at the insignificant towns of Damietta and Rosetta. (Herodotus, seeing this triangle formed by river and sea, coined the term "delta" from the Greek letter Δ in the fifth century B.C.) The Nile squeezes out of innumerable openings besides, coaxed into a gentle expiration there by man. Of all the places where the Nile relinquishes Africa, it best deserves the farewell that Alexandria can bestow, even if its waters there go by the name of the El Mahmûdîya Canal. Here is a history that alone can match the Nile's. Here Cleopatra slew herself. Here Alexander the Great's remains might be found if anyone dug deeply and carefully enough at a crossroads now overlooked by a sleazy hotel and a Pâtisserie Egyptienne. This is not a spectacular ending for a river that has come 4,160 miles from the pyramid on a hilltop in Burundi, a river that nourished one of the earliest civilizations on earth. It is a subtle ending, a perfectly proper one, facing the continent of Europe, which has been mesmerized by the Nile ever since rumor of its mysterious power first spread across the sea.

Near its source in Lake T'ana, the Blue Nile drops in the rocky waterfall of T'īs Ābay, the "smoke of the Ābay," in western Ethiopia. Now and then a crocodile rears its head or a hippo breaches with a snort in the broad, mile-long lagoon above the 150-foot-high cataract. Monkeys scamper over the crags, looting eggs from the nests of birds that rear their young behind the foamy veils.

A pair of sure-footed Ethiopians (above) hike up their robes and wade through the water of a slippery causeway. People fording large rivers risk not only a dunking but a rude welcome on the other side. The Blue Nile and its tributaries make natural boundary lines, often separating groups of people with differing ways and with dim views of their neighbors across the water.

Candleglow burns a hole in the gloom of Kiddus Istifanos (above), the Christian monastery of St. Stephen on an island in Lake T'ana. Here in glass-sided coffins rest the bones of kings whose dynasty ruled Ethiopia from the 13th century until revolution in 1974.

On a nearby island a priest displays an illuminated manuscript at a church called Narga Selassie (opposite). A figure of an archangel guards the door to the Holy of Holies, the inner sanctum of Ethiopian Orthodox churches. This faith traces its roots to fourth-century missionaries from Syria.

A corner of a shawl hides the shy smile of an Ethiopian woman (right) near the town of Bahir Dar, where Lake T'ana pours out the Blue Nile.

S entinel in a sorghum field, an Anuak farmer (left) perches on a platform to shoo away birds. In this drainage area of the Upper Nile, sorghum ranks as a staple. Anuaks brew it into beer to quaff from a gourd.

A woman at Lake T'ana (opposite) balances a water jug and steadies herself on a skiff of reeds called a tankwa. Such a boat may rot in weeks, but new ones are quickly made. Reed boats have sailed the Nile for ages.

Flowing to Sudan, the Blue Nile cleaves western Ethiopia (above) and defies boaters and hikers to follow. Angry rapids wait to batter boats; mile-deep gorges deny even a toehold.

Pages 50-51: Egrets go one way, elephants the other near Kabalega Falls in Uganda. The Victoria Nile flows over the falls to link Lakes Victoria and Albert.

49

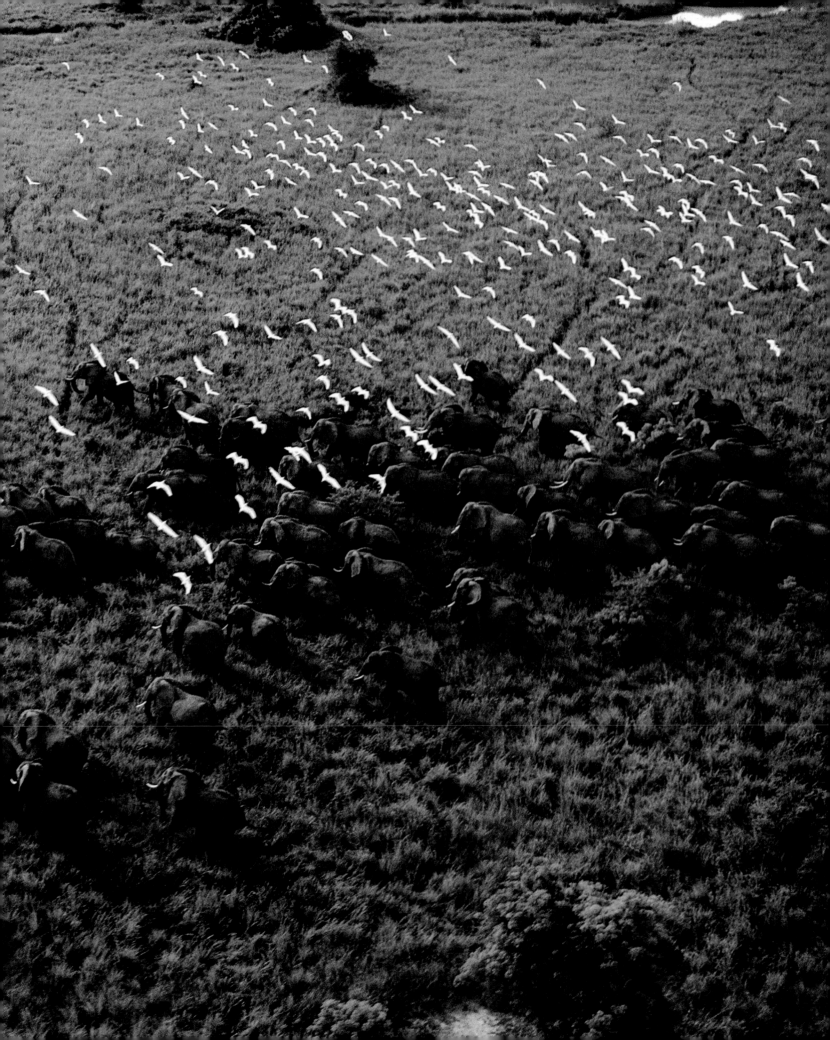

The chunky paddle steamer Hurriya (opposite) chuffs northward down the White Nile as the river flows through southern Sudan, and passengers loll on the foredeck. Boxy barges lashed to the ancient steamer tag along for a trip that may take a month to cover 900 miles.

Crowds jam the bank near Juba (above) as one of the barges nudges the shore. A helmsman (right) guides the ungainly assemblage of vessels. In some stretches of the river, captains often ram the banks to pivot around sharp bends.

S hadowy Nuer herdsman wanders in a thicket of horns (opposite) in the lush, swampy Sudd. These seminomadic Sudanese measure wealth in cattle, the source of meat, hides, milk, and the dung that smolders in great piles to keep the mosquitoes away.

A hollowed palm log (above), easily tipped, gives a risky ride to Dinkas crossing a Nile tributary. Here in the Sudd the Nile frays into a snarl of channels, lakes, and marshes, home to Dinkas who tend herds and plant crops on high ground in the rainy season and migrate with their herds to the lowlands when the waters recede near year's end.

Fish abound in the Sudd. A Nile perch rides (right) atop a Nuer fisherman, who finds its eye sockets a handy grip. Ancient Egyptians worshiped this fish, a voracious predator that often outweighs a man.

S iphon tubes sip from a ditch to water mile-long furrows of sugarcane (above) in Kenana, a flat region between the Blue Nile and White Nile just above their confluence at Khartoum. Sugarcane flourishes in soils laid down by thousands of Blue Nile floods. A network of dams and canals has increased the fertility and extent of arable land in this 80,000-acre plantation.

Nuer women move water the old way (opposite) while a mammoth excavator digs the Jonglei Canal. It will detour a fifth of the river's water around the spongy Sudd. Some people fear the canal will disturb climate, animal life, and old human ways in Sudan.

T wo Niles arrive but one departs at Khartoum (below, at left of picture), city overlooking the confluence of the Blue Nile and White Nile in central Sudan. Minarets of Omdurman (top) spike the sunset sky and look down on not one city but a trio called the Three Towns: Khartoum, Khartoum North, and Omdurman. Khartoum lies on the Blue Nile's southern bank, at left in the aerial view below. Graceful arches of the Blue Nile Bridge skip over the water to Khartoum North. The river forks around Tuti Island, then curls into the White Nile at distant Omdurman.

At a souk, or market, in Omdurman a textile merchant peers through his wares (opposite). More than half the city dwellers in Sudan live here in the Three Towns, clustering about the capital, Khartoum.

Pages 60-61: Downriver from the great confluence spread the ancient, shadowy kingdom of Meroë, whose masons and quarrymen reared this flat-topped pyramid as a tomb for a dead monarch. Egyptians 4,000 years ago knew this land as Kush and its people as formidable warriors who once humbled mighty Egypt and challenged the legions of Rome. The Meroitic kingdom flourished from the sixth century B.C. to the middle of the fourth century A.D., then fell at the hands of conquerors, probably Ethiopians.

I mages of mighty Ramses II (right) tower over the twilit waters of Lake Nasser. As the Nile filled this lake behind the Aswân Dam in the 1960s, it threatened to drown the pharaoh's statues and the rock-hewn temple of Abu Simbel behind them. Experts from many nations cut the entire temple into huge blocks and reassembled it on higher ground.

Symbol of the pharaohs' power, the falcon-god Horus (above) stands before a temple entrance at Edfu, its half-human image also cut into the pylon behind.

Along the Nile's green banks, ancient Egyptians farmed the fertile land and forged a civilization that endured for 3,000 years. Annual floods laid down a rich bed of silt but idled thousands of farmers whom the pharaohs put to work on pyramids.

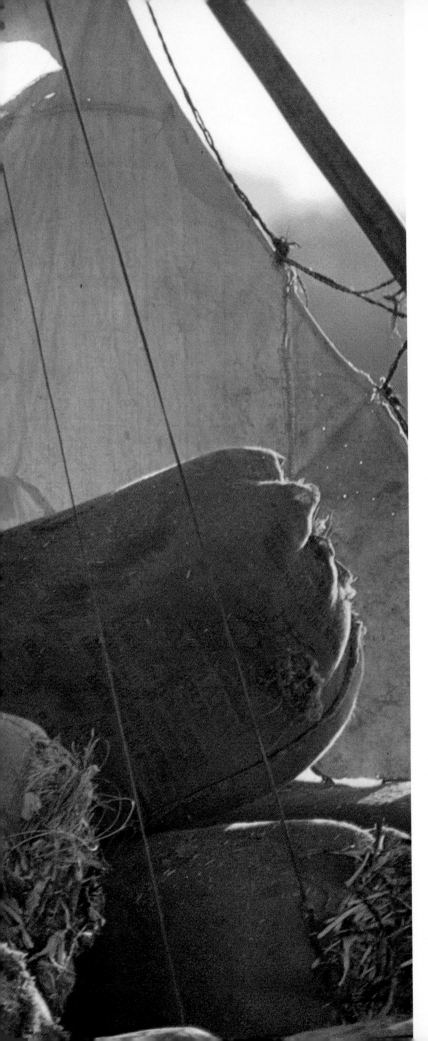

nder a tattered sail an Egyptian felucca (left) skims the Nile. In the days of the pharaohs two words meant travel: khent, "to go upstream," and khed, "to go downstream"—even if the traveler trudged on land.

The bales hold crushed straw left over from threshing; it may be used to feed animals or to make mud bricks like those that ancient people used in dwellings.

Paintings on tombs show farmers of 3,500 years ago dipping up river water with a shadoof. Today at the river's edge a farmer wields the same nodding wellsweep (below).

Thomas J. Abercrombie, National Geographic Staff. Left: Farrell Grehan

n the banks of the Nile at Cairo modern buildings rise over the 26 July Bridge (right) that angles across the river to Gezira, named from the Arabic word for "island." Here the Nile flows slowly from right to left as it forks around islands and heads for the delta and the Mediterranean Sea.

The river's bounty fills a Cairo fruit market (below) as it filled the granaries of pharaohs. Yet the Nile waters only a twentieth of Egypt; the rest of the land shimmers in hot desert.

With nearly a fifth of Egypt's population—some nine million people—Cairo is the largest city in Africa, and one noted for its color, vibrancy, and cosmopolitan flair. Twelve miles below this modern capital the river unravels into myriad watercourses that lace the sprawling delta.

Don Briggs

66

THE ZAIRE

Text and photographs by Georg Gerster

I had reached the village of Mumena, in Zaire's copper-rich Shaba Province, after a day's bumpy ride through highland savanna. A rusty sign on the dirt road indicated the source of the Zaire River, 50 meters away. But my guide haggled with Kaindu, a village elder. It seemed that the god of the river demanded an offering in coins. With inflation ravaging Zaire, I had not yet spotted such a thing as a coin. My companions argued that even gods should bend to reality and accept paper money. Kaindu relented and led us through elephant grass that waved over our heads. We entered a luxuriant grove that shaded a muddy pool with hardly a trickle running from it. *"Voilà la source,"* he said.

Speaking French, Zaire's official language, and a legacy of Belgian colonialism, Kaindu advised me to placate the god with a few bills and to bid him a hearty *bonjour.* "You had better ask for protection and for luck on your trip," Kaindu admonished. "Use any tongue—the god will understand you."

A giant springs from the slimy puddle in that holy grove 4,700 feet above the sea. The Zaire arcs 2,900 miles through Africa's heartland, drawing from a catchment area of 1.4 million square miles, swallowing river upon river, until it carries enough water to discharge an average of 1.4 million cubic feet per second into the Atlantic Ocean, a volume inferior only to the Amazon. Since the river touches the lives of so many among Zaire's 250 ethnic groups, it bore a variety of names. In 1971 President Mobutu Sese Seko, striving for national cohesion of the former Belgian Congo, renamed river and country Zaire, a version of *nzadi,* a local word meaning "river." The chief traditional name, Congo, persists in the neighboring People's Republic of the Congo.

As a young captain on the Congo, Joseph Conrad likened it to "an immense snake uncoiled, with its head in the sea . . . and its tail lost in the depths of the land." Portuguese mariners chanced upon the estuary in 1483, but roaring rapids a short distance upriver closed off the newly discovered artery for nearly four centuries. In 1867 David Livingstone struck the Chambeshi, and in 1871

A Luba fisherman salts and dries his catch on a papyrus island in Lake Kisale on the upper Zaire River. He will fish here only until the dry season ends. When the rains come, high water sets the papyrus islands adrift.

the Lualaba. He believed both to be headstreams of the Nile. Henry Morton Stanley fused bits of knowledge into the concept of one huge river system, linking the Lualaba to the Zaire's mouth on the West African coast. In 1876-77 Stanley traveled down the river, detoured by cannibals and cataracts.

At Bukama, a busy market town, I boarded a tattered launch, the *Boule de Défense*, which ferries passengers to Kikondja, a large village on Lake Kisale, and returns to Bukama loaded with salted fish.

The Zaire has fought its way to Bukama through the steep, rocky gorges of the Shaba plateaus. Downstream it meanders through swamps and marshes, hemmed in by reeds and rushes. Kingfishers hover over the water, an osprey perches on a solitary tree, egrets and herons wade among papyrus stalks. In this broad pan, the river intertwines with shallow lakes.

The kingdom of the Luba lasted from the early 17th century until the 1880s. Archaeologists have discovered Iron Age graves that contain jewelry, drink and food for the deceased, and money. Luba people had long believed these burials to shelter the remains of a different society. When archaeologists opened the tombs the Luba saw similarities to the style and use of their own jewelry. Then they embraced the dead as their forebears.

At a necropolis near Lake Kisale, I stood among Luba people to watch Nkulu Ngoie conduct a trial dig for the Museum of Lubumbashi. In years past these Luba blamed archaeological work for epidemics, linking measles and cholera to vengeful spirits from the violated graves. And now four new cases of cholera had erupted. The anxiety of my fellow onlookers was palpable. And so was the perplexed relief when we left.

"They expected us to take the bones," explained Nkulu when we were safely back on the *Boule de Défense*. He had collected artifacts from three burials but filled in the earth again on the skeletons. "I heard them say we have machines which can make the bones talk and betray all the secrets of Luba society. For sure, removing them would have incited a riot."

The first long navigable stretch of the Zaire ends at Kongolo. The river's volume has swelled sixfold from Bukama. A bridge for infrequent cars and trains spans a river 1,600 feet wide. There is no bridge across the Zaire for the next 1,740 miles. Below Kongolo lurk the vortices called the Gates of Hell. From there on, more rapids alternate with navigable reaches until the swirling finale, a 60-mile-long sequence of cataracts that Stanley named after himself. The last of these (now the Boyoma Falls) thunders within earshot of Kisangani.

I ran the the last cataract in a dugout manned by 26 chanting Enya paddlers. The Enya brave the roar of the river to inspect the fish traps that hang from precarious scaffolds above the foaming water. They recovered only a few small fish, and I joked that obviously I was to be their catch of the day. Few visitors come to Kisangani. The city of 340,000 has been in an economic tailspin ever

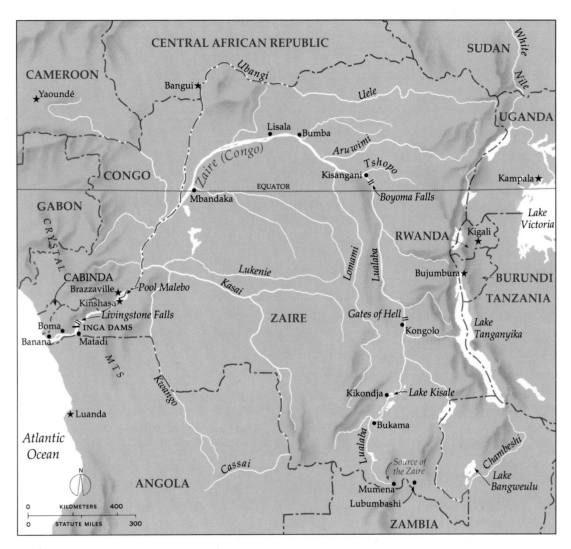

since the early years of independence. The pirogue pilot protested that it was fish they were after, not tourists. But catches have diminished. He blamed the low water of a dry year—and the Lokele downriver.

The enterprising Lokele roam the river with their nets and harvest fish below the falls. In their canoes roofed with palm straw, Lokele families live for weeks on the river. Lokele brides used to be more highly valued than other Zaire women. Their industry, their cunning, and their endurance are legendary, so that other women indict their Lokele sisters for thieving their men with magic.

A floating market on the Tshopo, a Zaire tributary, attracts Lokele pirogues to Kisangani's back door. My powerboat driver approached too briskly. Waves rippled, swaying boats and people. Angry voices decried our rudeness, and the protest of two women rose above the clamor. One accusingly waved the pieces of a broken paddle, the other bemoaned the near loss of her life. In fact, the paddle was already damaged, and the near loss of life was nearer a soak in the river, but I handed over a few bills. I teased the one who had shrieked so shrilly. *"Citoyenne,"* I said, using "citizen" to address her, as decreed by the government, "Citoyenne, I understand you Lokele women are bewitching beyond measure. Why are you berating us so?" She smiled sweetly. "But I am not Lokele, monsieur," she said. "Not everybody in this market is."

At Kisangani the Zaire swings westward. The middle Zaire, navigable for its entire length, is the most important of Zaire's waterways. Dozens of tributaries enter now. I caught the *Colonel Ebeya* at Mbandaka, bound for Kisangani. The boat was not one ship but seven: six barges for passengers and cargo were lashed to the bow and side of the diesel-powered *Ebeya*. I shared this convoy, complete with priest for Sunday services, with 632 other passengers.

F ive days into the journey the *Tshatshi,* sister ship to the *Ebeya,* passed us, limping downstream on one propeller. The *Ebeya,* too, was handicapped. A deformed propeller blade slowed us to about 5 miles an hour. Captain Mombila w'Alongo was a wiry veteran of 30 years on Zaire's rivers, although in loafers, blue jeans, and checkered shirt he hardly looked the role. During our journey the water level sank close to the all-time low. Tension on the bridge mounted each time Captain Mombila crisscrossed the river in search of a safe channel. His second in command perched atop one barge to fathom the waters visually, judging depth by color. He transmitted his findings by holding up two or three fingers. Ocher clouds swelled in the water when the *Ebeya* scraped a mudbank. We stopped for the night when fog foiled the searchlights.

My fellow passengers were a joyous lot who sometimes nearly gagged on their giggles. But we also talked seriously. From a Mongo man, Ekakia Lisenge, I learned a custom: Greeted with *"losako!"* an older man must offer a younger one a personally tailored maxim. Next morning, instead of bidding my Mongo friend "bonjour," I greeted him with "losako!" In surprise he replied, "Don't waste your time with idle chat, go and see for yourself."

I did. Most passengers on the *Ebeya* and the barges, it turned out, were traders, making round trip after round trip on a floating marketplace. River villages and encampments sent pirogues out to meet the *Ebeya*. The canoes would lie in wait upstream and then skillfully maneuver alongside. At times the convoy grew by dozens. No entertainment surpassed watching the boatmanship of arriving piroguiers, grasping anything to lock onto the *Ebeya* without dunking their goods. And if some fledgling oarsman took a dip, losing canoe and paddle, he would pretend that he had done it just for fun.

The visitors spent hours on board acquiring goods from bread and beer to cameras and comics. After hours of happy barter and banter the visitors loaded up and jettisoned themselves from the convoy to paddle home.

Above Mbandaka the Zaire breaks into scores of waterways amidst thousands of islands. Water hyacinths choke the channels. In *Heart of Darkness*, Conrad said, "Going up that river was like traveling back to the earliest beginnings of the world, when vegetation rioted on the earth and the big trees were kings. An empty stream, a great silence, an impenetrable forest. . . . You lost your way on that river as you would in a desert."

Here the river is nine miles across, but its might is lost on the traveler who sees only the nearest island. Where the river is wide, it looks narrow. Where it narrows in its rocky bed toward Kisangani, it paradoxically grows wide. On both banks looms dark and mysterious the equatorial forest.

Piroguiers offered me, for pets, snakes, crocodiles, and a young chimpanzee, and, for food, live grubs cultivated in rotting palm trunks. There was always manioc. Fish included the heavyweight champions of the river, *kambas*, up to 200 pounds apiece, ferocious tigerfish, and fat *mbotos*—all native to broad floodplains. As the forest closed in, we began to see smoked monkeys sold for food. Every day a woman sat just below my window with a heap of them, dressing the carcasses for market.

At intervals Captain Mombila slowed down just enough that passengers could jump on or off, amidst a frenzy of trading and greeting. Full stops, with pirogues as lighters, were the exception. Joy swept the *Ebeya* when the captain nudged the boat into its berth at Kisangani. For the first time in full regalia, with bars and stars, Captain Mombila bid me farewell on the quay. He would commence his return within hours.

I flew to Kinshasa. It faces Brazzaville where the river enlarges to form Pool Malebo. Because Pool Malebo has always been the end of navigable water, settlements sprang up on its shores.

Near Kinshasa, a sprawling city of three million, are many remnants of grandiose dreams shattered by economic realities. The town of Kinkole is one. President Mobutu founded Kinkole in 1967 as a showcase of urban and economic planning which included a fishermen's cooperative. It has fallen on bad times. Marinas, swimming pools, apartment houses exist only on a dusty display model reluctantly shown to visitors. Worse still, the spirit of the cooperative, some fishermen say, has given way to the old aggressive individualism.

Rail and road connect Kinshasa with Matadi, Zaire's major seaport. Between Kinshasa and Matadi the river is its most forbidding. Within 220 miles are the 32 rapids and cataracts collectively known as Livingstone Falls. The river winds amid green wooded mountains. It threads through rocky narrows where it flows, so to speak, on edge—fathomless. Again and again, voracious eddies create boils and crosscurrents. Stanley on this last leg of his journey had seen his party worn out and discouraged. A months-long portage made him realize that the riches of the Congo were worth hardly two shillings without a railroad to bypass the murderous rapids.

Where Stanley despaired, hope today shines bright. At Inga, the Zaire, in a 15-mile stretch, brutally drops almost 250 feet. The Zaire's most terrifying water to a white-water expert, these rapids are the stuff of dreams for hydroelectric planners. "One of nature's fairy tales," an Inga dam engineer exclaimed. The river's annual average flow is strong and dependable. And the terrain makes it possible to harness the river in stages.

Inga I and II are working, Inga III and Grand Inga exist on paper.

I visited the powerhouse of Inga II. A facade of abstract design in colored Plexiglas faces downstream. Blue symbolizes the river, red and orange the energy gleaned from its fall. Many visitors feel an almost religious awe. But critics see this cathedral of technology as a monument to a pipe dream. Surely nobody yet born will live to see the Grand Inga. And even Inga I and II yield far more energy than Zaire can absorb.

Just downstream from Matadi the river bends abruptly, creating a large whirlpool, the Devil's Cauldron. In the estuary, with mountainous constraints disappearing, the Zaire breathes freer. Low islands stud much of its final course. Swamps of mangrove line wide coastal plains. The left bank of the estuary belongs to Angola; the right to Zaire.

On both banks people share the ethnic heritage of the Kongo kingdom. This great society so awed 16th-century Portuguese seafarers that the kings of Portugal and the Kongo for a time were on "Dear Royal Brother" terms.

I drove along the river, through strung out villages, and past the cemeteries with their brightly colored tombs built in the shape of houses. Each time I asked to wander among the graves, custom demanded that I buy beer to be poured on them, for the dead to drink.

At Banana, at the river's mouth, I spent the day searching the mangroves for the *nzombo,* a lungfish the size of a man's arm. Shungu Talutena T'undu, my Kongo guide, insisted that the nzombo climbs trees. But my search had been in vain. Perhaps the river god had not wanted me to see a climbing fish this time. Disappointed, we bobbed in our small launch in the surf off Banana Point.

"This is the gate of entry," Shungu mused aloud.

"Entry?" I asked. Off Banana slave ships had waited to carry men, women, and children to the New World. Shungu had told me that his grandfather lost eight brothers and sisters to the slavers. Some of his family must have left through Banana. For sure, this was a gate of departure.

"A gate of entry," Shungu repeated. "Here the Portuguese entered, in the vanguard of white people who brought us misery and humiliation." After a pause, he added on a forgiving note, "But let us relegate history to history."

Amen, I thought. May forgetting bring forgiving.

age 75: Enya fishermen suspend traps near the Boyoma Falls.

The Tshatshi, *lashed with heavily laden barges (above), ferries between Kinshasa and Kisangani. On this 1,074-mile navigable stretch, the Zaire's longest, a crewman consults a chart (right) but must also watch out for shifting shoals. Entertainment aboard the* Ebeya *(opposite) often turns political with drumming, clapping, chanting, and dancing in praise of the "great helmsman," President Mobutu. Such sessions boost the cause of Zairian nationalism.*

Pages 78-79: "Sandy islands rose in front of us like a sea beach," reported explorer Henry Morton Stanley on reaching the lower river's 15-mile-wide expanse known as Pool Malebo.

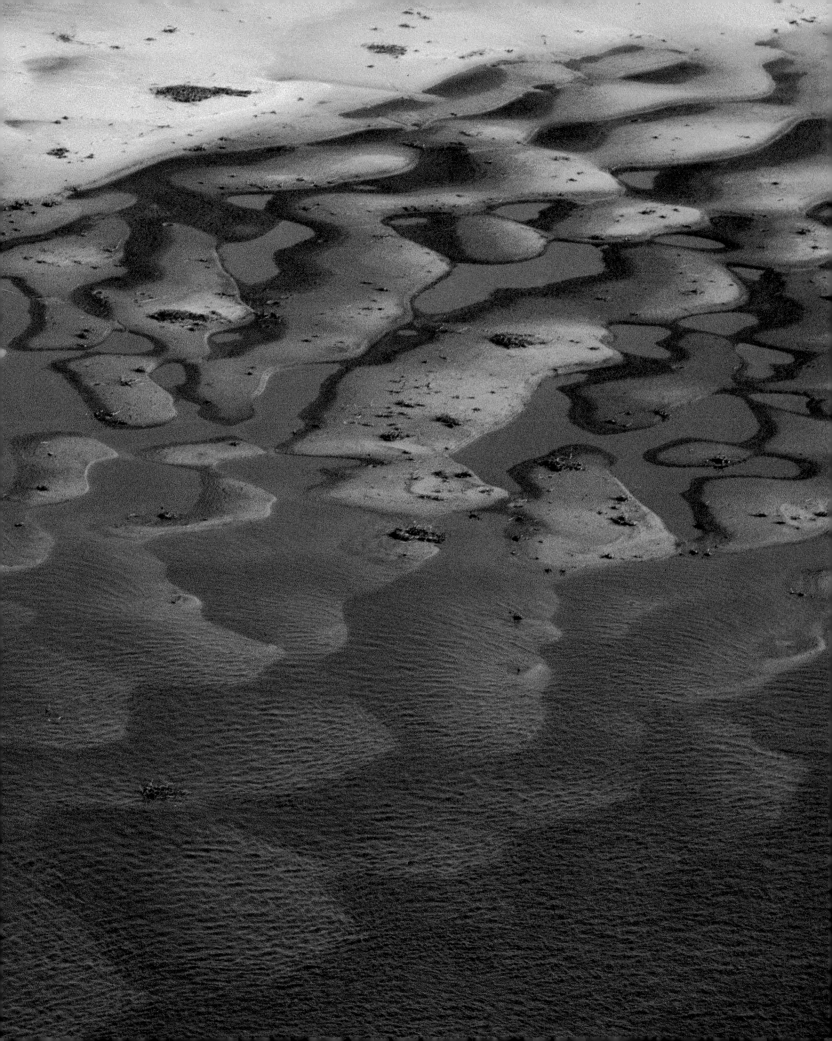

Distinctive hairstyles (right) reflect the move toward national and cultural authenticity, while Kinshasa, Zaire's gleaming capital (below), links the country to the modern world. River traffic begins and ends at this fast-growing city of three million. Between here and Matadi 220 miles downstream, cargo moves only by rail and road, for the treacherous Livingstone Falls covers most of that distance. At Inga, a particularly savage 15-mile stretch, the government has built two dams (opposite) and plans two more. If ever completed, the four dams could double Africa's current power yield and spark an African Ruhr on the lower Zaire.

A sandy spit called Banana Point (left) feels the force of the mighty Zaire as the river flows into the Atlantic Ocean at a rate of more than ten million gallons a second. Here at the mouth, only relics—rusty cannons and slave chains—remain from Banana's days as a slave market. The Republic of Zaire, in association with Japan and several European companies, plans to build an aluminum smelter in this port area as one means of using power from the Inga dams upstream.

Impenetrable swamps of red mangrove, with their aerial roots (right), line the banks of the estuary upstream to Boma. In this region live the Kongo peoples, descendants of one of Africa's most powerful civilizations, some six centuries old. In Kongo cemeteries, considered doorways between two worlds, elaborate tomb art reflects the deceased's achievements and hopes for immortality. The spirit of the mythic Kongo also permeates newer tombs made of concrete. On a tomb built in 1957 (above), both the Christian cross and traditional Kongolese symbols join images of the dead man in several stages of his life.

THE RIVERS OF EUROPE

A 14th-century toll station watches over the Rhine at Kaub, West Germany. By Christian Möller.

I n the year 885, a fleet of 700 ships brought 30,000 Danish Viking raiders up the serpentine bends of the Seine to Paris. After a 13-month siege, the raiders were bought off with 700 pounds of silver and permission to sail—and pillage—farther up the river. This was only one of many Viking invasions, chiefly along the river valleys, that France suffered during these years. "From the fury of the Northmen deliver us, O Lord," prayed the French. Finally in 911 King Charles the Simple ceded to these Nordmanni the coastal land which came to be called Normandy. From this base, 155 years later, the Normans invaded the land of the Angles and Saxons across the English Channel and put the Norman leader, William the Conqueror, on the English throne.

The rivers of Europe are not large; there is no Amazon. But their channels and banks have been the field for events that influenced or determined the course of history throughout the world.

Geographers disagree about where Europe ends and Asia begins. But, for convenience, many of them place the northeastern boundary of Europe along the Ural Mountains. From the base of these low peaks a broad plain arcs westward across the Soviet Union, Poland, northern Germany, Denmark, the Netherlands, Belgium, and France, south to the Pyrénées. Fringes of the plain reach into Britain and Scandinavia. The rivers of this North European Plain have carried cultures, or served as barriers to them, since human beings ranged the continent from the south on the heels of retreating glaciers some 15,000 years ago. River valleys and passes furrow the mountainous regions of central and southern Europe, making highways that penetrate these ramparts.

Western and central Europe's major rivers radiate from the continent's higher points to seas on the perimeter. The Rhône flows south to the Mediterranean, the Seine northwest to the English Channel, the Rhine northwest to the North Sea, the Vistula north to the Baltic Sea. No other continent has a coastline with a comparable density of river roads interweaving into the land.

Barge and bargemen rise up a watery stairstep in this 17th-century engraving of a canal lock in Italy's Po Valley.

In eastern Europe great rivers flow toward inland seas: the Volga into the Caspian Sea; the Danube, the Don, and the Dnieper into the Black Sea. The direction of their flow turned the Viking raiders and traders south and east.

Europe's most important cities flourished because trade and conquest followed the waterways, creating settlements at strategic fords and confluences. Some eight centuries before Christ, a band of shepherds and farmers halted on the eastern bank of the River Tiber. The location of their settlement became the city—Rome—that ruled the Western world for a thousand years. In Gaul, Roman colonizers found a tribe called Parisii on a fortified island in the Seine, a site so favored that it developed into the city of Paris. London was the Roman Londinium, in the year A.D. 100 a metropolis that commanded the mouth of the Thames. During the ninth and tenth centuries, Vikings from Norway sailed the rivers of Ireland, ravaging monasteries and homesteads. In 841, at the ford of the Liffey, the Northmen stockaded the site of Dublin. On the Shannon they established a small settlement which became the city of Limerick.

The horned river god Achelous is depicted in a gold Etruscan pendant crafted 26 centuries ago in Italy.

One way or another, Europeans were users of their rivers. When Charlemagne, the great eighth-century monarch of the Franks, wished to pay homage to the Caliph of Baghdad, Harun al-Rashid, he chose for a gift a cloak woven by Flemish peasants. Renowned for their beautiful colors, these soft woolen cloaks, along with Rhine wines, had long been the chief commodities of a prosperous river trade along the Schelde, the Meuse, and the Rhine, a commerce interrupted as Viking raiders began to ascend the rivers of the continent to plunder from every port their ships could reach. From the ninth century onward, Swedish Vikings plowed longships across the northern seas and down the rivers toward the magnets of Oriental markets. To the east they took amber, honey, wax, furs, and slaves. They carried homeward silver coins from Samarkand, gold and silks, spices and carpets.

By medieval times, European traders and travelers chose river routes over land passage whenever they could. In spite of tolls, boats carried heavy, bulky products such as salt far more cheaply than a donkey train could, and more safely, avoiding the robbers who infested highways.

In 15th-century Lombardy, farmers diverted streams to irrigate pastures that nourished the sheep and cows that gave milk for Gorgonzola and Parmesan cheese, products that, in those days before refrigeration, could travel as far as boats could carry them. By then, rivers and streams all over Europe had been at work for centuries, turning wheels to grind grain, crush stone, drive the blacksmith's bellows, beat cloth in fulling mills, saw wood, and accomplish scores of tasks. "The place that Nature has provided with a river or stream," observed Georgius Agricola, a 16th-century mining engineer from Saxony, "can be made serviceable for many things; for water will never be wanting and can be carried through wooden pipes to baths in dwelling-houses; it may be carried to the works, where metals are smelted; and . . . diverted into the tunnels, so that it may turn the underground machinery."

Throughout history, Europe's rivers have served as political boundaries as well as channels of conquest and commerce. The Rhine and part of the Danube once bordered the northern Roman Empire. Today the Rhine provides a boundary between France and West Germany. The Danube, now a highly international river, courses through the capital cities of Austria, Hungary, and Yugoslavia, and periodically serves as boundary for Romania, Bulgaria, Yugoslavia, Hungary, Czechoslovakia, and the Soviet Union. But Europe's riverways have been so drastically modified and interconnected with canals that the natural river paths have become much less important. Canals commonly

Ralph J. Santibanez

enhance the usability of natural channels, but others create new waterways; massive canal systems connect one river to another, in a continent-wide network of natural and artificial waterways. The construction of this complex network required the cooperation of many nations. They also work together in regulating river commerce. Barges laden with grain, coal, building materials, tractors, and computers cross the continent in every direction. So do travelers and tourists, pouring millions of dollars into national economies.

One of Europe's most popular tourist attractions is the Loire River of France. The river's source lies high in the Massif Central, a watershed called the water-tower of France because it sends rivers north, south, and west. The Loire runs through pasturelands, cascading through narrow gorges and past small villages where, for centuries, farmers have watched topsoil wash downstream to the fertile plain below. Below Nevers the Loire picks up as much as two-thirds of its volume from a major tributary, the Allier. Some 600 circuitous miles from its source, the Loire wanders to its end in the Bay of Biscay.

The Loire Valley is almost a mythical world, so well preserved in imagination and in architectural restoration that even modern cities and nuclear power plants cannot dispel it. In this valley, the early history of France spun itself out. Tours was already an important crossing by Neolithic times, and the Cher a regular route for river traders who carried the region's choice flint throughout Europe. For English or French power seekers of the Middle Ages, sites like Orléans, Blois, Tours, and Saumur all were bridged crossings (inherited from the Romans) that had to be fortified, defended over and over, and developed agriculturally and economically.

During the Hundred Years' War, beginning in 1337, battle after battle left bloodstained riverbanks. When it was over, the new king, Charles VII, and powerful noble families made their homes in the Loire Valley. Gradually the fortresses were turned to a new purpose. Architects remodeled dank castles into open, airy palaces with formal gardens, balconies, elaborate staircases. Under the patronage of the court, the arts flourished. Writers immortalized the *Val de Loire* in voices as varied as the lyricism of Pierre de Ronsard and the bawdy satire of François Rabelais.

During the Renaissance, Italian and Dutch engineers built extensive canals. In 1516 King Francis I invited the Italian genius Leonardo da Vinci to Blois to discuss building a canal to link the Loire and the Saône, the major Rhône tributary. Not until 1794, however, was this Canal du Centre realized. It became part of the first inland waterway to use the Seine and the Rhône system. In the meantime, another great engineering feat, the Canal du Midi, was completed in 1681. It connected the Atlantic and the Mediterranean.

The 16th-century château Azay-le-Rideau glows in the mirror of the River Indre in France's Loire Valley.

When the English agriculturalist Arthur Young toured France in the late 1780s he praised the canal network. But for agriculture, he gave the prize to the Po Valley in northern Italy. This river basin, a lifeline for the Etruscan civilization six centuries before Christ, then for the Celts, and then the Romans, Young called the "finest farmer's prospect in Europe." But today the fair prospect is dimming. Parts of the Po plain still produce the rice, corn, wheat, fruit, and dairy products vital to the nation, but industry and housing have taken over much of the farmland. Chronic severe flooding, worsened by the deforestation of the Po's Alpine headwaters, jeopardizes much of what remains. Almost every autumn, floodwaters rush down to the Adriatic Sea, carrying silt that piles up on the riverbed and builds an ever changing delta. Over the ages, the advancing delta has created lagoons on the coast and made cities such as Venice both lovely and vulnerable.

Other rivers throughout Europe have also been drastically changed by industrial development and the needs of a modern population. In Rome citizen concern arose in 1979 when a man died after swimming in the waste-polluted, rat-infested Tiber. When the building of a sixth dam proved disastrous for the Dnieper River, Soviet scientists pledged "to do everything possible to preserve the flow, purity and beauty" of the river.

The Rhine supplies drinking water to some 20 million Europeans. It is also Europe's most heavily trafficked and one of its most polluted rivers. With two-thirds of West Germany's chemical industries located along the Rhine and its tributaries, the water became "a smelly, turbid brew." Now authorities from France, Luxembourg, the Netherlands, Switzerland, and West Germany have banded together to clean up the overworked river.

In London, when the Thames froze over, it was time for the frost fair. As English scholar John Evelyn described the festivities of January 1684, the ice was "planted" with booths and shops; there were races, bowling, tippling, and more, "so as it seem'd to be a bacchanalia." Later that year, on the water, a fireworks pageant "as had not ben seene in any age" celebrated the Queen's birthday. In Evelyn's time, Europeans lived intimately with their rivers. No less do they today, with a new vigilance.

At a spring in France, first-century Celts placed this oaken image (left) for the goddess Sequana. From her spring flowed the River Sequana, the modern Seine.

Landmarks of Paris—the arching Pont St. Michel and twin-towered Notre Dame—look down on the Seine in Honoré Daumier's 19th-century painting.

THE DANUBE

THE MARCH OF EMPIRES

By Ross S. Bennett / Photographs by Adam Woolfitt

The tall young Hungarian guide at my side pointed across the Danube at the smoky industrial town of Štúrovo on the Czechoslovakian shore. "Most of the citizens there are Hungarian," he said somewhat dutifully. My wife, Vera, and I were standing at the parapet of a medieval fortress on Castle Hill in Esztergom, Hungary, a place revered by history-minded Hungarians. Here their first king had been crowned a thousand years before. But I was more intrigued by an old bridge, the only one in sight, just upriver. The central spans were missing and two naked stone piers curled the water in midstream. What a pain, I mused, for the people of these two towns. A recent accident, perhaps? No. Nazi troops had blown the bridge on their retreat to oblivion in the waning days of World War II. Forty years! A long wait for repairs.

I later learned that plans are in the works to rebuild the bridge, but for the time being those stone piers struck me as symbols of shattered dreams of conquest. The bridge had been built at the turn of the century during the twilight of yet another power, the Austro-Hungarian Empire. As I stood there above the Danube I imagined the march of many empires—down the river came the Christian armies of Charlemagne and then the Habsburgs, up the river came the soldiers of Allah, the Ottoman Turks, all of them stirring the ghostly remains of the earliest empire, Rome. For the Romans this frontier river held back barbarian hordes to the north.

For most of its 1,760-mile journey across south-central Europe, the Danube flows as graceful and dignified as a waltz. It dances out of the Black Forest in West Germany, across the Bavarian Plateau, and down the Great Hungarian Plain. In Yugoslavia it heads east for the Iron Gate Gorge, reaching depths of 177 feet and hitting 11 miles per hour, then rushes through a massive hydroelectric dam wedged between the mountains. Crossing the broad Danubian Plain, it forms the border between Bulgaria and Romania, meets the Dobruja Plateau and runs north to Galaţi. There it turns right and, entering a broad reedy marshland, reaches for the Black Sea with three great arms.

Austria's Aggstein Castle, fortress-lair of medieval robber barons, overshadows the Wachau Valley of the Danube River—central Europe's oldest avenue of commerce and conquest.

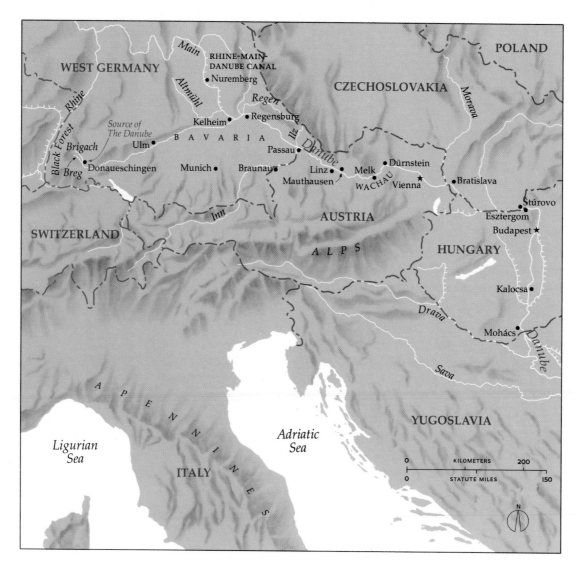

Though the Danube links East with West and ties eight countries together, historically, as I was reminded at Esztergom, it has ruptured old cultures. After the Roman frontier crumbled in the fifth century, Huns, Avars, and Mongols came and went. Franks, Slavs, and Magyars came and stayed—and tried to sort themselves into nations. I came to see how they lived, these old people of the river who showed the world how to build cities like Vienna, Budapest, and Belgrade and also how to wreck them in wars—the same people who added energy and strength to the melting pot of America.

Our first stop was Donaueschingen, a hilly little Black Forest town below which two streams, the Breg and Brigach, unite to form the Danube. Parking my car in the tiny *Platz*, I asked noonday diners at a sidewalk café the location

of a spring that is unofficially honored as the river's source. Down the winding street, behind a church, among some trees beside a palace I found the richly ornamented Donauquelle, a clear shallow pool spangled with the votive coins of modern pilgrims.

Salt springs made Donaueschingen a place of resort—Marie Antoinette slept here—and the seat of the Fürstenbergs, one of those durable families that provided the muscle for the Habsburgs and probably for the Holy Roman Empire. Rudolf, the first Habsburg to ascend the imperial throne, granted the Fürstenbergs a license to make beer in 1283, and the liquid gold still streams out of a bright modern brewery. One old custom has died. To announce a noble birth to the peasants, a salute was fired, 105 times for a prince, 15 for a princess.

We felt compelled to tour the Fürstenberg's baroque palace. Later we discovered that it typified the palaces—and the cathedrals and monasteries—along the Danube. It is really a museum, a treasure house of priceless art. The library preserves an original codex of the *Nibelungenlied,* Germany's early 13th-century folk saga, by an unknown author, of treachery and murder among courtly ladies and impassioned knights.

From Donaueschingen we headed for Ulm. The two-lane road keeps to the river, which flows gently through fields of grain and corn and potatoes. On this July day solitary women, their heads tied with scarves against the sun, bend to the harvest, scything wheat near a horse-drawn wagon. Acres of hops grow in thickets that break up the mosaic of fields, the hop vines twining up strings attached to 20-foot poles cut from conifers that put the black in the Black Forest.

At Ulm, first mentioned in chronicles dated 854, trade routes intersected the river at the point where it deepened enough to take 100-ton cargo boats, and by the 14th century the town had become an important commercial center. The town burghers grew so wealthy they financed the construction of their great cathedral without help from the imperial coffers. It's still the tallest cathedral in the world—528 feet to the top of its main steeple.

For us, just getting to the *Dom,* as Germans commonly call cathedrals, was not easy. Searching for a parking space in narrow streets crowded with fashionably dressed shoppers and white-aproned tradesmen. Sidestepping streams of small cars and cabs. Weaving through the open-air market, with its ranks of wooden stands sagging under mounds of fruits and vegetables. Finally reaching the door, we puffed up the spiral stone stairway, each of the 768 steps cupped by the tread of millions of feet, up past the gargoyles and the bell platform to where the colorful canopies of the market stalls in the square below diminished into tiny patches.

T he day was clear, and watching the river meander off to the northeast out of town I conjured up armies hurrying toward collision about 50 miles away near the village of Blenheim in one of the most decisive battles in military history. There in 1704 an allied army under Englishman John Churchill and Austrian general Eugene, Prince of Savoy, routed the forces of France's Louis XIV which were en route to attack the Habsburg capital of Vienna. The French bid for mastery over Europe would not be repeated until a century later, when Napoleon defeated the Austrians and in 1806 abolished the Holy Roman Empire.

Charlemagne, the Frankish king who laid the groundwork for the Empire in A.D. 800 in an attempt to unite Europe, had an earlier idea—a canal that would link the Rhine and the Danube. In 793 he set 5,000 men to digging a Fossa Carolinga. Only a ditch remains, at Graben, south of Nuremberg. In 1837 Bavarian King Ludwig I began a 100-mile canal connecting a headwater of the Main with the lower Altmühl River, which enters the Danube at Kelheim. It took ten years to complete, then was made obsolete by the coming of the railroad.

The latest attempt at a Rhine-Main-Danube Canal, begun in 1966 and near completion, will short-cut shipping from the Black to the North Sea by more than 2,000 miles.

Northeast of Kelheim, the Regen River joins the Danube at Regensburg, a Celtic settlement enlarged by Emperor Marcus Aurelius in A.D. 179 and named Castra Regina. The tributary deepens the Danube for heavier barge traffic, and the flags of Soviet Bloc countries flutter on many a long, flat boat. Drying clothes wave on lines strung from the cabin aft. A small flower garden brightens the drab deck. A bicycle for ready transportation leans against the rail.

Now the current turns east and snakes toward Passau, where the broad blue Inn from the south enters the narrower gray Danube. From here Soviet cruise ships set out on week-long trips to the Black Sea, a luxurious experience recommended by all, but we kept to the road. Swinging down past tidy farms beside the Inn, we crossed into Austria at Hitler's hometown of Braunau and rejoined the Danube at the haze-hung industrial city of Linz. I wanted a look at what Hitler had wrought at Mauthausen, a concentration camp just down the river.

For the drive to Mauthausen our guide, Helmuth, took the wheel after somehow folding his skinny six-foot-six-inch frame into my small car. A journalist who had studied political science at Linz's Johannes Kepler University, he typified all the guides we were to meet—pleasant, forebearing, encyclopedic. I sensed a measure of obligation on his part as he pointed out the workers' apartments built during the days of the Third Reich, mostly gray and almost barrack-like. They set the mood.

Mauthausen is a monument to despair. A stone-walled compound with a capacity of 114,000, the labor camp began its grisly work in 1938. Before U. S. Army tanks rolled up in May 1945, 200,000 men, women, and children from a score of countries had entered, half of them never to leave. Though not officially a death camp, it dispatched its share of victims in a small gas chamber or in a special closet with a shot in the back of the neck. Prisoners mined rock from the nearby quarry and built the walls of their own prison. Walking down the treacherous 186 "death steps" to the quarry, I felt helpless rage.

A common reaction, but not always helpless. Weeks later in Yugoslavia our guide Marina told us she had once accompanied 16 busloads of survivors and relatives from Belgrade to Mauthausen for the annual memorial day. As the people assembled inside the gate, an official mounted a platform to greet them—and was shouted down in a chorus of protest at the sound of German.

Downstream from Linz the Danube breaks free of close confines, passes Melk and its imposing baroque monastery, and draws the unsuspecting traveler into 25 miles of enchantment—the Wachau Valley. Probably the most unrelentingly picturesque of all the beautiful stretches on the river, the Wachau is a realm of castle-crowned crags and vineyards terracing down slopes to tidy villages pinned in place by stately churches.

One midday we searched out Willendorf, home of the Venus of Willendorf. She's a famous sandstone figurine, a 20,000-year-old fertility goddess. I drove up the village's narrow main street—about the width of a New York City alley—between two-story stucco houses neatly painted in pastels. Suddenly lost in a maze of side lanes seemingly devoid of people, we were abruptly rescued by an aging man, lean and lively, wearing a lopsided grin, velvet knee britches, an alpine hat at a jaunty angle, and a small leather holster on his belt that held an emery stone. Karl Kappelmuller, retired woodworker, now a self-appointed one-man chamber of commerce, insisted on taking us on a tour of the village. He hobbled a bit, like Walter Brennan, and talked like him too, except in German. Eventually he steered us to the spot where the four-inch Venus was discovered in 1908, just above the village along the railroad tracks. A six-foot replica of the naked, pot-bellied, balloon-breasted goddess with no face stands on a concrete block. From a patch of weeds and grass she gazes out over the river and its gently curving course down the mile-wide valley. Herr Kappelmuller animatedly demonstrated that it was his job to keep this memorial to the Stone Age culture of the upper Danube neatly trimmed; he used the emery stone to sharpen his sickle.

"East of Vienna, the Orient begins," someone once said. Today the imperial city of the Habsburgs still bears the scars of close encounters with Eastern ambition. Our guide Angela, a young matron who this day dressed in a red-and-white dirndl, pointed out a Turkish cannonball embedded in the wall of the House of the Golden Dragon as we drank Turkish coffee and saw Saracen crescents in our croissants. "The cannonballs are all over Vienna," Angela said.

After crushing the Byzantine Empire at Constantinople in 1453, the Turks marched up the Danube and besieged Vienna first in 1529, again in 1683. For two months the walls held, while imperial forces gathered strength and then routed the enemy. The Turkish tide would slowly ebb, until by the end of World War I the Ottoman Empire had virtually disappeared.

Vienna's Ringstrasse, a circling boulevard of chic shops and expensive car showrooms, follows the line of those famous walls, pulled down in the 1850s to let the city expand and become the "Paris of the Danube." Angela pointed out her city's incredible diversity with such verve that her accent often slipped into full German. Glittering music halls, a giant Ferris wheel, a palace that houses a school for horses that do the four-step to Beethoven and Schubert. In St. Stephen's Platz, she ran her hand over an outside wall of the cathedral where a line and a circle, scored in the stone, served as a medieval bureau of standards: "If shoppers in the marketplace had a dispute about the size of the cloth or the bread they had just bought, they measured the item against these marks and a magistrate gave judgment on the spot."

Sitting on the edge of the platz, eating a Sacher torte in a konditorei—a traditional coffeehouse serving the drink introduced by the Turks—built over the remains of a Roman settlement named Vindobona, and watching such a civilized and happy people stroll up and down the fashionable Kärntnerstrasse, I mused on one more irony: While Habsburg royalty now are all ordinary citizens of Austria, the dead of this colorful dynasty still reign in the city, where one old church contains Habsburg bodies while another preserves their hearts, and where, in the 18th century, Empress Maria Theresa rattled around in a summer palace of 1,440 rooms in the course of birthing 16 children.

One morning we drove downriver with Dr. Heinrich Eder, a doctor of history, graduate of the University of Vienna, and explored the stony ruins of Carnuntum, capital of Rome's Pannonia Province. In the distance, opposite the mouth of the Morava River, rose the Braunsberg, a popular lookout hill. We went to look. At its base lay the village of Hainburg.

"In 1683," said Dr. Eder, "when the Turks devastated the region, they slaughtered the 8,000 inhabitants of Hainburg. But six men hid in a chimney and survived. One was a grandfather of Joseph Haydn." Haydn, 18th-century master of the symphony, composed the melody that became Austria's national anthem. So appealing was it that the Germans borrowed it and burdened it with the message, *"Deutschland, Deutschland über Alles."*

T he Morava, which flows from the north, separates Austria from Czechoslovakia and changes the Danube's political color from democratic blue to Communist red. Barbed wire fencing and gray guard towers stalk the Czech shoreline, startling otherwise carefree tourists on the hydrofoil run to Bratislava, 35 miles east of Vienna. A great square castle rebuilt by the Hungarians in the 1430s announces the city on the left, but by now I was more interested in the city's new stainless steel bridge, the only single span bridge on the Danube.

A funny old Czech guide who refused to smile greeted our small group. "I speak German, French, and American, but not English," he said, adding in a confidential tone, "It was your President Wilson, you know, who helped create our country in 1918." On the bus tour through the city up to the marble shaft commemorating 8,000 Soviet soldiers who died liberating the region from the Nazis, he pointed at the *Pravda* office and said, "That's the most important newspaper in town." We all smiled. But I could tell he was righteously proud of the satellite city going up across the river. Some 5,000 flats are added each year to these high-rise apartments. By the end of the decade they will house 80,000 workers for the area's chemical and textile factories.

Bratislava is the capital of Slovakia. Since the end of World War I the province has been politically united with Bohemia and Moravia to form Czechoslovakia. But Slovakia is more culturally connected to Hungary, whose princes dominated the region for centuries. From 1541 to 1784, with the Turks holding Hungary most of that time, Bratislava served as the Magyar capital.

The Magyars were the last of the tribes to arrive at the Danube. Nomads from the east speaking a non-Slavic tongue, they reached the Hungarian Plain in 896, liked the water and the soil, and established a base on Czepel Island, now the southside industrial section of Budapest. The Magyars never lost their identity even under the Habsburgs, who joined them in the Dual Monarchy of the Austro-Hungarian Empire in 1867.

East of Esztergom the river turns sharply south at the scenic Danube Bend, heading past the town of Szentendre, just above Budapest. The artist colony at Szentendre, a warren of house galleries scattered among steep, narrow lanes and stone stairways that lace an old Serbian settlement, draws thousands of visitors. My favorite collection was the 312 pieces by Margit Kovács, sculptor in potter's clay who died in 1977 at the age of 75. Her art captures the spirit of a people in the most poignant and heartwarming way. Dr. Imre Mailáth, curator of galleries, spoke almost reverently of this artist. "Everyone loves her work," said the white-haired 79-year-old former jurist as he guided us through the gallery rooms of an old house. "Her range of interests had no limits. She was—is—very popular with the people." Vases, dishes, reliefs, murals, figures run the spectrum of human condition and emotion. In "Woe!" a seated woman bent over in abject despair, her head and arms hanging limp between her spread legs, the tips of her fingers almost touching the floor, seems to plumb the depths of Hungary's struggles down the centuries, including the revolution that failed against Soviet domination in 1956.

Eight bridges connect the flat modern business district of Pest, with its lacy, domed parliament building, to the history-encrusted hills of old Buda—even the ultramodern Hilton Hotel is built around the stone ruins of a medieval monastery. Invading Mongols devastated the area in 1241 and killed half of King Bela IV's two million Hungarians. After the Mongols left a year later, the king built at Buda a castle now being restored as the Royal Palace museum.

Far south of Budapest, in a village near the Yugoslavian border, white-haired Janos Sardi welcomed us into his household compound and demonstrated a dying craft—*kékfestő*. He was in his work clothes—blue bib overalls with no shirt. Long ago he had converted his barn into small rooms with vats and drying racks and rollers. He demonstrated how he dyes cloth blue after pressing in various designs with copper pins stuck in wood blocks and dipped in acids that won't take the dye. His handkerchiefs, tablecloths, scarves, and wall hangings are all a rich blue. Now in his 50s, he complained that there was no one to carry on his art. "There are only nine of us in Hungary," he said. "None of the youngsters seem to show any interest in this sort of work anymore."

Mr. Sardi told us the craft originated in Germany. So did many of the ethnic enclaves in this part of Europe. After the Turks laid waste the land at the close of the 17th century, the Habsburgs sent German colonists from the crowded west to the lower Danube. In the volatile late 1930s, Nazi agitators stirred up nationalist sentiments among the ethnic German settlers in what were then newly independent Balkan states, creating deep resentment among the Germans' Slavic and Magyar hosts. When Nazi troops retreated from these regions late in World War II after years of brutal occupation, whole villages of ethnic Germans in Hungary, Czechoslovakia, Yugoslavia, and Romania fled or were driven westward to homes their ancestors had departed centuries earlier.

The southbound Danube enters Yugoslavia and captures one of the largest of its 300 tributaries, the Sava, at Belgrade. Though the site has a history that goes back 7,000 years, no house now standing is more than 150 years old. War has devastated the city about 60 times. Devastating for me was the printed word— it came in multiple languages and both Roman and Cyrillic alphabets, the latter used by the Serbs, whose kings once ruled here. Our guide Marina did not have to remind me that it was a Serbian youth, intent upon uniting all the South Slavs, who shot the Habsburg's Archduke Ferdinand in 1914 and set off World War I, a conflict that doomed the Austro-Hungarian Empire.

ast of Belgrade the river grinds through the Iron Gate Gorge; until a dam was completed in 1972 with locks on either side, this was the most treacherous and difficult passage on the Danube. Farther along, the river breaks its rocky shackles and becomes the Bulgarian border near the port town of Vidin, a place bustling with urban development. We inspected one of the largest businesses, the Vida shirt factory. The manager, 12 years in his position, showed off the plant's self-sufficiency: gardens and hothouses to supply the cafeteria; courts for tennis, basketball, and volleyball; a youth club and recreation rooms; an infirmary with free medical care; discounts on produce and shirts. Workers could even have the kitchen rustle up supper at half price to take home in a box at night—a good way to use up leftovers.

On the half-day ride by car from Sofia over the Balkan Mountains our guide, Donka, had rattled off Bulgarian history, recounting the centuries-long struggle to shed the Turkish yoke. I noted that she never mentioned Soviet Communism. "It was the *Russians* who drove the Turks from our land in the great War of Liberation in 1878," she said, "and we are grateful."

Donka took us to Novo Selo—"new town"—just north of Vidin, where we met the ruddy-faced young "mayor." At the town vineyards, irrigated by Danube water, Penko of the tractor brigade was cultivating rows of grapevines. "Penko was an orphan," Donka explained as the curly-haired youth climbed down from his tractor and shyly shifted from foot to foot. "The mayor took him under his wing and taught him how to drive a tractor. Penko is doing well. He has a family and earns 400 leva a month," twice as much as a mechanic.

Back in town our entourage (it had grown by four more officials) filed through an arbor and invaded the home of Nely, an apple-cheeked mother of two, for glasses of wine and grape brandy. Nely, a bookkeeper at the winery, disappeared into a bedroom and returned holding up an intricately embroidered red-and-white tablecloth. "Young girls make many of these for their hope chests, and when they marry they hang them out on a long string," Donka said. "When the couple has a boy child, the father begins making wine and buries 400 bottles in the dirt in the cellar. When the boy marries, the wine is dug up for the wedding party." I asked Nely if fathers didn't sneak out a bottle or two ahead of time—20 or 25 years is a tempting wait. Nely smiled while Donka translated, "Maybe that's why they bury the bottles deep."

Armed with gift bottles of Bulgarian wine, we sped eastward, dodging horse-drawn wagons loaded with Gypsies, trucks carrying harvested hay, groups of women road workers shouldering shovels like rifles. At the port city of Ruse I prowled the deserted waterfront early one morning and spotted a lone fisherman—a gray-haired old man in rumpled pants and long-sleeved plaid shirt—casting his net from a small boat a few yards from shore. I hunkered down well back on the bank between two bushes to wait and watch, camera in hand. He stood with his back to me and threw the net with a sweeping sidearm motion. When he drew it in, the net came up empty. He cast again and again, keeping his balance like a tightrope walker.

The sun rose like an orange balloon and burned off the mist obscuring the wooded Romanian shore across the river. A towboat came and went, pushing a string of barges loaded with logs. Ripples from the wake rocked the boat, but the fisherman never wavered.

My legs were beginning to feel numb when he finally scored. He hauled in a solitary fish, about a foot long. Carefully he extracted it from the net, then slowly turned toward me and held it up by the tail in the time-honored manner. I could just make out the smile on his face as I clicked off a couple of shots. With a wave of my hand, I walked away, amused that he had known I was there.

Upriver in the Ruse dockyard I found towboat captain Vasil Borissov. He was a tanned, bald, robust 45, nattily dressed in leisure clothes with his boat's manifest papers in hand. The Danube was in his blood—he was the son of a Danube captain and himself father of a sailor. A proud native of Ruse, he said the city had one of the best shipyards on the river, equal to any in Austria. "My ship was built here. It's 13 years old." Typical of the towboats that ply the river, it carries a crew of nine and cranks up 1,500 horsepower that can push a raft of barges with 58 cars and fully loaded trucks.

"We work in brigades," he explained, "eight or ten to a brigade. Two weeks on the river, then another brigade takes over and we're off for two weeks. My ship is the *Nikola Yanko Vasala*. It's named for a Bulgarian poet, a revolutionary killed fighting the Fascists in 1942."

Leaving Ruse, we crossed the Friendship Bridge into the southern Romanian district of Walachia, where broad fields of grain and corn are stabbed by the nodding noses of oil-well donkey engines. Here on this plain Vlad Tepes, a 15th-century prince, battled the Turks. Once he cut off the noses of 20,000 captives and sent them back to the sultan.

Vlad was a man of his times and not much worse than other noblemen, I was repeatedly told, but he suffered from poor public relations—even before novelist Bram Stoker turned him into the vampire Dracula. He devised a unique poverty program: Inviting all the poor to a big dinner in a makeshift building, he burned it to the ground. When the town of Braşov in Transylvania refused to pay him tribute he impaled 14 of the town councilmen on a nearby hill.

R omania's real vampires are not Transylvanian bats but the mosquitoes of the Danube Delta. They attack in battalion force—but only in the dead of night. Fishing villages dot the vast reed-choked delta that splays out from Tulcea. So we rented a speedboat, with a skipper, to delve its mysteries. Every morning leathery-faced men row out in black wooden boats to their fish weirs, empty the traps into their boats, cover the fish with reeds to protect them from the sun, and pole their catches to places like the Caraorman fish station near the Sulina Channel, the middle arm of the Danube that reaches for the sea.

We tied up at the dock as a few fishermen rowed in and sorted their catch into wicker baskets on the wharf. Inside the thatch-roofed building the workers iced and salted the eight species of fish for an hour, then poured them into round plastic jugs bound for Tulcea and export up the Danube.

Later that day we raced past huge freighters and dredging barges to the busy little port of Sulina. A hundred years ago its lighthouse stood at the channel mouth. Now the lighthouse is a few miles back from the sea, left behind by land-building silt.

Our skipper wouldn't take us beyond the lighthouse—we didn't have the right papers—but he agreed to put us ashore for a visit. From the town dock we walked down dusty back streets to the Black Sea, past a strange complex of cemeteries—English, Jewish, Eastern Orthodox. In the distance "No photographs" signs warned us away from radar dishes.

Young laughter rippled through the air. Hundreds of school kids on holiday overtook us and went trooping across the wide, sandy littoral toward the surf. I fell in behind one boy wearing Adidas, black shorts, and a white T-shirt. The printing on the back read J. R. EWING. DALLAS. Now there's an empire.

The legendary Danube loops among the limestone hills of southern Germany near the river's source in the Black Forest. Europe's second longest river (after the Volga) wanders 1,760 miles, bordering or passing through eight countries on its way to the Black Sea—a *Schicksalsfluss, a river of destiny.*

Stone Age hunters roamed the Danube's wooded banks more than 20,000 years ago. Farmers and herders from Asia Minor, migrating through the Balkans, settled its fertile plains and valleys around 8000 B.C.—and introduced to Europe wheat, barley, sheep, goats, and cattle.

Metalsmiths, brewers, and salt traders set up a thriving commerce with the Mediterranean region along the length of the Danube and many of its 300 tributaries. Ancient Greeks knew the lower Danube as the Ister. The Romans called it Danubius, after a river god, and wrested an empire from the Celts and restless Teutonic tribes that lived in the area.

As barrier and battleground, the Danube hosted the legions of Trajan and Marcus Aurelius, Julius Caesar and Attila the Hun, Charlemagne and Suleiman the Magnificent. Its castles, cloisters, and crumbling ruins make it a setting fit for elves, sprites, gods, and heroes—the fateful route of the Nibelung warriors who journeyed to destruction at the court of King Etzel, as recounted in the German epic saga of the Nibelungenlied.

P ast gabled roofs, half-timbered houses, and sprightly blossoms, the Blau River purls through an old section of Ulm enroute to a rendezvous with the Danube. A key trading center since the 14th century, the walled city lies at the head of navigation on the Danube. Its cathedral (above), a bastion of Protestantism since the Reformation, claims the world's highest spire—528 feet. Outside the cathedral (left) vendors display their wares on the Platz, square, just as they have since medieval times when a town's cathedral served also as a focus of trade and commerce.

ommerce smudges the skies and crowds the docks at Linz, one of Austria's leading industrial cities. Belching stacks of a giant petrochemical complex, Chemie-Linz AG (opposite), attest to a continuing demand for the plant's output, chiefly fertilizers but also pharmaceuticals and pesticides. Other factories turn out iron and steel, heavy machinery, and textiles—some six million tons of goods are shipped on the Danube each year.

At the warehouse district (above), large diesel tugs from Eastern bloc nations nest together in self-imposed isolation to discourage crew defections. Here they wait for barges like the one being loaded by an Austrian dockworker (left). While moored, their crews do "chores such as washing and repainting," notes the photographer, "and hide from the camera when possible."

M elk Abbey crowns a wooded promontory above the Danube. A soaring expression of baroque art and architecture, the massive structure has been a Benedictine monastery since 1089. Because the abbey stands on a site once occupied by a castle of Austria's first ruling dynasty, the Babenbergs, it has been called the cradle of Austria. Rebuilt in the 1700s as we see it today, the monastery's vineyards and its labyrinthine cellars a century later supplied Napoleon's troops with 6,000 gallons of wine a day.

The ornate library (right), a trove of more than 85,000 books and manuscripts, included a Gutenberg Bible, which was sold in the 1920s to raise funds for renovation of the abbey.

Pages 116-117: Joseph J. Scherschel, National Geographic Photographer

B irthplace of the waltz, the Wiener schnitzel and the Sacher torte, Vienna still conjures the glorious days of empire when it reigned as music capital of the world. Couples at the Concordia Ball (opposite), held annually at the Rathaus, or town hall, twirl to lilting melodies composed by three generations of the Strauss family and a host of other musicians.

Mouth-watering confections including chocolate rolls and wedge-shaped tortes garland one of Vienna's many pastry shops, while a river nymph (left) lends romantic luster to Schönbrunn Palace, a summer retreat of the Habsburg emperors.

Pages 116-117: Budapest's 860-room Royal Palace, converted to a museum and culture center since ongoing restoration after World War II, blazons the night above the Danube.

115

S hedding clothes and woes, bathers relax in a Turkish bath—one of several fed by mineral hot springs that have won renown for Budapest as a city of soothing waters. Here, at the Király Fürdö, *King's Baths,* a vaulted dome built by Turkish conquerors four centuries ago shelters those who seek relaxation or relief from aches and pains.

Youthful marchers in Budapest (above) carry the red flags of communism—a new kind of empire—at a May Day rally in honor of the international labor movement. The annual event is marked by parades, speeches, and concerts in most communist nations.

The nimble fingers of a skilled embroiderer at the Folk Art Cooperative in Kalocsa keep alive decorative traditions passed from mother to daughter.

T he Danube separates Yugoslavia (at left) and Romania as it shoulders through the Iron Gate, a gorge in the Transylvanian Alps once notorious for seething rapids and whirlpools. A dam completed downstream in 1972 now floods the gorge, making it safe for river traffic.

Scowling image of Suleiman the Magnificent—carved in oak and strung with severed heads—commemorates the crushing defeat of Hungary by the Turks at the Battle of Mohács in 1526; 25,000 Hungarian soldiers died in one afternoon. A legacy of the slaughter lives on in a gibe used to squelch complainers: "More were lost at Mohács."

Pages 122-123: A shepherdess leads her flock of sheep and a goat along a rivulet on the Danube Plain, the heart of Bulgaria's fertile agricultural region.

The rolling hills and fertile, well-watered plains that mark the Danube's course as it approaches the Black Sea make large areas of Romania and Bulgaria prolific producers of grains, fruits, and vegetables. Windblown, loamy soil, much originally from the Transylvanian Alps, formed thick deposits later enriched by organic matter from great forests that once grew here.

Rippling cornfields near Lom produce a major Bulgarian crop. Both countries also profit from the industry of a tireless field hand, the honeybee (left).

In Romania, workers at a farm cooperative near Călăraşi (opposite) ready ripe plums for shipment. Many are destined for export; others will make ţuica—a plum brandy that serves as the national drink.

T he Danube Delta, a watery labyrinth the size of Delaware, ranks
as one of Europe's chief wildlife
breeding areas. Its myriad lakes,
lagoons, forests, and floating
reed islands shelter some 300
bird species, including the purple
heron (above). Five major fly-
ways converge here, bringing
migrant birds in spring and fall
from the farthest reaches of Europe, Asia, and Africa. Wild
boars prowl the shadowy forests
and thickets; so do wolves and
smaller mammals such as mink,
otter, and ermine.

More than 100 fish species—
including the catfish landed by
these fishermen—spawn in the
brackish waters of the delta.
Sturgeon lay their eggs here,
producing some of the world's
finest, most expensive caviar.

isty dawn greets the Danube as the river nears the end of its journey to the Black Sea. These men fish near the Sulina Channel, the shortest and straightest of the three major waterways that fan out to form the 1,700-square-mile delta—a wild, hauntingly mysterious land.

Constant dredging keeps the Sulina Channel open, for as the river slows to meet the sea, it drops its burden of sediment—up to 3,000 cubic feet of soil a minute. Each year the delta in some places pushes seaward as much as 250 feet, marooning far inland lighthouses built at the ocean's edge during the last century. When Ottoman Turks held sway over the area they kept the channel clear by dragging sunken vessels along the bottom.

Ancient historians, including Herodotus, Polybius, and Strabo, described the delta—then far smaller than it is today. King Darius I of Persia journeyed through the region; so did Philip II of Macedonia and Alexander the Great. The Roman poet Ovid spent years of exile nearby. And, outside the old town of Babadag, near Tulcea, local residents proudly point out an iron ring set in rock. Here, tradition says, Jason and the Argonauts moored their vessel while searching for the golden fleece.

THE VOLGA

A HERO RIVER FLOWS

By Margaret Sedeen / Photographs by Cary Wolinsky

In the oldest city on the longest river in Europe stretches a point of land known as the *strelka*—the arrow—honed by the meeting of the Volga and its tributary, the Kotorosl'. On this headland of ancient Yaroslavl', I stood one October day in the belfry of a 12th-century monastery. Below me was a beach with a park where a shabby Aeroflot plane had made its last stop, to live out its days as a children's theater. The gilded domes of the monastery cathedral licked at the sky like the tongues of holy fire their creators imagined them to be.

I was at the end of my journey on a river that Russians call *Matushka*, little mother. It is the heart and soul of their nation. And at every place I had visited, I found the same uneasy but natural yoking of Russian past and Soviet present that I saw here in Aeroflot plane and onion dome. In those two images, ages of history and geography coalesced.

A fierce wind swept the beach, where summer had abandoned rows of faded pastel umbrellas. A spitting snow lashed my face. The Volga flowed swiftly, and the Kotorosl', past the water gate where monks and merchants used to call at the monastery. I knew that soon the rivers would freeze three feet thick and, until April, people would tramp across the ice from one part of town to another, and great trucks would make it a highway.

The strelka has been home to human beings for almost 2,000 years. Legends say that a bear-worshiping tribe inhabited the thick forests there early in the 11th century, when Yaroslav' the Wise, prince of Rus', vanquished them and built a wooden fortress—a kremlin—on the high right bank of the Volga, opposite the flatland of the left bank stretching away to the east. This strategic use of the prominent shore would be imitated in the founding of many cities along the river. Thus does geology make politics.

By the middle of the 13th century, the Tatar hordes of Genghis and Batu Khan had swooped down on the Volga, then finally subdued all Russia. By 1557 the khans had fallen to Tsar Ivan the Terrible, who captured their river strongholds as far south as Astrakhan', gaining control of the entire Volga.

Pathway to five seas, the Volga runs past the busy port of Volgograd. One of every four Soviet citizens lives on the Volga or a tributary.

No part of the 2,290-mile-long main channel today resembles the Volga that khans and tsars coveted. By the time it reaches Yaroslavl' it has worked its way through three of the twelve hydroelectric stations that make up the Volga-Kama Cascade, as Soviet hydromaniacs prettily term the dams and enormous reservoirs. From its source spring in the Valdai Hills, the Volga trickles through an area of woods and lakes once glaciated like northern Minnesota, broadening until it receives its two greatest tributaries, the Oka, at Gor'kiy, and the Kama, near Kazan'. Below the scenic Zhiguli Hills the landscape changes to bare, almost treeless steppe, bright and green in the brief spring, scorched bone dry by midsummer.

As the Volga runs south through its floodplain, it breaks into looping, interconnected channels separated by low islands. At the 3,850-square-mile delta is a world-famous wildlife preserve, one of several regions of the Soviet Union now closed to foreigners.

In Yaroslavl' I was to attend the Sunday service at the Church of the Fyodorovskaya Virgin. Father Georgi greeted me at the altar steps. He was tall, a hale, barrel-chested man with a gray beard. On a chain around his neck he wore a crucifix that snagged at the lace on his green and gold brocade vestments.

The faces of the throng gathered in the 300-year-old church made a tapestry of old Russia, beautiful and intricate. Some were wrinkled and coarse, some luminous and fine featured. Most were old women, scarved-head babushkas, whose eyes had seen revolution, war, famine. A few young parents had brought their children to be blessed by the priests. Opposite me, on the far side of the altar, a fine choir sang a capella. In a small chapel just behind me, the bodies of three old women lay in open coffins as mourners listened to a priest intone prayers for the dead. On the altar, as acolytes and priests in gilded robes chanted the liturgy in old Church Slavonic and swung burning censers, a crew of old women in continual motion tended the tiers of slender brown candles in half a dozen tall candelabras.

Later, at dinner at Father Georgi's, I asked the size of his congregation. "We don't count them," he replied, affirming the official policy. In all things, the Russian Orthodox Church tries to keep a low profile, a requirement for survival in what one ecclesiastic delicately terms "a distracted world." Believers may number 15 to 20 percent of the adult population, but no one can know. Russia watchers dispute the intensity of the official campaign against religion but agree that it works. However, a resurgence in churchgoing includes even young people, perhaps hoping to mend their culture's broken links with the past. But no one in town seems to know how many of the churches are open for worship. When I asked at the hotel, the answer was "one." Over dinner Father Georgi assured me there were seven.

We ate in a tiny room in a small house on a narrow dirt street not far from

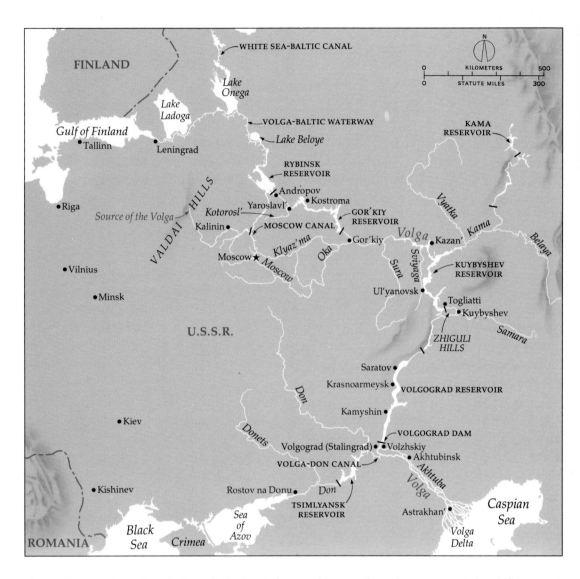

downtown Yaroslavl'. Small Oriental rugs lay on the glossy varnished floors. A little office held a bare desk and a glass-front cabinet containing two or three elegant miters. The kitchen was spic-and-span. Every other Russian home I'd been in was packed with life's clutter, but this, obviously for entertaining visitors, had the sparseness and tension of a stage set.

Our host set a splendid table: endless rounds of *zakuski*, including sausage, cheeses, tomatoes, cucumbers, delicious caviar, and white bread; soup and a meat course; dessert of sugared sour red berries; tea, cognac, and convivial toasts. Two women dined with us. One, small like the house, was presented as Father Georgi's housekeeper. The identity of the burly one was vague. She sat facing the priest, at the foot of the table. When he responded to my questions, the words were for me, but his eyes sought her approval.

On the other side of town, in a converted warehouse, a cheery band of boys and girls makes amateur movies under an elfish director, Rem Alexandrovitch Ustinov, and his wife Nina, "the president of the samovar." Arriving on a bright afternoon, I blinked as Rem and Nina led me across the dark, rambling studio, where we stepped over cables, ducked under cameras, and stumbled through tight corridors. We ended up in an enormous room where Rem bustled around explaining that we would see two movies the club had made. *The Little Meadow* starred the small brown and white dog who scampered at our feet. Druzhok was his name—"little friend." It was a lovely film, with the message that every life needs a flowery meadow. The second movie, *The Same Sun Shines Over Everybody,* had been made with a Finnish group, to promote friendship and understanding, Rem said.

The lights came on and we moved to a huge table, where Nina began to draw endless cups of tea from her samovar. Looped above our heads like popcorn on an invisible Christmas tree were great skeins of the ring-shaped, rock-hard cookies known as *bubliky.* Young filmmakers joined us at the tea table: 12-year-old Vova, the chief animator; Yura, who wants to photograph his mother at work as an X-ray technician; Grisha, who's filming a glassblower. The tea was hot and delicious. When I bit into the bubliky, fearing for my teeth, the cookie cracked deafeningly in my ear. Nina told us how the film club had worked for three years to renovate the warehouse, how used projectors had been scrounged from theaters, how she and Rem strove to help youngsters develop their imagination. The talk turned to peace, friendship, and isms. Rem said, "You and I can be friends. Can we help our governments?" I wish I knew, I thought. The problem's as tough as the bubliky.

T he middle Volga is where it all began, where the father of the Big Ism was born, in a town called Simbirsk—until its name was changed to Ul'yanovsk to honor this famous citizen, Vladimir Ilyich Ul'yanov, who had already changed *his* name to Vladimir Ilyich Lenin, being on the run from the tsar's police. Lenin's leadership in the Socialist Revolution of 1917 launched the Soviet state. The deification of Lenin helps keep it afloat. Everywhere in the U.S.S.R., amidst the barrage of political and industrial slogans, posters, and banners, are those proclaiming, "Lenin lives, Lenin is living, Lenin shall live."

I saw two Ul'yanovsks. One was the city of monuments, which preserves four of Lenin's boyhood homes. Three are enshrined inside an opulent, marble memorial complex with museum, concert hall, a "house of political enlightenment," an 18-foot-tall statue of Lenin shrouded in somber organ music, gardens, and flaming torches—all on a high hill overlooking the river. On nearby Lenin Street stands the neat, comfortable home where the intellectual-bourgeois Ul'yanov family lived, one supposes, a little longer than they'd stayed in the other places. Lenin's father was a school administrator, his mother a talented pianist. In the schoolroom where the boy Ilyich distinguished himself, his desk still sits, last in the row by the window. Every autumn, on the first day of school, each first grader gets a precious moment to perch on little Lenin's chair, as our earnest guide explained, "for their first lesson in life."

The other Ul'yanovsk is a fast-growing industrial and shipping center of almost 500,000 people. A ten-minute walk from the memorial led me into the real world. I was high on the right bank, 500 feet above the river. Railroad tracks traced the shoreline. The channel, 24 miles wide just upstream, here narrows to 3 miles. Lean, slate-colored cargo ships, sleek white hydrofoils, oil tankers, chugging motor launches, huge cruise ships moved upstream and down, silent in the distance. Across, far to the east, lay farmland and villages. From where I stood, river, land, and low sky spun out a blue-gray ribbon.

I was in a neighborhood of dirt lanes. On a corner, children drew water from a hand pump. Leaves rustled, and a dog barked. Suddenly I knew I stood in the 19th-century country town that Ul'yanovsk had been. The wooden houses of soft greens, browns, and faded pastels wore elaborately carved window frames. Tall board fences at the edge of the brick sidewalk hid yards with small garden plots, fruit trees, and—so much for my reverie—now and then, a car.

A woman, middle aged, arrived home on a bicycle. As she parked it in her yard, we talked. She shares the house—it is at least 100 years old—with two other people. One room is hers; the kitchen, toilet, and yard are communal. She's worried by rumors that her street will be razed to put up apartment buildings. "They won't take it!" she protested. I wondered how she likes living on the bank of the Volga (with a river view, I was thinking, that an American would pay a couple of thousand a month for). Her matter-of-fact reply: "On summer evenings, it's beautiful. In the winter, it's windy and cold."

Old Simbirsk began as a Volga fortress in 1648. Ul'yanovsk still confronts the river. Cottages swarm over the great slope, tall buildings command the heights, so that even residents of the often dismal Soviet-built apartment blocks have a view of the river and the busy port. On a choice riverfront site, a Communist youth group, the Young Pioneers, have a splendid new Pioneer Palace, an outside-of-school-hours community center where the adult leaders see to it that over 2,000 boys and girls have absolutely no spare time. One group of seven-year-olds, making stuffed toys to decorate New Year trees, spontaneously showered me with little animals to bring home to my grandchildren.

On the flight south to Volgograd we followed the river, and I looked down upon a devastation of erosion. Deep ravines cut the dry land of the west bank, and I pictured the scarce but intense rains of this drought-prone region flooding down the gullies into the river. Some of the gullies have, in fact, developed into small tributaries. Ages of careless farming are to blame for the erosion, as are the *sukhovey*, hot dry winds that sear crops and drive dust storms across the steppe. Famines and poor harvests are the inheritance. Later I talked with scientists and citizens of Volgograd who work to reverse the gully erosion. As our plane neared Volgograd, I saw evidence of their labor—grasses and shrubs grew in ravines and greenbelts freshened the landscape. One ravine called the Tsaritsa Gorge, miles long and 200 feet deep, cuts across the city.

The ravines and the river shaped this city that strings itself 45 miles along the bank. In 1942, when the world knew it as Stalingrad, they nearly brought its end. Hitler's troops advanced toward the Caucasus and threatened to sever the Volga lifeline at Stalingrad. The city's shape made encirclement impossible, and the Nazis forced Russian backs to the river.

alentina Petrovna Slobina was 18 years old when she joined an anti-aircraft battery. With 30 other girls, she'd come to Volgograd from her home in Bykovo, "the watermelon village," 75 miles upriver. August 23 was a sunny day, Valentina told me. People felt calm, unaware that German tanks had reached the riverbank north of town. Suddenly the bright blue sky blackened with a cloud of German planes. Hundreds of incendiary bombs rained down. Heavy bombs hit homes, factories, hospitals, boats. Oil tanks near Mamayev Hill exploded, and blazing fuel cascaded onto the river. "The soil burned . . . the water burned . . . burned . . . burned."

When the planes came, Anya Aronovna Shanina was standing on the slope of the Tsaritsa Gorge, where General Yeremenko had his bunker headquarters. Anya had grown up in Volgograd, studying medicine, swimming and picnicking along the river in summer, playing ice hockey in winter. Now that war had come she was a surgeon in a military hospital. With her at Tsaritsa was a medical school classmate. "She was a poet. She wore her hair in a beautiful braid." Anya saw her friend's eyes widen, then watched a piece of shrapnel tear off her head. Anya apologized for her tears as she told me how her friend's head rolled into the gorge, and the body stood for seconds before it fell.

In Anya's apartment we quietly discussed the battle that cost a million lives before the Germans cracked and surrendered in February 1943. From her tiny balcony—as in most Russian apartments, it was spare pantry space—we could see the house on Solnechnaya Street where Sgt. Jacob Pavlov and a few men stood for 58 days between German tanks and the Volga. Amid the jars of preserved plums and strings of drying fish, Anya described her war months in a dugout hospital on the right bank and, often under fire, ferrying wounded to the left bank on small boats and rafts.

For the wartime valor of its citizens, the Soviet government named Volgograd a Hero City. Every day, pilgrim veterans from all over the country return to the streets and squares where they fought hand to hand. One veteran I talked to wore medals for campaigns from Leningrad to Berlin. But he was equally proud of his decorations as Hero of Socialist Labor for construction work on the Volga-Don canal and the Volgograd dam.

Lenin's assertion that "Communism is Soviet power plus electrification of the whole country" has been more than an empty slogan. At Volgograd the largest hydropower station on the river stores water in a reservoir 370 miles long and as much as 12 miles wide. This brings the blessing of irrigation to farms that grow grains, sunflowers (for oil), mustard, melons, vegetables, and many other crops. The dam construction created a city, Volzhskiy, now an industrial center noted for the youth of its population. In addition to powering factories in Volshskiy and Volgograd, the dam sends electricity to Moscow. And it bears a mighty symbolism. "A spark from the Volga," one hears, lighted the eternal flame at Volgograd's Square of Fallen Heroes.

The dams have changed for all time the life of the sturgeon, the monarch of Volga fishes and, because of its caviar, a treasure in foreign currency. Once they swam far upstream. Now they stop just below the dam at Volgograd, their ancestral spawning grounds beyond reach. The dam has fish elevators, but people say that even the small fish won't use them.

Islands in the channel have come to the rescue. A picnic one day with some Volgograd friends on a flat, rocky island in sight of the busy city, showed me a sturgeon hatchery firsthand, so to speak—I sat on it. The hundreds of thousands of adult sturgeon that winter in the reservoir find acres of these specially graveled beds, which, flooded with spring's high water, resemble the river bottom their species used to know. They lay their eggs on the rocks and return to the sea. Tom Yanin, a conservation-minded Volgograder (whose marvelous briefcase spilled forth cheese, meat, fish, bread, pickles, and vodka) expressed his philosophy that "social patterns should be in harmony with patterns of nature." Tom said that the hatcheries each cost more than a million dollars, money gladly spent to preserve fish "suffering from civilization."

On one of my last evenings in Volgograd, I dined in the apartment of a journalist colleague, Stanislav Golubov. With us were his blond wife, Ludmilla, an ideal Russian beauty, and their two shy, pretty daughters, bravely testing their schoolbook English on the American visitor. The girls showed me their stamp albums, embroidery, favorite books. Slava demonstrated his stereo with American rock and Volga folksongs. He showed us pictures of Los Angeles and New York he'd taken on a memorable visit to the United States. Ludmilla's dinner included vegetables and melons from her mother's garden plot on the Volga bank. We talked of our families and daily life—matters that cross political boundaries. The Volga had brought us together. It had done its work well. I might even call it a Hero River.

ranes of the modern port of Yaroslavl' mingle on the skyline with the domes and bell tower of St. John Chrysostom. The 17th-century church stands on the headland of the thousand-year-old city, at the confluence of the Volga (in the distance) and its tributary Kotorosl'. Like many other monuments in the wealthy city-state of Yaroslavl', St. John Chrysostom was built by a merchant family.

At a small church in the city of Ul'yanovsk (above), a worshiper lights a votive candle. People buy their candles for a few kopeks in the church vestibule and often pass them forward hand to hand through a densely crowded congregation, to be lighted at the altar or at an icon along the way.

Old houses lavish with decoration line many quiet streets of Ul'yanovsk, called Simbirsk in tsarist days when the Soviet leader Lenin was born there in 1870. Windows present bits of household beauty—plants, flowers, dolls, crystal—to smile on passersby.

Two of the Soviet Union's twenty million Young Pioneers puzzle out a chemistry experiment in their Ul'yanovsk community center, where boys and girls study ballet, gymnastics, zoology, music, pantomine and many other subjects. Chess clubs, stamp collections, ham radios, and serious political and patriotic sessions also fill their time. The Scout-like Pioneer movement grew in the 1920s to educate the children of unschooled peasants and workers. Being a Pioneer is sometimes the first step to membership in the Communist Party.

The high right bank of the Volga at Ul'yanovsk overlooks the flat left bank across a channel widened and deepened by downstream damming at the Kuybyshev Reservoir. Extensions on either end of the bridge show the difference between the width of the new Volga and the old, where steamboats used to get stuck now and then in low water.

A professor at the Ilya Ul'yanov Pedagogical Institute (above) describes some of the 59 species of fish that now live in the Volga. The beluga, at a top weight of 2,500 pounds, is the largest of the sturgeon species. The three-pound sterlet is the smallest. In between are the sevryuga and one known simply as sturgeon. Before the dams beluga swam at least as far upstream as Kalinin to spawn. Now the dams block them from their ancestral spawning grounds.

144

A blue-ribbon cook presents crayfish from a Volga-filled canal on the state farm where she works in Volga-irrigated onion fields. At left, milkmaids collect milk that will go to market in nearby Volgograd and Kamyshin. All the cows wear painted names, as well as numbers so they'll be milked in turn. Some have pretty names like Snowflake and Willow. Two of those opposite mean business: They're Profit and Foreign Currency.

At left, in the farm day-care center, cupboard shelves sprout the colorful footgear of children whose parents work in the fields and barns. The U.S.S.R. worries about the low birthrate of its Russian population, but the farm director boasts that the day-care center and the school both need to be enlarged.

145

T he city "is like a medal on the chest of the earth," wrote Soviet veteran Sgt. Ivan Bratchenko after the battle for the Volga city then called Stalingrad. On Mamayev Hill, high above the river, Mother Russia exhorts her children to defense (opposite). A Young Pioneer (right) joins the honor guard at Volgograd's Square of Fallen Heroes where an eternal flame burns on the graves of soldiers who defended the city in the revolution of 1917 and in World War II. As veterans' groups approach this monument, tourist crowds hush. In a silence broken by murmurs, the shuffle of feet, a muffled sob, the veterans present their flowers. It is a ritual observed all over the Soviet Union but most reverently here at the site of the 1943 victory on the edge of the Volga.

Red is beautiful to the people of Volgograd when it pours from furnaces of the Red October Steel Mill, named for the 1917 revolution that established the Soviet state. During World War II soldiers fought even in the mill shops. Now the Red October helps make the U.S.S.R. a leading world producer of steel.

The elaborate staircase leads to the Volga embankment in the rebuilt city. A circular restaurant tops a new river station for the multitudes of travelers who cruise the river on huge three-deckers. An enthusiastic corps of city planners dreams of a soaring Volgograd of the future. The city's vitality owes much to the hardworking river. At right, a fisherman pulls a sturgeon from the Volgograd reservoir. The fish will be inspected to monitor the water quality.

A n official at the Volgograd reservoir cooks for guests to celebrate the successful cleanup of the water. Here it is clear, sparkling, and drinkable. The island will flood in the spring, and sturgeon will lay eggs on the rocks. When the water recedes, the picnic ground will again welcome skilled campfire chefs to skewer fish chunks or make ukha, an aromatic fish soup.

The boat (above) waits in a small shipping canal at the Volgograd dam, near the new city of Volzhskiy. Downriver 30 miles, the Volga links with the Volga-Don canal. At the first lock another Volgograd satellite city thrives on land that 35 years ago was open steppe.

Cary Wolinsky, Stock, Boston

152

THE THAMES

T H I S   W A S   M Y   R I V E R

By Cameron Thomas

For one brief moment, as I trod the worn stone steps from the bridge at Richmond to the river below, I was 12 years old again, starting out once more down the towpath on another excursion with other boys. The old bridge seemed much the same, a little weatherworn perhaps, but 50 years does that to us all. Life moved at a slower pace then, and our needs were few and simple. With little more than a few slabs of bread and jam to sustain us, and an upturned boat to provide shelter for the night, we roamed the river at will. It was our summer playground, an escape from the drab streets of London, and a place where we let our imaginations wander as we became the heroes of our favorite stories.

To Londoners the Thames is more than a great river. It is a way of life. We meet it in the first nursery rhyme, "London Bridge is falling down," and are made increasingly aware of its presence through the stories of Charles Dickens, Kenneth Grahame, and Jerome K. Jerome. It was such literature that enticed me to the riverbanks in my youth.

This river's greatness lies not in its length—indeed it measures only a little over 200 miles from source to mouth—but in its long history. Roman legions camped by its banks and founded a port they named Londinium. Celts, Romans, Saxons, and Danes fought for its crossings, and from Wallingford, William the Conqueror marched on London. A river of pomp and circumstance, pollution and decay, and an astounding rebirth. A highway for kings and commoners alike, workplace for millions, and playground for many others. It was the lifeblood of a great empire, and a path to glory for a ragtag flotilla of naval vessels, pleasure craft, and cockleboats that sailed from its sheltered waters to cross the Channel and pluck over 300,000 troops from the besieged beaches of Dunkirk in 1940. German bombers used it as a pathway to London in the blitz, and from the sea to the Tower Bridge the great docks were home to the largest mercantile marine in the world, and back in the thirties this was my river.

It rises, somewhat reluctantly it seems, as there are often periods when there is no water at all, at Thames Head in the Cotswold Hills. There are still those

The Tower of London shimmers on the Thames. Through the notorious water gate at left, Sir Thomas More, Queen Elizabeth I, and other notables sailed to their imprisonment.

who support the Seven Springs theory, which holds that the river begins near Cheltenham. In February 1937 Parliament debated the claims for both sources, Thames Head winning out. A portion of that debate went like this: Mr. Perkins in whose constituency Seven Springs lies: "Is the right hon. Gentleman aware that the source known as Thames Head periodically dries up . . . ? An Hon. Member: Why don't you? (Laughter)."

The river becomes navigable at Lechlade, about 20 miles from the source, though it is possible to go as far up as Cricklade in a canoe or rowboat. A wharf existed at Lechlade once, handling a wide variety of cargo brought down the Thames and Severn Canal, now extinct. Tall-masted Thames barges would take the freight from Lechlade to London and beyond. Now a boatyard sits where the wharf once stood, and ever present and always inert fishermen dot the banks below the bridge. One to whom I spoke expressed great joy at catching two large eels, a delicacy he hadn't seen for some time. He said the eels' return was due to the new cleanliness of the river. I later learned that it was probably due more to his ineptness as an angler, as the major pollution had plagued the lower reaches, and that I was the recipient of yet another fishy tale. There has been, however, a vast cleanup of the lower Thames, and over a hundred species of fish have returned to the river, which almost died in the fifties. The real victory came in 1983 when Russell Doig, an auto mechanic, won the prize for hooking the first salmon in 150 years. The prize was presented, appropriately enough, by Mr. Hugh Fish of the Thames Water Authority.

Below Lechlade the river wanders through hills and flat pastureland, then suddenly takes a great loop north to Oxford. Oxford was a world as unattainable as mythical Camelot to youngsters of our plebeian background, and we found it difficult to comprehend that the annual fee for the education of these begowned, bike-riding, privileged few would more than equal the annual wage of any of our working fathers. So I left the university to the scholars and historians; my business was at Folly Bridge, with Salter Bros. Ltd. Launch and Boat Builders, whose steam launches have ruled the river since the *Alaska* first went into service in the 1880s. It ran from Oxford to Kingston upon Thames, making the 182-mile journey down and back in five days. An advertisement in an 1872 guidebook offered a four-oar rowboat for one week for the sum of three pounds ten shillings, which sum also included cartage back to the boatyard from your destination. Many Salter's boats still use the river. I noticed that even their slatted wooden seats remain, with the only nod to progress a change of power from steam to diesel. These were like the launches we would see, and try to stay clear of, while flailing away on a makeshift raft, being Huck Finns or Robinson Crusoes as the mood took us. On my return visit, all these years later, I took a short afternoon ride on one of these old launches, and though the passage was smooth and comfortable, slatted seats notwithstanding, I think

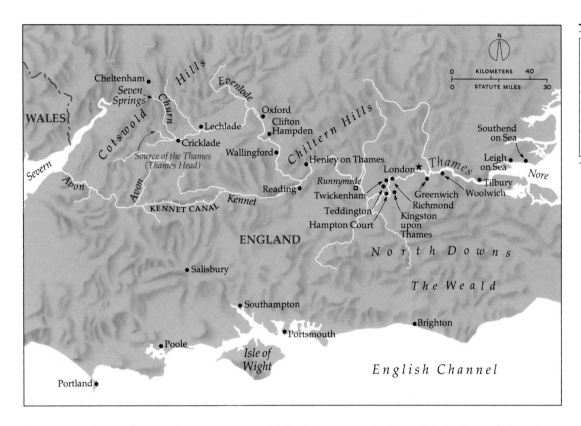

the precarious float of my youth still holds sway. I also think that if the time ever comes when there is not a Salter's boat on the Thames, it will be because the river has dried up.

I fulfilled a boyhood dream as I followed the river to Clifton Hampden and lunched at the Barley Mow Inn, where, it is said, Jerome K. Jerome wrote *Three Men in a Boat*. He became in turn a railway clerk, schoolmaster, actor, and journalist. *Three Men in a Boat*, the book that brought him great fame, described a camping journey upriver, in a skiff, with two companions and a dog. Published in 1889, it became a best-seller. The vivid descriptions of their adventures and misadventures, read and reread in my formative years, initiated a love affair with the Thames that continues to this day. The inn at Clifton Hampden, damaged by fire in 1975, has been faithfully restored. I saw it just as Jerome described the place back in 1889. "It is, without exception, I should say, the quaintest, most old-world inn up the river. It stands on the right of the bridge, quite away from the village. Its low-pitched gables and thatched roof and latticed windows give it quite a story-book appearance, while inside it is even still more once-upon-a-timeyfied." And so it is today.

Crossing over the little bridge, I noticed a backwater and wondered if it led to one of those delightful ponds we boys would find while searching for the source of the Nile. Those ponds held a special fascination for us. We would lie on our stomachs in the muddy grass at their edges, noses a few inches from the water, and watch the antics of the inhabitants: Tiny fish not yet an inch long, darting about through the weeds, wheeling in unison in shiny, silvery groups; the ever present tadpoles; the water strider on its fragile legs; the water boatmen; and the ugly bottom crawlers, which would shortly become gossamer-winged dragonflies, skimming the surface. And all around, the buzz and bite of gnats. The buzz of gnats, alas, has given way to the harsher buzz of the outboard motor—a fumy replacement for the skiffs and punts of old, pushed aside by the demands of modern-day river travelers, forever in such a hurry.

The past came flooding back again when I arrived at Henley on Thames, home of the Royal Regatta. It was here we would see river life at its most affluent. Steam launches, decks crowded with glass-in-hand spectators, vied for room on the water with private cruisers and sleek, polished motorboats. Blazered men and fashionably gowned women sipped wine as they watched the efforts of the oarsmen. Sometimes it seemed, from the snatches of conversation we picked up, the passengers were more interested in the vintage in the glass than the rowers in the boats. Today their sons and daughters bedeck themselves annually in striped blazers and organdy gowns in an effort to recapture, if only briefly, the feeling of those golden days, a pastime made all the more difficult as today's jetliners roar overhead, giving lie to the yesterday beneath.

I remember crawling out from our temporary abode one morning at Runnymede, and dabbling my fingers in the cold water in reluctant deference to personal hygiene. Through the early mist you would swear you could hear the voices of the barons as they hammered out the Magna Carta. In our young minds we became part of whatever circumstances we found ourselves in, though at Runnymede, I recall, nobody wanted to be King John. No such romantic daydreams affect today's youngsters, eating their lunch of Kentucky Fried Chicken from a nearby take-away. "No" they say, when I ask if they know the history associated with this stretch of the river. They've "never 'eard of no barons" and "was it on the telly?"

The closer you get to London, the more you can see where the hand of "progress" has touched the river of my youth: Sleepy riverside towns have become mini-cities, their still narrow streets choked with pedestrian and automobile alike, the very narrowness necessitating a one-way traffic system that confounds the visiting driver. Such a town was Twickenham, a couple of miles upriver from Richmond Bridge. In my youth horse-drawn carts plied its quiet thoroughfares, and ice cream vendors pedaled their tricycle businesses and did a roaring summer trade in penny snow fruits. Len Smith's, school and sport outfitters, still follow their trade there, now cheek by jowl with the "golden arches." It was here I took the towpath again, retracing my route of yesterday. The footbridge leads to Eel Pie Island, named, according to legend, after the delicacy cooked there for Henry VIII. He would stop for a snack before proceeding to Hampton Court Palace for yet another amorous encounter. Below the footbridge sits the Riverside Inn. I remembered this place well, a "must" stop on our youthful excursions. Here we could beg a drink of water, knowing full well that the landlord's wife would take pity on us and more often than not offer us a frothy glass of lemonade or ginger beer. I was given a warm welcome by John Masterson, temporary landlord of this charming 400-year-old inn. But I could not help but notice at the same time the wails of a video machine against one wall, and the *clunk, clunk, clunk* of coins dropping into an electronic jackpot machine as young hopefuls endeavored to line up three of a kind.

Nearby at Hampton Wick, the timber firm of Gridley Miskin & Co. was still doing business after 120 years. I was tempted to call and see if they had ever missed the few planks we had "found" and used for our raft one early morning all those years ago. Across the river, office workers were lunching in the sun on the red brick embankment above the bridge, while a circle of ducks floated below. Near the bridge itself a bunch of kids took the advice of Kenneth Grahame and simply messed about in boats.

The silted incoming tide turns the water a muddy brown as we approach the city of London. On the South Bank the great smokestacks of Battersea Power Station no longer spew their white smoke skyward, and the new Covent Garden Market sits on the site where once we watched, fascinated, the operations of the railway yards at Nine Elms, a short bike ride from home—too short a ride, as it turned out. A few years later the power station and the railway became prime targets for Nazi bombers as my youth was ending and reality began. An errant bomb missed its target and hit our street, demolishing in one blow both my home and my boyhood. At 16 I was a man. I went to a recruiting office, lied through my teeth about my age, and joined the Royal Air Force, finishing up as a Mosquito bomber pilot in Burma.

Above Westminster Pier, Big Ben stands ghostlike, one of the most venerable figures of London, shrouded by a tent of plastic and iron scaffolding as workers restore this age-blackened clock tower and the Gothic buildings surrounding it. Only the famous clock face peeks out from an opening in the covers. At the pier's end tour boats constantly come and go, carrying their hordes of holidaymakers with cameras. It was from this same pier that the old Belle Line paddle-wheelers would take the London worker and his family on their one-day-a-year holiday. No vacations with pay in those days. The paddle-wheelers would glide, streamers flying, down the river to Southend on Sea or Ramsgate, all the men in the bar, all the women on deck, trying to keep the kids from falling over the side. At the seaside the men would again head for the pubs. Their wives were left to amuse the children on the pier or to eat sandwich lunches on the sand until time for the return trip, during which the whole scene would be repeated, men drinking, women tending children. Today these children take their annual paid vacations on the Continent and cruise the Mediterranean in sleek chartered ships.

Below Tower Bridge, St. Katharine Dock, once a thriving center of seagoing commerce, has been transformed into a residential and marina complex. An old warehouse, which held tea and wool, wines and spices, has been converted to a Dickensian pub, and some half dozen or so of the old Thames sailing barges lie moored in the basin, hospitality centers catering to meetings and private parties. Tilbury excepted, most of the great docks are dead now, their towering cranes idle, but like St. Katharine they will be born again, reincarnated as housing and recreation centers.

As the docks fell into disrepair and decay, the old riverside pubs lived on, and will no doubt be here long after the river traffic is gone. The Prospect of Whitby at Wapping still dispenses ale as it has done since 1543. Pirates and smugglers haunted the place, also a fertile recruiting ground for the infamous press gangs, who would drop their drunken victims through a trapdoor in the floor of the barroom. A waiting longboat below would conduct the groggy recruits away for forced induction into the Royal Navy. This same pub was a watering hole of Samuel Pepys, the diarist and secretary to the admiralty who, on his own confession, drank "liberally" at meals and "for the most part of the wines that are reckoned strong, viz—Greek, Italian, Spanish and Portuguese and at the small Bordeaux claret."

I doubt if his impressed sailors fared as well.

Across the river another old inn, the Angel at Southwark, was in business when John Harvard left his home here and sailed to the New World in the early 1600s to become a patron of the university that bears his name.

Something new has been added to this stretch of the river since the old Belle steamer days: the silver sentry boxes of the Thames Barrier, the flood control system recently completed at a cost of some 700 million dollars. No floods have come yet, but the first tests of the system, during February 1983, showed that the massive flood-control gates, the biggest of which weigh more than 3,000 tons each, snapped smartly into place to block the incoming tide, just as they were designed to do. With the barrier in place, it seems unlikely that the great river will ever rise again and enter Westminster Palace where, after a 13th-century surge "men didst row with wherries in the midst of the Hall."

I ended where I began, gazing over the parapet of Richmond Bridge. The years have changed Old Father Thames, and there seems little room for schoolboy romantics now, but I can still see a bunch of scruffy kids pedaling down the towpath in search of Treasure Island, and I know that this is still my river.

O. Louis Mazzatenta, National Geographic Staff. Page 159: Gordon W. Gahan (also above)

O. Louis Mazzatenta, National Geographic Staff. Below: Gordon W. Gahan

age 159: A barge cruises the peaceful meanders of the upper Thames between Oxford and Lechlade. Until the mid-1800s commercial boats, towed by horses or by men called halers, carried goods up and down this part of the waterway.

At Henley on Thames (above), punting enthusiasts enjoy a lull at the annual Royal Regatta. Near Oxford, a footbridge draws a couple to sun-dappled waters on a stretch where some bridges date from the 14th century. A barge (opposite) that once served as a clubhouse for rowers becomes lodgings for Oxford students who help with a major refurbishing project. At left a Thames fisherman angles for chub near Northmoor Lock.

*V*ictoria Tower and Central Tower *soar above the Houses of Parliament beside London's Thames. The Gothic-style buildings, rebuilt after a fire in 1834, serve as the seat of English democracy. In East London, the Thames winds past wharves, warehouses, and the haunts of Charles Dickens. Like many London pubs, The Grapes (above) claims connections with literary history: It may have been the Six Jolly Fellowship Porters in Dickens' novel* Our Mutual Friend. *At Greenwich the* Cutty Sark *(opposite) sits silhouetted beneath a ghostly moon. The speedy ship gained fame in the late 19th century for breaking records on runs for Australian wool.*

Gordon W. Gahan

A worker steam-cleans cockles at Leigh on Sea, a town once famed for its cockle fleets. These mollusks and other aquatic life almost disappeared from the badly polluted river. In the 1950s, a major cleanup began. Now more than a hundred species thrive in the tidal waters. Visitors to Leigh and nearby Southend on Sea buy cockles, whelks, and jellied eels at outdoor stalls.

Another herculean project, the Thames Barrier (opposite), takes shape at Woolwich. Now completed, the pier-and-gate structure protects London from massive surge tides. Ten gates lie on concrete sills on the riverbed. When danger threatens, the gates rise on arms in a 90° arc, presenting a solid, 60-foot-high wall to oncoming water.

THE RHÔNE

B O R N   I N   A   G L A C I E R

By Mary B. Dickinson / Photographs by Farrell Grehan

"Vineyard country," said people who had visited the Rhône Valley. "And Roman ruins in Arles. It should be gorgeous in September." I decided to begin my river journey in the south, reaching Avignon at grape harvest time.

I would be following a well-traveled route northward. By land or by water, the Rhône Valley has always provided access from the Mediterranean to the heart of Europe. Today a new canal from the river to the Gulf of Fos links France's premier port, the huge Marseille-Fos "Europort du Sud," to the end of a modern river highway. Navigable as far as Lyon, the Rhône feeds through its chief tributary, the Saône, into a network of continental waterways.

East of Lyon, navigation ends. The Rhône twists through the Jura Mountains to the Lake of Geneva, a hollow scooped out by an ancient Rhône glacier. River and lake merge in the city of Geneva, to separate again at the lake's southeast tip in the Swiss canton of Valais. And in northeast Valais, France's most powerful river is born in a glacier 6,000 feet up a Swiss Alp.

At the river's mouth I drove through the bleak, beautiful salt marshes of the Camargue. Water glinted on every side. Black-and-white magpies flapped clumsily by, and the famous white horses grazed in quiet groups. The river splits into two branches here, the Grand and Petit Rhône. They embrace a sprawling national park and wildlife preserve, a haven for millions of migrant birds each spring and fall, and home of Europe's largest flamingo colony.

At the apex of the delta stands the ancient port of Arles. The Phocaeans, Greek traders from Asia Minor, settled in Marseille about 600 B.C. and later established a post at Arles. Then the Romans came in the first century B.C. Arles retains a lot of its Roman flavor, as do other towns along the old route up the Rhône Valley. Orange, Vienne, Lyon, all have well-preserved Roman remains. I sat and dreamed for a while in the stone open-air theater in Arles.

From Arles I traveled to Avignon through the golden Provençal countryside, dotted with mellow stone or stucco houses roofed in red tile. Tall avenues of poplars, cypresses, and plane trees serve as windbreaks against the mistral, a

Streetlights cast dazzling reflections across the Rhône as it flows by Avignon's fortresslike Palace of the Popes, where 14th-century pontiffs held lavish court.

fierce wind that funnels down the narrow Rhône Valley from the northwest. In Avignon, J. Jonker, a young Dutch motor barge captain, had moored his 360-ton *Adrianto* with other craft below the massive walls of the medieval city. His boat carries cargoes via river and canal between southern French ports, like Sète or Port-St.-Louis, and Germany or Holland. "But there's not very much work," he told me, "so we're waiting, huh? Everybody has his turn here."

In the morning I drove 15 miles north to Châteauneuf-du-Pape. Vines have been cultivated there, off and on, ever since 14th-century popes took over the "new castle" as a country residence. Most important vineyard area on the Rhône, Châteauneuf-du-Pape lies in the southern group of Côtes du Rhône estates, whose collective name proclaims their location along the river. Hermitage is the best known in the northern group between Valence and Vienne.

Jean Abeille showed me around the Domaine de Mont-Redon, the largest Châteauneuf estate. "Domaines" here are like "Châteaus" elsewhere, many bottling their own wines on the premises. Mont-Redon's rambling stucco buildings house immaculate modern facilities and a long, cool cellar where the best wines age in huge oak casks. Smaller vineyards form village cooperatives. One of my guides, Isabelle Carsol, took me to her father's place near Rochegude. Edmond Carsol was picking in the field with his workers. "I'll probably help my father pick grapes this weekend," said Isabelle. In Rochegude we saw members of the cooperative drive up and dump their purple loads.

North of Avignon, a new riverscape takes over. People refer to Donzère-Mondragon in one breath. A 20-mile diversionary canal, with dams, a lock, and a hydroelectric plant, joins the two towns. A nuclear power plant occupies 1,700 canalside acres. Donzère-Mondragon is the most ambitious of 20 engineering projects that are converting the Rhône into a giant watery stairway descending from Geneva to the sea. A canal usually diverts most of the flow to a new channel and through the turbines of the electric plant, while the old river bed receives a "guaranteed" minimum. But sometimes the Rhône bed carries only a muddy trickle, while its jaunty rival brims to overflowing. The Compagnie Nationale du Rhône runs these projects from its base in Lyon.

Valence is on the way to Lyon. "Ah . . . Pic!" sigh gourmets the world over when Valence is mentioned. Jacques Pic, one of France's famous provincial chefs, runs a three-star restaurant there. His huge black Briard sheepdog wandered over and flopped down where we sat talking. "We use fresh local produce when we can," said Pic, "mostly fruit and vegetables—and herbs, of course. But we get our fish from Brittany. We couldn't use fish from the river, with all those factories and motorboats."

As I entered for dinner that evening, I could see through large windows the gleaming stainless steel kitchen. The Pics greet everyone at the door. Waiters and sommelier hover, ready to discuss a dish or a wine. Pic had recommended

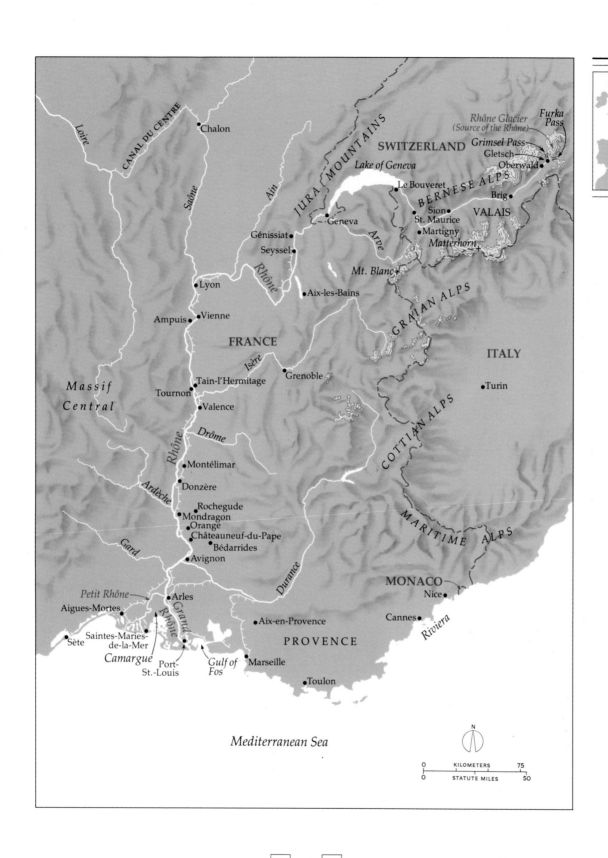

Loire

CANAL DU CENTRE

Saône

Ain

JURA MOUNTAINS

Rhône

•Chalon

SWITZERLAND

Rhône Glacier (Source of the Rhône)

Furka Pass

Grimsel Pass
Gletsch
Oberwald

Lake of Geneva

BERNESE ALPS

Brig

VALAIS

Le Bouveret

Sion•
St. Maurice
•Martigny
Matterhorn+

Génissiat•

Geneva•

Arve

Seyssel•

Lyon•

Aix-les-Bains•

Mt. Blanc+

GRAIAN ALPS

Ampuis• •Vienne

FRANCE

Isère

ITALY

*Massif
Central*

Tain-l'Hermitage•

•Grenoble

•Turin

Tournon•

Valence•

COTTIAN ALPS

Rhône

Drôme

Ardèche

•Montélimar

•Donzère

•Rochegude
•Mondragon
•Orange
•Châteauneuf-du-Pape
•Bédarrides

MARITIME ALPS

Gard

•Avignon

Durance

MONACO

Petit Rhône

Arles•

Nice•

Aigues-Mortes•

Grand Rhône

•Aix-en-Provence

Cannes•

Riviera

Sète•

Saintes-Maries-
de-la-Mer•

Camargue Port-
St.-Louis

*Gulf of
Fos*

•Marseille

PROVENCE

•Toulon

Mediterranean Sea

N

KILOMETERS
0   75
0   50
STATUTE MILES

a selection for me. Each portion was exquisitely arranged with accompanying vegetables. I sat in heaven in the pink and gold dining room, while lobster in fresh tomato purée, duck liver in raspberry sauce, sea bass with caviar, pigeon wings with fresh morels passed in blissful succession down my throat. At one point, *"Monsieur vous propose un petit sorbet,"* and a delicious sherbet refreshed my palate. Meantime the sommelier uncorked with a flourish a Hermitage white and red, sniffed the corks, and tasted the wine with a silver scoop that he returned to the pocket of his long, dark green apron. By the time the waiter offered the cheeses in their wicker basket, I could only sample my favorite regional goat cheese, *banon,* wrapped in chestnut leaves. And then, "But madame *must* taste the cold orange soufflé. It's a *spécialité de la maison!"*

In Lyon I wandered along the loading docks of Port Rambaud on the Saône, where river boatmen line up for cargoes. The captain of one large motor barge, the *Offaly,* invited me aboard and showed off his snug family quarters—lace curtains flapping at the windows, pot-au-feu simmering on the stove. He and his wife had raised four children aboard. An extra double bunk now awaits their visits, with a shelf at its foot just big enough to hold a grandchild.

At the headquarters of the Compagnie Nationale du Rhône, I spoke with Pierre Gilibert. "The Compagnie has a threefold responsibility," he said. "First, hydroelectric power; second, navigation and the locks and port zones; third, irrigation. That's to say, we keep the river's level high enough to supply the pumping stations along the Rhône." The river's power plants provide 20 percent of all hydroelectric power in France and underwrite the Compagnie's construction costs. Gilibert pointed to the map: "This little road will allow you to follow the Rhône to Geneva and see the power plants that are being built."

As the road twisted with the river's course, I could see in places that the bed was a bare storage area for cranes, bulldozers, and building supplies. I stopped at a dam construction site. Onlookers were enthusiastic. "They've built a huge lake upstream," said one man. "It's beautiful, and you can fish there. They had a big opening with boat rides and all." And Yves Colin, former director of the 340-foot-high dam at Génissiat, waxed eloquent about its present capacity and the future of energy and navigation on this stretch of the Rhône.

But at Seyssel, just below Génissiat, I stood for a few quiet moments at the river's edge. "It's too calm," said a voice behind me. I turned in surprise. "The river," snorted an elderly woman. "The Rhône used to be beautiful. It was impetuous. It was, so to speak, the brother of the Rhine. But now it has been domesticated." She gestured upstream to the small local dam: "The dam has ruined it. It has sacrificed our river."

One of the Rhône's chief functions in Switzerland is to maintain a scenic water level in the Lake of Geneva. In the heart of the modern city of Geneva, a hundred-year-old trio of dams still does a creditable job. Downstream another century-old facility, a pumping station in a lofty raftered building with graceful arched windows, propels water from the lake through the entire canton of Geneva. Foreman Chalut was passionate in his admiration for the ancient pumps that thumped through the building like a gigantic heartbeat. "That's what we are, the heart of the city. Because without water there's no life," he said. "And it's all free! The river does everything!" But I was told that more efficient machinery would replace the dams and pumping station within ten years.

I could only marvel that the Rhône had created the 45-mile-long Lake of Geneva, the largest Alpine lake in Europe. Skirting its southern shore, I arrived at Le Bouveret, where the Rhône becomes the lake. Not far out, the green, muddy river disappeared, swallowed by the clear dark blue waters of the lake.

As I drove through Valais from Le Bouveret to Martigny, the snowcapped mountains on the periphery of my vision drew closer. At St. Maurice the now youthful river swirled along in frothy eddies through a narrow gorge. And at Martigny that night, a lighted chalet and floodlit castle floated high in the air outside my window. In the morning I saw vines terraced way up the mountain. Protected by encircling ranges, the canton's central plain enjoys plenty of sunshine and mild temperatures—ideal for growing vines, fruit, and vegetables.

The mountains press ever closer after you cross the German-language borderline west of Brig and approach the steep valley leading to the river's source. In Brig I took the little red narrow-gauge train up the valley to Oberwald, last stop before the Rhône Glacier at Gletsch. The railway runs by the river, clinging to the mountainside. The windows were open. I could smell cow manure and hear melodious cowbells near villages we passed. The snowy peaks, which had looked so remote before, suddenly seemed only an afternoon's walk away. The view was dizzying where the glistening river wound far, far below. At Oberwald I set out to hike the final three and a half miles to the glacier.

As I climbed, it got colder and the wind whistled through the pines. Several inches of ice cloaked the bottoms of mountain rivulets. I glanced across at a bleak slope scattered with glacial boulders and realized that I was above the level where people lived. It was strangely quiet without the cowbells.

I hitchhiked the last mile. An obliging gnome picked me up in his sturdy car. He wore a Tyrolean hat and jacket and an earring in one ear, and I could understand only two words he said. He was going "nach Grimsel"—to the Grimsel Pass. He took me nach Gletsch on the way, then sped on, leaving me alone.

And there I stood, gazing up at a patch of bluish ice—that feeds a river, that makes a lake, that turns back into a river, that becomes a giant, that flows down to the Mediterranean 500 miles from where I was standing. The Rhône was purling along nicely here in its shallow bed, green and clear and chuckling around pebbles. So I said goodbye, aloud.

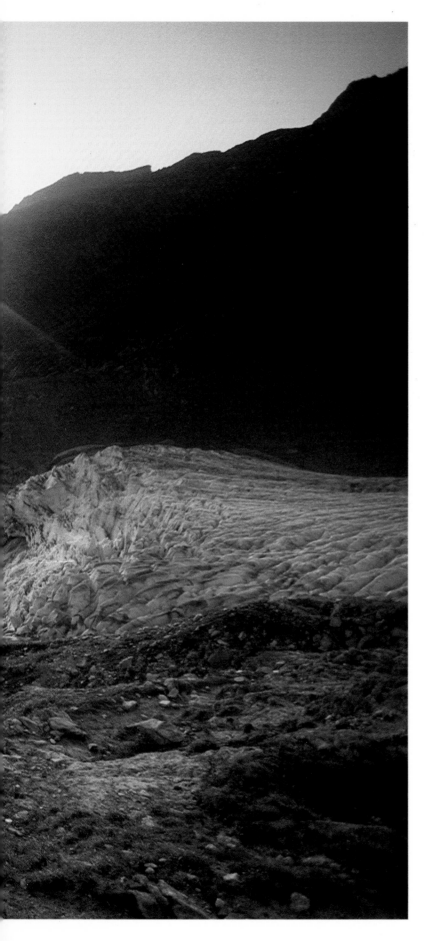

An evening sunburst illuminates the Rhône Glacier, the river's birthplace in the Swiss Alps. A century ago, ice covered much of the basin below, where the Rhône loops away in braided channels. A winding mountain road climbs past the historic Hotel Belvedere (center) and the visitors' entrance to an icy grotto.

Seasons govern the glacier's runoff, with highest annual flow from June to August and daily peaks when the sun is hottest. The milky surge takes a day to reach the Lake of Geneva some 130 miles downstream.

Seasonal rhythms dictate life, too, in the upper Rhône Valley. Families harvest potatoes near Oberwald (above) and tend sheep and cows on Alpine pastures. Hiking is popular in this scenic valley, and winter snows turn it into a skiers' wonderland.

173

irror image of the Quai St. Vincent silhouettes a fisherman beneath a footbridge on the Saône in Lyon (opposite). Farther south the Saône flows into the Rhône, almost doubling its volume.

Townsfolk joke about their "third river," Beaujolais wine. Flocking to street cafés (above), bistros, and three-star restaurants, they endorse Lyon's reputation for fine cuisine. Chefs use local ingredients: chicken, pork, fish, and cheese. From the Rhône Valley come fruit and vegetables, here heaped in brimming containers on a street market stall.

Pages 176-177: Châteauneuf-du-Pape vines bud out in early spring. "Rolled stones" are a gift from the Rhône that tumbled them down from the Alps eons ago. Reflecting the hot sun onto grapes, they ensure high sugar content—hence potent wines.

ôtes du Rhône vineyards prove the adage that "a vine likes to see the river but it doesn't like to get its feet wet." Grapes grow fat and sweet in the sunny climate alongside the Rhône.

A young worker near Ampuis (opposite) braces his pannier beneath cascading clusters of Syrah grapes in a Côte Rôtie vineyard, where grapes ripen on a steep "roasted slope." Muscle power matters here and at other northern vineyards such as Hermitage (left), where men load emptied tubs onto a truck for refilling. Hillside terraces require backbreaking manual labor.

Once picked, the grapes are pressed and processed at wineries. The Châteauneuf-du-Pape estates may blend thirteen grape varieties for full-bodied red wines, like the one being tasted in a cellar at Bédarrides (above), but most choose only six or seven.

C rowd pleasing dates back 2,000 years in Arles' Roman theater and amphitheater (top picture, right and left), where orators and gladiators starred. Today colorful festivals pack the theater, and amphitheater patrons cheer bullfights: Spanish-style corrida or Provençal course à la cocarde.

At a nearby arena (right) in Saintes-Maries-de-la-Mer, competitors strive to snatch the cockade (a red ribbon) from between the bull's sharp horns with a hooked comb. A flying leap to safety is no disgrace, even if you leave your comb in midair.

Thumbs-up sign comes from Fanfonne Guillierme, a local bull rancher. In her 80s now, she has herded bulls for 50 years in the Camargue. And in that mysterious, salt-encrusted marshland, the Rhône ends its journey, gradually yielding to the blue embrace of the Mediterranean.

THE RIVERS OF ASIA

Burma's Gawdawpalin temple looms over the Irrawaddy River. By Inger Elliott, Photo Researchers.

sia's rivers spring from the continent's core, a 5,000-mile-long belt of plateaus and mountains. Tumbling down these slopes, powerful streams flow south or east into the forests and swamps of monsoon lands. Others drop north of the core crossing the Siberian taiga. Still others course into steppe and desert country, fortifying the land with life-preserving oases.

Of all these giants, China's Yangtze runs the greatest distance, some 3,900 miles from the Plateau of Tibet to the East China Sea. A workhorse, the broad, swift-flowing Yangtze carries most of China's inland cargo.

But the Huang Ho, or Yellow River, most stirs Chinese passions. Known as China's sorrow, the Huang Ho has caused more disastrous floods than any other river in the world. It cleaves a serpentine course from the Tibetan highlands through a cold, mountainous region, settled sparsely by shepherds and goat herders. It loops north across the Ordos Desert, then turns south to traverse the Loess Plateau. Here the Huang Ho sweeps up enormous amounts of loess, the rich silt whose yellowish color gives the Huang Ho the name more familiar to Westerners. Geologists think the loess rode winds from Central Asian deserts to the plateau long ago. A load of silt equal to that filling all of North America's rivers winds up muddying the Huang Ho.

As the river continues south through gorges, then northeastward across low plains, much of the silt settles to the bottom and often raises the water level above the surrounding farmland. If it were not for protective dikes and levees, the Huang Ho would more often overwhelm its banks. Before intensive modern flood prevention programs, catastrophes occurred: In 1889 a flood swept away some 1,500 villages, killing and injuring one million people; 22 years later, unchecked Huang Ho waters either drowned or led to the starvation of some 3,700,000 Chinese.

Today, well-maintained levees guard the main channel. Reservoirs in the middle basin snare much of the silt that might cause trouble downriver. In addition, the government is encouraging citizens to terrace fields, build check

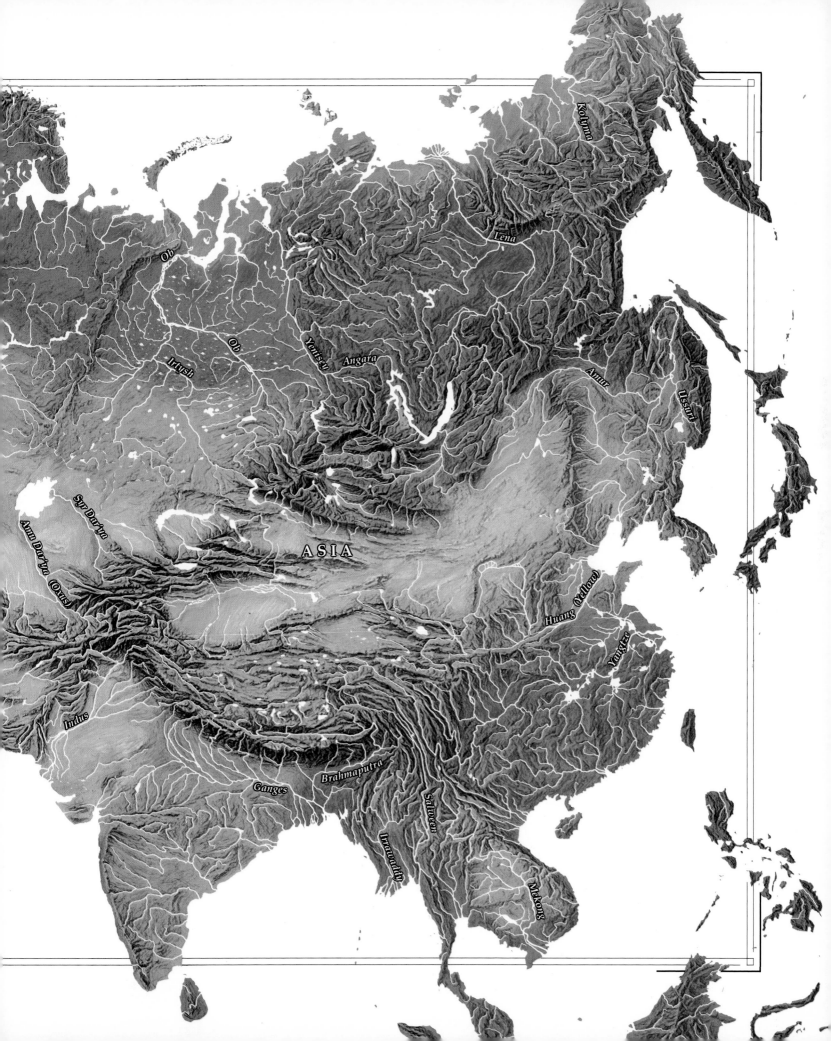

ASIA

Kolyma

Lena

Ob

Ob

Irtysh

Yenisey

Angara

Amur

Ussuri

Syr Dar'ya

Amu Dar'ya (Oxus)

Huang (Yellow)

Yangtze

Indus

Ganges

Brahmaputra

Salween

Irrawaddy

Mekong

God ushers Adam and Eve into Eden in a 1503 woodcut. Four rivers gush from gargoyles.
Two of them, the Tigris and Euphrates, embrace ancient Mesopotamia.

Opposite: A clay boat model sails the seas of time. Ancient mariners called Harappans
shaped it—and sailed its counterparts on the Indus River and out to sea 4,000 years ago.

dams in gullies, and plant trees to try and halt soil erosion, the cause of the silt problem. And the huge San-men Gorge Dam, southeast of the Ordos Desert, reduces the threat of flood upstream. Engineers promote some flooding to coat desert land with the fertile loess. In the plain of the lower Huang Ho, such irrigation has allowed for the area's first rice fields. Irrigation also enriches the farmland of Ningxia, where the Huang Ho curves north to the Ordos Desert. An ancient saying celebrates the river's work here: "The Huang Ho brings a hundred sorrows, but there is prosperity in the bend."

Sorrows and a push for prosperity also tell much of the story of the Mekong River. This 2,700-mile-long waterway drains more than 300,000 square miles from the Plateau of Tibet to the South China Sea. It bounds or traverses six nations, a region historically ravaged by war. To the farmers who work the plains and delta of the lower basin, this strife has again and again wreaked ruin. Most of these people—largely poor Thais, Khmers, and Vietnamese—tend paddies along the river. Until South Vietnam's fall to North Vietnam, the countries of Thailand, Kampuchea (then Cambodia), and South Vietnam had worked together to better the farmers' lives. Aided by a United Nations commission, they founded the Mekong River Development Project, whose aim was to boost rural economy by harnessing the Mekong. The project's accomplishments were many: building irrigation and hydroelectric facilities at both Nam Pung and Nam Phong in Thailand, erecting a power plant on the lower Done tributary in Laos, and improving methods of flood forecasting. But the Vietnamese invasion of Kampuchea in 1975 slowed further advances. Today an organization called the Interim Mekong Committee struggles—often in vain—to realize further water management plans.

West of the Mekong, and roughly paralleling it, flows the beautiful Salween. What makes the Salween scenic also makes it perilous. Rapids crash through narrow gorges, and dangerous backwaters swirl around jutting reefs. The rainy season sometimes swells its waters to flood levels.

Like the Mekong and Yangtze, the Salween has its headwaters in the Tanggula Range of eastern Tibet; 1,750 miles later, it empties into the Gulf of Martaban. After striking south through the gorges of China's Yunnan Province, the Salween slices across Burma's Shan Plateau. Along this choppy run, summer rains can raise the river level 50 feet and more. So Chinese and Burmese along the river build their villages on high ground. Little worked to date, these upper rapids could one day power irrigation and hydroelectric systems. Not surprisingly, vessels cannot navigate much of the Salween's frothing middle and upper reaches. But south from the Shan region, people raft teak and rice to the narrow delta for export from Moulmein harbor.

The Irrawaddy flows 1,200 miles through Burma from its mountain headwaters on the Burma-China border to the Andaman Sea. Villages dot its banks, serviced by steamers that push a thousand miles upstream. In the dry zone of its basin, from Mandalay south almost to the delta, farmers grow millet, rice, cotton, and beans. The Burmese government is building more canals, dams, and reservoirs to increase crop production.

In the past the dry zone set the pace for Burmese life, but today the delta fuels Burma's economy. Across those 12,000 square miles of raised levees and marshland, rice is king. Irrigated plots stretch to the horizon, keeping Burma near the top among the world's rice exporters. Next to this staple, fish winds up most often in Burmese cooking pots.

Remnants of past settlements are sprinkled along the Irrawaddy's basin. Just north of the delta lie the 2,000-year-old brick ruins of Shrikshetra, the first capital of Pyu settlers who brought Indian culture to Burma. Farther upstream, pagodas stud an eight-mile sweep of the river—impressive remains of Pagan, the capital of the empire of the Burmans, forbears of today's Burmese. More than 2,000 of an original 5,000 pagodas still stand, all built before the late 13th century A.D.

On the subcontinent of India, where Hinduism counts over 500 million believers—some 70 percent of the population—the faithful worship Ganga Ma, or Mother Ganges. They believe that bathing in the river cleanses the soul of sin. The Ganges also sees to their physical well-being. It irrigates rice and wheat fields, powers hydroelectric plants, and provides drinking water for about 17 percent of the land area of the subcontinent.

In Pakistan's Indus Valley, one of the world's earliest civilizations took root around 2500 B.C. Countless peoples have settled in the valley since that first Indus culture; foreign invaders have swept through as well, among them Alexander the Great in 325 B.C. The river that has lured so many begins its journey as melting snow in the mountains of Tibet. On its 1,800-mile trip to the Arabian Sea, the Indus flows across dusty plains in Pakistan. It drains an area a little smaller than the country of Egypt. Perhaps no river has been tapped more thoroughly by farmers. Canals have carried water across the basin for millennia, but the 19th and early 20th centuries have seen many more. Following Pakistan's separation from India in 1947, food shortages aggravated by surging immigration led to crisis for irrigation planners. Large-scale projects followed. The Bhakra Dam and Canal System soaks the once stubborn soil of the Rajasthan Desert, while dams and canals in both India and Pakistan enrich millions of acres in the Sind, Punjab, and western Thar Deserts. Most impressive is the

The demon king Ravana (right) squares off against two monkeys in a timeless pantomime photographed in Cambodia more than 70 years ago. Today this nation bears a modern name—Kampuchea—yet still looks to an ancient culture nurtured by the mighty Mekong River, lifeline of farming and commerce.

Indus Waters Treaty, painstakingly negotiated between India and Pakistan. This scheme diverts western Pakistan streams as irrigation sources to offset Pakistan's loss of water to India as a result of boundary claims. Thirty-four million acres soak up water channeled along the world's most extensive network of canals. The irrigated parts of the valley usually stay lush even through the driest months. In this country agriculture—wheat, rice, sugarcane, and other crops— accounts for 70 percent of the export trade.

In Soviet Asia the Amur River defies the rule for Siberian waterways by feeding chiefly on monsoon rains—not glaciers or snow—and draining into the Pacific—not the frigid Arctic or an inland lake. Threading along a mineral-rich and fertile valley, the Amur creates a pathway long traveled by settlers, traders, and soldiers. It also forms a lengthy stretch of the uneasy border between China and the Soviet Union.

From its source at the confluence of the Argun and Shilka Rivers on the

ights turn night into day—and water turns desert into cropland—along the Kara Kum Canal (above) in the Soviet republic of Turkmenia. One of the world's longest canals, this irrigation channel snakes nearly 700 miles through Central Asia's Kara Kum or "black sands" Desert. The waters of the Amu Dar'ya surge westward through the canal to fill reservoirs, and irrigate farms and greenbelts through once barren steppe. Workers labor day and night to widen this part of the watercourse for freight-carrying boats. East of

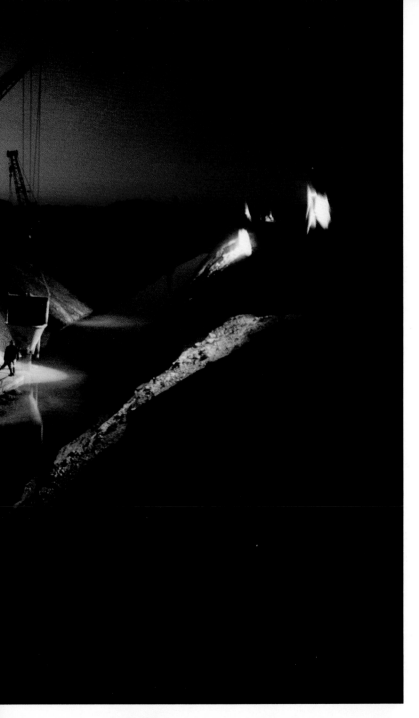

the Kara Kum Desert, north of the Amu Dar'ya as it traces the border of Afghanistan, Uzbekistan soil drinks from irrigation ditches to produce a bounty of crops. A worker in Dushanbe (opposite) forks bolls of cotton to dry in the sun. From the world's northernmost cotton region this crop keeps the U.S.S.R. among the world's top three cotton producers. Market days bring fruits and vegetables to Bukhara (left) and mounds of melons (above) to the feet of the 14th-century Bibi Khanum Mosque in Samarkand.

191

Chinese-Soviet border near Mongolia, the Amur first falls from high plateaus through deep, forested gorges. At Blagoveshchensk, it splits and then begins to weave across lowlands on its way to a level marshy plain and its broad Tatar Strait estuary, with islets and sandbars cluttering the bed. The Amur has been an asset to travel and commerce in this isolated corner of Asia. Navigable over its entire length, though ice-choked for half the year, the waterway connects remote taiga outposts to the coast. Oil from Sakhalin Island travels upstream while Siberian timber, grains, and machinery come downstream.

A century ago, Amur waters swollen by summer thunderstorms often submerged lowland areas. Today dams and levees protect the basin, and enrich cultivated plots. Both the Chinese and the Soviet Union profit—farms on both sides thrive. The two nations also benefit from stores of coal, petroleum, iron, and copper. The valley's wealth has provoked border disputes since Cossacks first settled here in the 17th century.

Development came much earlier to the Amu Dar'ya in Soviet Central Asia. Known in antiquity as the Oxus, the river courses 1,630 miles from the Pamir mountain ranges northwest to the Aral Sea. To the northeast spreads the Kyzyl Kum Desert; to the southwest, the Kara Kum. The Syr Dar'ya parallels much of

Dragon boats thread a rock-rimmed river on an 18th-century Chinese plaque. Even today, annual races of these fierce-headed craft honor Qu Yuan, poet of the third century B.C. who chided his era's weak kings, then drowned himself in despair in the Miluo River.

Inflated sheepskins buoy a load of dates on China's Yellow River in 1932.

the Amu Dar'ya's course, cutting a rich loess valley across Turkistan.

As early as 1200 B.C., farmers channeled irrigation water from the Amu Dar'ya's lower reaches. But no irrigation project yet undertaken here can rival the far-reaching and still uncompleted Kara Kum Canal, with its wide, deep channel, reservoirs, hydroelectric plants, and subsidiary canals. The Kara Kum begins just upstream from Chardzhou in a region that has been irrigated for centuries. By 1985 it should reach Krasnovodsk on the Caspian Sea.

Farther southwest, across Iraq and Syria, spreads the ancient "fertile crescent"—although its most fertile years may be past. The lifeblood of the many cultures that thrived here—Sumerian, Babylonian, Assyrian, Persian, and Turkish among them—flowed from the Tigris and Euphrates Rivers. Most of these peoples built dams and canals to make the rivers work. Many traveled the waterways through the inhospitable desert. Towns flourished along the riverfronts, crowned by the splendor of Baghdad, a 1,200-year-old city that survives as Iraq's capital. Centuries of irrigation have deposited too much salt into too many acres; stripping of forests has sped the erosion of topsoil. The Iraqis must irrigate—after oil their chief exports are farm products such as dates, barley, wheat, and rice. Water projects abound, among them the Kut Barrage on the Tigris, which serves some 900,000 acres by way of the Gharraf Canal. And 35 miles north of Mosul, a dam across the Tigris stands as the world's fifth largest. The lake it creates sends water to some 2,250,000 acres.

Obviously, to speak of the rivers of Asia is to speak in superlatives. These waterways drain one third of the land surface of the globe. More than half the human race lives in Asia, depending on the cultivation of food crops and, thus, on these great rivers. Now, channeled and dammed, they serve the most agrarian continent on Earth. The past has made great demands on Asia's overworked rivers. The future is likely to be no different.

THE GANGES

Text and photographs by George F. Mobley

The axis deer bolted. Moments later, a tiger crept into the clearing below my watchtower. The tiger sniffed the air, then melted into the dense mangrove swamps. Hoping the tiger would return, I waited in the afternoon heat and reflected on the river that created the Sundarbans, this ever shifting maze of waterways and islands in the largest river delta in the world.

The Ganges rushes from a Himalayan glacier and boils through deep gorges, cutting away rock and soil, and capturing streams. After reaching the broad Ganges Plain, the river flows gently during the dry season, rages like a sea during the monsoons, and gathers strength from scores of tributaries. Near the Bangladesh border, the Ganges divides. The main channel, now called the Padma, flows east to join the Brahmaputra in Bangladesh; the other, briefly called the Bhagirathi, then the Hooghly, flows south past Calcutta. After the split the Ganges also fans out, carving channels through the jungle and depositing silt to help form the huge delta. Saltwater marshes and tidal estuaries stretch along the coast from the Indian state of West Bengal nearly across Bangladesh.

Ganga Ma—Mother Ganges, as Hindus revere the river—is the heart of India and the Hindu faith, one of the world's oldest religious traditions. The waters of the Ganges and its tributaries mean life itself for the 300 million Indians and Bangladeshis who live in the Ganges basin and depend on the river for irrigation, electric power, and drinking water. To Hindus, the Ganges is the most sacred river, a goddess they have worshiped since long before the time of Christ.

Hindus believe bathing in the Ganges washes away sins. The water plays an important part in rituals to purify body and soul. Pilgrims from far away carry Ganges water home to use in weddings, births, and funerals. Hindus generally cremate their dead, ideally on the banks of the Ganges, believing the practice releases the soul from its temporary bodily abode.

I had come to India to trace the Ganges from its tropical mouth in the Sundarbans to its glacial source. The pilgrimage had begun in my childhood

Sunlight glints on the bearded face of Gangotri Glacier high in the Himalayas at the source of the Ganges. Many Hindus believe the goddess-river fell from heaven, tamed by the god Shiva, who trapped her Earth-threatening torrent in his matted locks.

as my father read me Rudyard Kipling's tales of holy men and Himalayas.

In the past three decades, Indians and Bangladeshis have pushed back the jungle in the Sundarbans. Settlers have built dikes, cleared and drained land for farming, cut forests for lumber and firewood. At the same time, the saltwater crocodile and Bengal tiger populations were threatened. With help from World Wildlife Fund, the Indian and West Bengal governments have established a crocodile farm and an animal sanctuary for the tigers, axis deer, wild boar, and countless smaller animals that inhabit the Ganges Delta. Bangladesh shares in conservation efforts.

I visited the Sundarbans aboard a 37-foot launch belonging to West Bengal's Forest Department. From the fishing village of Basanti, southeast of Calcutta, I had motored with a guide into the swamps before stopping at the watchtower where I had spotted the tiger.

It never returned. I climbed back on board the launch, and we wound south through tidal creeks, deeper into the animal preserve. At dusk a full moon rose over the mangroves, painting a silvery path in our wake.

"A honey collector was killed there last month by a tiger." My guide pointed to a narrow inlet. "His friends had gone into the bush. They heard the commotion, but by the time they reached the water's edge, he was dead."

In the Indian Sundarbans alone, I was told, tigers kill 25 to 30 people a year. Most victims are honey collectors, wood gatherers, or fishermen. "Fishermen are not supposed to come here, but they have such a hard time making a living where it is crowded," my guide said, wiping his sweaty brow. "They come a long way, and it's dangerous. They take their fish from the tiger's mouth."

The air was still oppressive when we dropped anchor after midnight.

On the third night we reached Sagar Island. Every January pilgrims flock to this flat, marshy island for a festival that celebrates its role in the mythical descent of the Ganges from heaven to earth. But now the island was quiet; the Kapilmuni Ashram Temple held only a priest and two visitors. From there the half-mile walk to the shore led across a deserted beach. Windblown sand hissed over broken bits of earthenware discarded by pilgrims.

On the Hooghly, at the head of navigable water for seagoing vessels, East India Company agent Job Charnock established the first permanent English settlement in 1690 to open the interior of Bengal for trade. The settlement grew into the city of Calcutta, capital of British India until 1912. With access to abundant supplies of jute, tea, and indigo, Calcutta flourished during the 19th and early 20th centuries. Then, during World War II, famine drove masses of refugees into the city. Thousands starved in the streets. In 1947 India became independent from Britain and divided along religious lines into two nations. The central and southern portions of the country retained the name India; the predominantly Muslim northeastern and northwestern portions formed the new

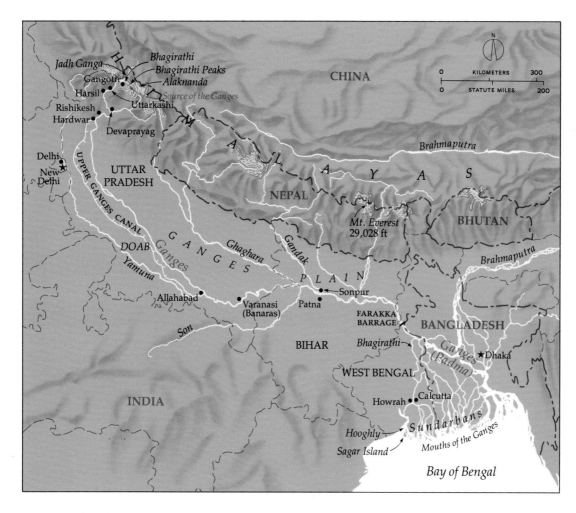

nation of Pakistan.

The partition brought religious riots and more refugees as East Bengal became East Pakistan and then, after a bitter struggle with West Pakistan in 1971, the independent nation of Bangladesh.

Although Calcutta's harbor once accommodated the largest ships afloat, the Hooghly is too shallow for modern bulk carriers. As the Ganges shifted more of its flow into the eastern channel, silt began to clog the Hooghly. To divert more water down the Hooghly, India built the Farakka Barrage 11 miles from the Bangladesh border although there had been no previous agreement with Bangladesh nor with East Pakistan. The 1971 dam sparked a feud over water rights and has failed to reduce siltation in the Hooghly.

Calcutta is crowded, filthy, chaotic, noisy, and hot. During my visit, the air simmered by 6:30 in the morning. My elbows rested in pools of sweat on the tea shop table. Before the monsoons begin in mid-June, the thermometer often reaches 105°F, and the humidity hovers near 100 percent. Ceiling fans and air conditioners have no value when the electricity fails—as it does nearly every day. Telephone and telegraph also suffer frequent interruptions.

But despite its shortcomings, Calcutta is a cultural center. Audiences pack theaters for movies, plays, concerts, and classical dance performances. Soccer fans line up early to get seats in the giant stadium on the Maidan, a large park in central Calcutta. City parks attract families for weekend outings. I spent a quiet afternoon strolling through shady trees beside the Rabindra Sarobar, formerly the Dhakuria Lakes. Cormorants dived for fish, and oarsmen propelled a racing shell across the water. Blue hyacinths bloomed along the fringe.

Calcutta's 11 million people live in everything from mansions to tin-and-cardboard shacks so small their occupants sleep outdoors. Often, several people rent the same room and sleep in shifts. Thousands are homeless.

Buses, trucks, cars, bicycles, and rickshas jam the streets. Traffic signals fail routinely. Even when the signals work, no one seems to heed them or other rules of the road. Drivers park where they please and often abandon vehicles that break down.

Sometimes I walked around the city. Blaring horns, racing engines, loud mufflers, and amplified music assaulted my ears. I jostled through the crowds, breathing diesel exhaust from buses packed to overflowing. Here and there, cows foraged in the mounds of garbage fermenting in streetside dumps.

Beggars waited at the hotel entrance. Men with twisted bodies and women with babies slung on their hips approached me, crying "Rupees, rupees." Others pleaded in silence.

L eaving Calcutta, I drove across the Howrah Bridge and north along the Hooghly through the lush state of West Bengal. Beyond industrialized Howrah lay a string of urban communities, each merging with the next, many retaining traces of their European colonial origins. Gradually the population thinned out. The towns became villages with mud huts, small brick buildings, mango and banana groves. Jute, rice, and pulses grew in the fields.

I followed the Ganges upstream and west into Bihar. I stopped at a sandy beach that sloped into the brown Ganges. An old man with a leathery face and dirty clothes stood alone beside the wide, lazy river. "Why have you come here?" he asked in a gravelly voice, leaning on a rough staff and waving his free hand as he spoke. "This is a cremation site. You are still living!" I drove on.

The rice, wheat, and pulse farmers of Bihar struggle under the plain's harsh rhythm of droughts and floods. In the villages, nursing mothers squatted on the porches of dried mud huts. Women with earthen jugs on their heads trudged through the dust to the wells. Men with ox plows scratched rough furrows in the hard soil. I drove five hours without meeting another car. But I heard the creak of oxcarts, the rattle of bicycles, the splash of oars in the river, and the whistle of a distant train.

In the state of Uttar Pradesh, halfway between the Bay of Bengal and the Himalayan source of the Ganges, stands the city of Varanasi, the holiest city of Hinduism for nearly three millennia. The British called the city Banaras.

In Varanasi vendors hawked goods sacred and profane from open stalls: painted clay idols, marigold garlands, incense, garlic, cinnamon, gingerroot, coriander, cartons of tea, a kind of lentil soup called *dal,* unleavened bread called *chapatis,* earthenware, cast iron pots and pans. The smell of sandalwood, curry, burning cow dung, coal and wood smoke, and sweet milky tea filled the lanes. Flutes and drums competed with loudspeakers.

The river was pale in the early morning light. Temples towered along the banks. Priests and their clients lined the ghats, broad flights of stone steps leading into the water. Thousands of people bathed in Mother Ganges. Holy men sat meditating, and bards were singing and reciting the Hindu epics, the *Ramayana* and the *Mahabharata.*

During my stay in Varanasi, I often sought quiet in the middle of the river. For a few rupees a round-faced boatman was always eager to row me there in his small boat. "Ask for Cheddi Boatman," he said.

As we drifted slowly downstream one evening, I watched firelight dancing on the water at Manikarnika Ghat. Smoke billowed from the funeral pyres, and burning wood crackled. Mourners haggled with wood sellers or immersed and garlanded the bodies awaiting cremation. Once preparations were complete, a mourner, usually the eldest son, circled the body several times, then lit the pyre with a sheaf of burning grass. When the fire had nearly completed its work, he cracked the skull with a long stick, thereby releasing the soul.

Varanasi's two cremation ghats have become a political issue. Mourners and attendants keep the fires burning 24 hours a day, cremating some 35,000 bodies each year and casting the ashes into the Ganges. Because firewood is scarce and costly, some bodies go into the river only partially burned. The very poorest people dump bodies directly into the water without any attempt at cremation. City officials want electric crematoriums, which are cheaper and more efficient. But the officials face stiff opposition from the *doms,* whose status as untouchables in the Hindu caste system is now outlawed. The doms are attendants who control the ghats, the right to burn bodies, and the firewood concessions. The doms argue—and much of the public agrees—that electric crematoriums would breach ancient Hindu traditions.

Cheddi Boatman rowed back to shore and jumped out smiling, his teeth red from the betel nuts he always chewed. He tied the boat next to a sewer that emptied into the river beside a bathing ghat.

Many people claim that Ganges water destroys bacteria. But at Banaras

Hindu University Dr. Katil N. Udupa disagrees. He told me the university's microbiology department had tested the water at several points along the river and found bacteria everywhere. Yet Dr. Udupa insisted that drinking Ganges water does not cause widespread disease.

"Millions drink it every day, and they don't get sick. Faith plays a very important role in this. It's psychosomatic. Many people say it's the mind that makes people fit or ill, and there is a very intense faith that Ganges water is good for you." He also pointed out that people tend to develop a tolerance for bacteria to which they are continually exposed.

Exploring the nearby floodplain, I came upon a mound of earth 350 feet across and 12 feet high. On it sat nine huts, the village of Bansi ki Pahi. Water buffalo grazed in the fields. In a faded sari an aged woman named Magna hunkered on the ground and waved her dark, wrinkled hand as she described life in the village. Men, women, and children clustered about her. Someone gave me a glass of water buffalo milk, boiling hot and creamier than cow's milk. The village's 80 inhabitants grow millet, wheat, chick-peas, rice, sugarcane, lentils, and guavas. For cash they sell buffalo milk in Varanasi.

"We're totally under the power of rain," Magna told me. "No pump. No well for irrigation, only one small well for drinking water. But the moment the heavy floods of the monsoons come, we are finished. Everything is finished."

The farmers must plant crops in the rainy season and hope that the flooding spares them for the harvest. Sometimes the floods are too great. The water rises into the homes, forcing the villagers to take refuge away from the river. When the flooding ends, Magna and her kin return to Bansi ki Pahi to rebuild and to till the fresh silt the floodwaters have left behind.

"Ganga is troubling us, wasting our crops, breaking our houses," Magna said. "In spite of the trouble, we don't hate her. She is our mother."

Upstream from Varanasi in the city of Allahabad millions of pilgrims gather (every 12 years or so, depending on the positions of stars and planets) for Kumbh Mela, a festival of a mythical battle between gods and demons.

The most recent Kumbh Mela, in 1977, was relatively uneventful. But in 1954 the crowd panicked and trampled to death hundreds—some say thousands—of people. Ashok Mohiley, a prosperous lawyer I met in Allahabad, was 19 years old at the time, but he remembers it well.

"My family and friends were returning from the river when a procession blocked our route," he told me. "We had to wait while the crowd poured in behind us. Suddenly people rushed forward to touch the feet of holy men, and the police forced them back. We were caught between the crowd pushing from the river and the crowd running toward it. We were literally lifted off our feet. People fell and were crushed. My legs were trapped among the bodies, and I fell. Several people ran across my back. Everyone was in panic, running, screaming. After I freed myself, I heard my mother crying under a pile of bodies. A friend and I pulled her out of the heap."

With D. K. Burman, a stocky government worker who had befriended me in Varanasi, I took a boat to the confluence, where the jade green waters of the Yamuna mingle with the silty brown waters of the Ganges and, according to most Hindus, with the invisible, mythical Saraswati. We docked at a platform out in the river and watched pilgrims come and go in small boats. Many people bathed and frolicked in the shallow water. But nearby, an old woman covered her eyes. Five men, their shaved heads a sign of mourning, argued with a priest about the price of a ritual for a deceased family member. The priest wanted twice what they possessed but finally settled for all they had.

"These people are poor and ignorant," D. K. said. "Some of these priests are sharp salesmen. They are worse than thieves. At least thieves come with known intentions."

I drove northwest through the Doab, the rich plain between the Ganges and Yamuna. The land was a patchwork of tiny fields, recently harvested. Piles of wheat and pulses lay in the yards. Villagers had dried cakes of cow dung in the sun, stacked them in dome-shaped piles, and plastered the piles with fresh manure to seal out rain. They sprouted everywhere like mammoth brown eggs poking up through the soil. In the months ahead the dung would serve as fuel.

The Doab used to suffer devastating sieges of famine whenever the monsoons failed. In the mid-1800s the British built the Upper Ganges Canal for irrigation. Today, during the dry season almost all the Ganges water is diverted into the canal, by a weir across the river, leaving a mere trickle over gravel in the broad main channel. The canal begins at Hardwar, where the flat monotony of the plains gives way to the Himalayan foothills.

In the 1,400 miles from the Bay of Bengal to Hardwar, the Ganges gains only a thousand feet in altitude. Then abruptly the course steepens. At Rishikesh, some 15 miles upstream from Hardwar, towering canyon walls confine the river, and it becomes a torrent.

In Rishikesh I found a smorgasbord of religious institutions—ashrams (retreats), yoga schools, medical centers, temples, and caves of holy men. I joined a new friend, Sanjeev Saith, a wiry man with a black beard, for the journey to the river's source. Sanjeev had studied economics in Delhi before becoming a mountaineer. We drove up into the Himalayas through the deciduous forests of the terraced valley. The narrow road clung to high cliffs. The trees gradually thinned out as we drove for hours uphill and downhill.

We stopped for the night at Devaprayag, where the Bhagirathi, the source stream, and the Alaknanda Rivers rush together to form the Ganges.

At Uttarkashi we bought food for the trip. The road climbed steadily beside rapids. Rain often causes landslides here, and we encountered several bulldozers clearing away rock and gravel. Once, debris knocked a hole in our oil pan. We plugged it with a bar of soap and went on our way.

An avalanche blocked the narrow road at Harsil, a village of wood and stone huts strung along the river amid budding apple trees. Abandoning the car, we climbed over the snow and broken trees and set off down a deserted gravel road through a valley bright with wild apricots. Below us, red rhododendrons punctuated the steep slopes. Pine trees and deodar cedars scented the valley. A red fox trotted along the hillside above us. It stopped and sat on a rock for several minutes watching us watch it. Finally it got up and casually trotted away.

We camped on the flattest, driest place we could find—a wooden bridge over the Bhagirathi. Night fell as we built a fire on the riverbank and cooked our supper of dal, chapatis, boiled cabbage, and tea.

Next day, to cross the deep gorge of the Jadh Ganga River, we plunged down a precipitous trail to the canyon floor. Rock walls towered above deep pools, roaring cataracts, and mossy boulders. We panted up the other side of the gorge. Continuing along the trail, by midafternoon we reached Gangotri, the village nearest the source of the Ganges. The tiny valley community's stone and wood huts flank a small temple that attracts thousands of hardy pilgrims each year. We crossed the river and followed a footpath to a rustic retreat, the Dandi Ashram, where pilgrims find food, lodging, and instruction. Swami Poornanand, a tall clean-shaven man with sparkling eyes, welcomed us with cups of hot tea.

The swami, whose name means Complete Bliss, came here on a spiritual quest 19 years ago and stayed. Now he teaches and oversees the ashram as a service to pilgrims.

"I came to find out who I am," he told me. "But if you don't recognize it at home, why should you recognize it here? Will the tree come here to look for its own shadow, or will it look to the sun? One is a form of the other."

He pointed to his saffron yellow cap and sweater. "Compare these. They seem different, but remove the thread and it's all the same. You look at the world and everything seems different, but at the heart of everything—at its essence—everything is made of one thread. At the heart of everything is God."

On the third day from Harsil, Sanjeev and I set out in five inches of fresh snow for our final destination, where, at an altitude of more than 13,000 feet, the Bhagirathi emerges from the Gangotri Glacier. Slush and rivulets soaked the steep trail. In many places rockslides had scoured the trail off the canyon walls or buried it with rubble. We made our own path, feeling for footholds. As the sun melted the ice and snow in the vertical wall of glacial moraine above, rocks came crashing down around us. We found a safe spot and camped. It would be better to climb in the morning while the ice was solid.

The moon still rode high over the frozen ridge when we set out. Just above camp we found snow leopard tracks and traced them for an hour before they turned off the trail. At last we climbed a ridge of snowy moraine and sat on a rock, savoring the view.

The river appeared from a hole in the snow near where it springs from an ice cave at the glacier's snout. The water disappeared under a snow bridge almost immediately, then reemerged a hundred yards downstream to continue its 1,560-mile journey to the Bay of Bengal. Beyond the river rose a greenish wall of fissured glacial ice. Above that towered the 21,000-foot Bhagirathi Peaks. Off to the right rose Mount Shivling.

Hot from the walk and eager to taste at last the water of the Ganges, we scrambled down from the ridge and drank directly from the stream. The water was ice cold, sweet, delicious, and vital. We pitched our tent on the moraine overlooking the glacier. Afternoon clouds poured over the mountains, and a light snow fell at dusk.

Sanjeev lay propped against his rucksack, halfway into his sleeping bag. A white terrycloth hat hid his eyes; his mustache and beard hid the rest of his face. Despite the cold, his fingers moved nimbly over a simple bamboo flute. Delicate notes rose into the night, blending with the murmur of the river, the gentle flapping of the tent, and the distant rumble of rocks down canyon walls.

When morning came, we explored the area and climbed a short way up the face of the glacier beneath an ice wall adorned with crystal icicles.

High clouds were moving in, so we made a late breakfast of oatmeal, then reluctantly broke camp. After a last drink of Ganges water, Sanjeev started down the trail. I sat alone on a rock atop the moraine and watched clouds swirl on the top of Mount Shivling and ice glisten on the Bhagirathi Peaks.

Maybe Swami Poornanand was right. Perhaps everything *was* of one thread. The water bubbling from the glacier was the same water that would wash away the sins of bathing Hindus from Hardwar to Sagar Island; would irrigate the Doab; would buoy the boat of the charlatan priest at Allahabad; would waste the crops and break the houses at Bansi ki Pahi; would swallow ashes, corpses, sewage, and marigold petals at Varanasi; would deposit rich sediment on the floodplains of Bihar; would clog the Hooghly with silt; and yet would taste as vital to the axis deer and the Bengal tigers in the Sundarbans as it did to me here at the source.

I drank in the beauty before me, and a strange, sad peacefulness came over me. It *was* a holy place.

 procession bears images of the warrior goddess Durga and other Hindu deities through the streets of Calcutta and down to the river (above). Each autumn the city turns out for Durga Puja, a nine-day festival celebrating the triumph of good over evil. Craftsmen work year round building images of Durga, placing a weapon in each of her ten hands poised to slay the demon Mahisha. First the idol maker smooths clay over a frame of lath, cane, and tightly packed straw. Then he adorns it with paint, flowers, tinsel, and thinly sliced white cork. Durga is the patron deity of Bengalis and is usually depicted riding a lion.

The festivities peak (right) as celebrants cast the images into the river.

The Howrah Bridge (above) spans the wide Hooghly, as the Ganges is called flowing past Calcutta, and links Calcutta with its sister city, Howrah, and the rest of India. The British built the cantilevered bridge during World War II. Along with buses, trucks, cars, rickshas, and bicycles, more than a half million commuting pedestrians cross the bridge daily. Calcutta teems with immigrants from nearby states. They add new ethnic customs to the city's diversity and impose a severe strain on the economy.

During Durga Puja, Calcuttans

gather at a pandal—a temporary neighborhood shrine featuring a clay tableau of the goddess Durga vanquishing the demon (top). The pandals are usually canopies or tents, but some have elaborate touches. A fierce mask of woven fiber (opposite) glares from a shrine in Mohammed Ali Park. Each neighborhood sets up its own pandal where worshipers can sing, pray, and offer sweets and flowers to the deities. Festivals mean a brisk trade for those who sell garlands and flowers used in worship (right).

priver from Calcutta, farmers harvest jute, which thrives in steamy West Bengal. Grandmothers care for small children (right), while other family members work in the fields. In the East India Company's day, jute first helped Calcutta prosper. The golden fiber remains the region's major cash crop. Farmers hack off stalks at the base, diving underwater if necessary, then submerge them in bundles (below) for as long as a month. After the outer bark rots, workers strip away long strands of the inner fiber (far right). Rinsed, dried, and baled the fibers go to jute mills to become goods ranging from ropes and burlap to imitation silk.

Pages 210-211: At dawn elephants lumber into the river at Sonpur. Their keepers will scrub them clean with porous stones, decorate them with paint, and sell them at the giant fair.

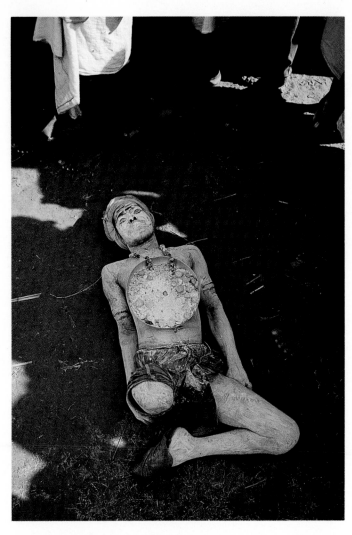

 indus throng to the confluence of the Ganges and Gandak Rivers to commemorate a mythical battle. Their hair glistening after a ritual bath in the Gandak, worshipers (right) jam the lane to a nearby temple, carrying pots of water to pour on an image that unites the forms of the great gods Vishnu and Shiva. A beggar with a plate of coins on his chest seeks alms (above).

In the battle legend, a huge and evil crocodile clamped his jaws on the leg of an elephant and began dragging him into the river. When the elephant cried out to Lord Vishnu, the god intervened and killed the aggressor. The religious event occurs during the Sonpur Mela, an annual month-long autumn fair. Highlights are the famous elephant and cattle sales. Indian fairs offer food, drink, movies, singers and dancers, and carnival rides.

ife and especially death in Varanasi center on the ghats—stone steps leading down to the Ganges. Funeral pyres blaze at Manikarnika Ghat (left), as bodies shrouded in red or white await the fires. Many Hindus hope to die in the ancient, holy city of Varanasi in order to escape the cycle of reincarnation and to achieve union with the Supreme Being. Residents and pilgrims from every walk of life bathe in the river to purify body and soul (above). Cupping water in their hands, bathers let it run through their fingers as an offering to gods or ancestors, and carry it home in pots for rituals. Pilgrims visit a nearby temple that slid into the river in the 19th century. Or they sprinkle water or flowers on a marble slab bearing Vishnu's footprints or bathe in a pool where Shiva is said to have dropped a jeweled earring.

P ilgrims cross the floodplain at Allahabad (right). Here the Ganges unites with its tributary, the Yamuna, and with the invisible, mythical Saraswati to form the most sacred confluence of the Ganges' course. Bathing in these waters brings many blessings, most during Kumbh Mela, a festival held by an astrological calendar—usually every 12 years. Here, also, people bring the ashes of their dead for immersion—a final goal of many Hindus. Even India's great leader, the secular Jawaharlal Nehru, requested this act as his "last homage to India's cultural inheritance. . . ." A sadhu or holy man (below) mortifies his body in a tradition recalling Allahabad's ancient name, Prayaga—"place of sacrifice." He controls his breathing using techniques of yoga.

A llahabad's bazaars bustle with commerce. Poverty, expensive gasoline, and national priorities in manufacturing make private cars scarce and cycle rickshas, buses, and motor scooters (above) popular. A fabric merchant (opposite) will unfurl bright silk, cotton, and synthetic saris to their full six-yard lengths for any customer who takes off her sandals and sits on the covered platform in front of his tiny shop. His assistant will fold the rejects. Nearby, a sidewalk grocer weighs peppers on a hand balance (left) as the goddess Durga oversees the transaction from a lithograph on the pillar beside him. The red onions, gingerroot, chili peppers, limes, and garlic he sells spice up a national diet that is more than 70 percent grain.

When the gods spilled the nectar of immortality on Allahabad, a drop also splashed onto Hardwar in the rich plain, the Doab. The city celebrates many religious festivals, including Kumbh Mela. On Baisakhi, the solar New Year, Hindus gather at Hari-ka-charan Ghat (right) to praise the goddess Ganga and sing into the night. Bathers may hang onto chains linked to a ghat or bridge for safety in the fierce current. Hardwar sits just below the head of the Upper Ganges Canal, at the mouth of the gorge that spews the Ganges onto the plain. A city more than 2,000 years old, Hardwar has established many traditions. Local laws ban consumption of meat, fish, eggs, alcohol, and drugs. Guidebooks admonish tourists against "hobnobbing" and announce that "Roughs and rowdys forget their disturbing activities on the pious land of Hardwar."

A Hindu family worships the god Shiva at a temple (opposite) on an old Ganges channel in Kankhal, outside Hardwar. Cloth and garlands drape a lingam, or phallic representation of the deity, while offerings of water poured on the heart-shaped stone run into the tank. Shiva's mount, the divine bull Nandi, guards the sanctuary. Sanskrit verses adorn the lintels. At right, a native of nearby Roorkee reads a devotional tract at the Mansa Devi Temple, on a peaceful hilltop above Hardwar and the river. In mountains to the north (below), the Bhagirathi and Alaknanda Rivers join to become the Ganges. At the confluence is the holy city of Devaprayag.

Pages 224-225: Terraced fields deck the slopes above Uttarkashi on the Bhagirathi.

R ushing through the village of Gangotri (above), the sacred river is less than 60 feet wide. An 18th-century temple built by a Gurkha commander to honor the goddess Ganga perches on the bank amid vacant market stalls. In winter the temple is closed, and only a few ascetics remain in the area. Outside his nearby hut, Swami Sundarananda (left) recounts his wanderings in the Himalayas. During summer, pilgrims flock to Gangotri. Hardy visitors trek another 12 miles to the river's source, stopping at a rest house or camping beside the trail. Mount Sudarshan (right) overlooks Gangotri Falls and the deodar cedars of the narrow gorge below the village. Through the centuries, water and ice have polished the granitic riverbed to a marble-like smoothness.

T he Bhagirathi River, considered by Hindus the headwater of the Ganges, bursts into the open (above), only to dive quickly under the snow. Late spring snows conceal the source of the stream—an ice cave at the snout of the massive Gangotri Glacier (center, above). Summertime pilgrims to Gaumukh, or "cow's mouth" as the cave is known, find a boulder-strewn terrain. Campers gather around a fire as the cold Himalayan night settles over the Bhagirathi Peaks.

SIBERIA

WILD & MIGHTY SHORES

By Ernest B. Furgurson

To think of Siberia is to see Katya, her flame red hair jouncing behind as she ran toward the cabin beside the lake—and then the lake itself and the piercing pure wind that blows 15-foot waves against the gray stone shore.

It is to hear Yuri again, bragging politely about how he earns twice as much as engineers back in European Russia, and how when the great dam began he braved mosquitoes flying so thick they clogged the nostrils.

To much of the world, Siberia is a legendary monotony of snow and ice and cruel prison camps. And those legends are true.

But to today's Russia, Siberia is the frontier. It is where eager young engineers, parachuting explorers, ambitious party apprentices come to build careers. That means challenging and developing immense north-flowing rivers, each on the scale of the Mississippi, the keys to gold, coal, oil, gas, timber, electricity beyond estimation.

Olekma . . . Tunguska . . . Amur . . . Ob . . . Lena . . . Irtysh . . . Siligir . . . Indigirka . . . Amga . . . Vitim . . . Kolyma . . . to fly across Siberia is to watch hundreds of rivers cut the mountains and plateaus sliding past. Like all great rivers, they are complex systems. But perhaps none is more complex in its geology, biology, history, and its future than the Angara-Yenisey, which surges out of Lake Baykal through the very heart of Siberia.

Some geographers maintain that mapmakers cheated the Yenisey River. Its true source, they say, is the headwaters of the Selenga, deep inside Mongolia. Measured thus, the Selenga, Angara, and Yenisey together would be 3,440 miles long—and the 2,540-mile-long river we call the Yenisey would crash through the gorges of the Sayan Mountains by some other name.

The Angara on its way to join the Yenisey is majestic on its own. It passes Irkutsk, long the unofficial capital of Siberia. To Irkutsk came Cossack fur traders in the mid-1600s, and, later, exiles from tsarist oppression. Settlers built thousands of traditional Russian cottages with elaborately carved eaves and window frames. There came the Trans-Siberian Railroad in 1898, main corridor of

Salekhard's harbor is icebound as the end of winter approaches. At this Arctic Circle port on the Ob River, shipping shuts down between November and March.

Russian development. And then came Progress: the first of the monster dams on the Angara in 1958. After that, bulldozers started ripping down the old houses of character as builders put up repetitious concrete flats. But still Irkutsk was the crossroads of Soviet east and west.

That is how Katya comes in, and Yuri and Irina and the callow young draftees we three Western journalists met at the Arktika Restaurant in Irkutsk.

Katya's hair was bright as the autumn sunset that lights the mountains running off toward Mongolia. The day after our arrival at Baykal we spotted her as our car swung around a curve and for the first time we saw the cold blue waters of the lake pouring between abrupt snowy hills into the Angara. Katya was plodding along the roadside, puffing steam. She seemed no more than 20 years old. She waved us down and, without asking, leaped onto our laps in the backseat, giggling.

"I'm from Omsk, where are you from?" (In Siberia everybody is from somewhere else.) "What are you doing here? How do you like our lake? Is it this cold in America?" Then before we knew what to make of this dreamlike gift, she stopped the driver and jumped out and ran away waving, down a packed snow path toward the lake.

It had lasted hardly minutes, but burned into my memory. Somehow Katya—young, bold, trusting, in a hurry—came to symbolize all the excitement of Siberia. We hypothesized about her as we wound into the village of Listvyanka and surprised the napping manager of the boatyard lunchroom by asking for a midafternoon meal. She was glad to thaw us out with thick potato soup and sliced onions, then pickled *omul* and fried *kharyus*.

That began our short course on the fauna, flora, and mythology of Baykal, source of the Angara, reservoir of one-fifth of the world's fresh water, a lake like no other. Omul and kharyus are salmon relatives. They are two of the 1,800 species of wildlife found at Baykal, 75 percent of them unique or endemic to this lake. Baykal is one mile plus 45 feet deep, fed by 336 streams and emptied by only one, the Angara. If all the inflow stopped at once, it would take 400 years to empty, if the water could run out at its present rate.

Such statistics piled up till they drove us outdoors, where the zero wind whipped across the shore and the boats, stacked bottom up, awaited spring. Icy spray coated the boats and dripped icicles down to the pebbly beach. But even in late November the lake's surface did not freeze, and would not till New Year's because of the lashing wind. Once the ice covers the lake, it becomes five feet thick and from 1903 until 1915 carried the Trans-Siberian Railroad eastward during the winters before a year-round roadbed was cut around the lake's south shore. In summer, ferries transported the trains.

Baykal is clear and pure, with life forms in especially delicate balance. Because of this it has been the center of the most public environmental struggle in

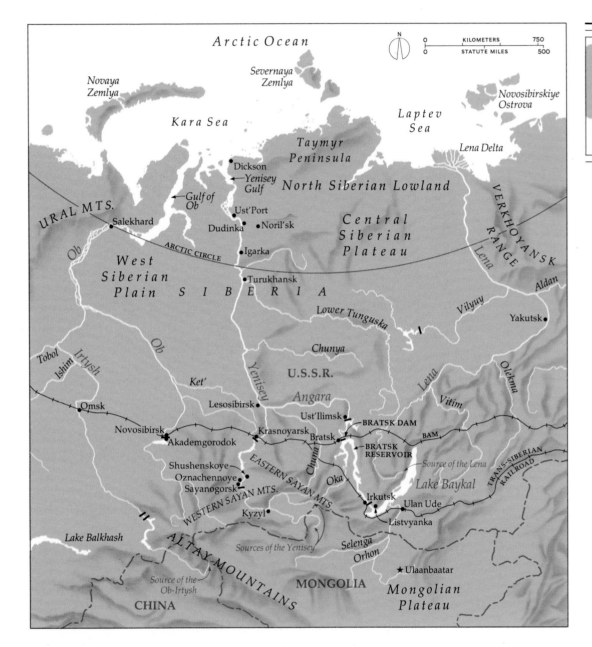

the Soviet Union. When the government built a pulp mill near the south end in the early 1960s, the alarm went up. Since then filters have been built that cost more than the original mill. Still there was pollution from construction of the new Baykal-Amur Main Line rail link until it was rerouted away from the lake's north shore, as well as from logging and tourism, and from Ulan Ude, biggest city on the Selenga.

One bitter night we stamped into the Arktika Restaurant on Lenin Street in

Irkutsk, and were starting in on bowls of *pyelmyeni* (Siberian ravioli) when three wind-burned boys at the next table heard us speaking English. One asked for a cigarette. A conversation ensued and the boys told us all about themselves. They were telephone linemen from the North Caucasus, freshly drafted into the Red Army and on their way to duty on the Pacific coast, whether Sakhalin or Kamchatka I have willfully forgotten. They started to tell us just what their duties would be, and where, and how wonderful Soviet radar was. Desperately, we offered toasts to peace and friendship, covered our ears, turned away. They couldn't understand why we really didn't want to know.

e flew through a near whiteout next day, more than 300 miles north to Bratsk and its massive dam, which was the focal point of all Siberia's pride. The poet Yevgeni Yevtushenko rhapsodized over it:

> *In the very heart of the Bratsk station*
> *climbing, almost like an acrobat, my eyes goggled*
> *at the hatches and the machines. . . .*
> *That, my brother, is technology—our ruler!*

But Yuri Solovyov was more practical than poetic. We had dinner with him after inspecting the insides of the dam, tomb cold at 25 below, guarded by thickly quilted, pistol-toting women. Yuri had spent six years in Moscow working on a mock-up of the mighty hydroelectric project before coming east to help build the real thing. Yuri and his wife Irina, an engineering economist, each made premium pay plus bonuses. He wore a sharp jacket tailored in Germany, and was on the list for a Moskvich car. They had vacationed without cost in Black Sea sunshine in Romania and Bulgaria. Despite these privileges, Irina wanted to go back to Moscow to raise their daughter. But not Yuri. Where would he go from Bratsk? "On up the river, to the next dam, and the next one."

The huge lake behind the Bratsk dam—the Bratsk Sea, they call it—supports a major aluminum plant and timber operations. It has moderated the climate around it, warming the area by several degrees in winter, cooling it slightly in summer. The same thing has followed each of the dams Yuri Solovyov looked forward to, the next and the next, each more powerful, on up the river.

Not all the workers who have settled Siberia are recruiting-poster volunteers. Through modern Russian history, before and since the Revolution, authority has prescribed the long trip east for political disrespect, religious dissidence, and other misdemeanors. Prisoners dug the immense goldfields on the northern reaches of the Lena River. Émigrés assert that even now thousands of religious and political offenders labor in pipeline camps along the Ob.

Vladimir Ilyich Lenin himself is believed to have picked his last name to substitute for the original Ul'yanov in tribute to political prisoners on the Lena. Twenty years before his revolution, he was exiled by the tsar's police for Marxist agitation. Leaving the then new railway, he forded the icy Ob on horseback in March 1897 and settled for three years at the Yenisey River town of Shushenskoye. Lenin gave exile an honored status in Russian tradition that helps sustain those sent for longer stays and less glorious offenses.

He also gave the Yenisey a proud place among Soviet youth, making its very name an attraction. It has pulled thousands of idealistic men and women east to help build the great dams and their satellite industries at Krasnoyarsk, and farther up the river near Sayanogorsk.

Roiling north beyond its junction with the Angara, the Yenisey broadens between rough mountains on its right bank and marshy flood plains on its left. Beyond the Arctic Circle it is rich with sturgeon and wildfowl. But its most spectacular product is the annual crop of ice.

In the short summer, ships run between Oznachennoye and the Kara Sea, using an elevator that lifts vessels via an inclined railroad past the great Krasnoyarsk dam. In winter, nuclear and diesel-electric icebreakers lead commercial vessels from Murmansk into the sea and the Yenisey estuary, where shallow-draft icebreakers take over, then river icebreakers. When ice is too thick for these boats to proceed to the timber and ore port of Dudinka, cargoes are loaded onto hovercraft to skim the surface on a cushion of air.

The Englishman Henry Seebohm hardly dreamed of such hi-tech travel when he set out to explore the Yenisey in the winter of 1877, eventually using a thousand horses, 18 dogs, and 40 reindeer. Until the end of May, he wrote, "the forces of winter had gallantly withstood the fiercest attacks of the sun." And then came "the battle of the Yen-e-say, the great event of the year in these regions, and certainly the most stupendous display of the powers of nature that it has ever been my lot to witness." The thaw was on its northward march.

The ice started to break on June 1, forming mountains and jagged ridges, and the water thus dammed made the river rise so fast it flowed backward, crashing up its tributaries. "At last the final march past of the beaten winter forces, in their fourteen days' battle, took place, and for seven days more the ragtag-and-bobtail of the great Arctic army came straggling down—worn and weather-beaten little icebergs, dirty ice-floes that looked like floating mudbanks, and straggling pack-ice in the last stages of consumption."

The Yenisey, split in its delta into winding channels between banks 47 miles apart, merges again at its mouth to spill an average 447 billion gallons of water per day into the chill Kara. The river is slightly more voluminous and longer than the Mississippi. Yet its wild shores, its abrupt mountains, its very cities and hydroelectric colossi are hardly visible to the rest of the world.

In that, they stand for Siberia—seeming so empty, though full of life.

A n ice-sheathed tributary of the Kolyma River cuts a course through the taiga in northeastern Siberia (right). In this fur-rich region, 17th-century trappers endured sub-zero winters. In Stalinist days, thousands of political prisoners succumbed in the Kolyma's gold mines. At Srednekolymsk on the Kolyma's midsection, ice fishermen (above) keep warm with the help of wood-burning stoves and vodka. Residents of Yakutsk (opposite, top), on the Lena River, stroll on a fog-shrouded street. The fog rises from exhalations of people and animals in winter temperatures that reach 70° below zero. In south-central Siberia, the Bratsk dam shimmers on the Angara (opposite, bottom). Completed in 1964, the dam's 350-mile-long reservoir serves as a beach resort in hot Siberian summers.

237

A Khanty reindeer-herding family warms by the stove in a hide-covered tent on a state farm near Salekhard (opposite). Among some 64 native groups of Siberia, the 21,000 Khants raise reindeer, trap, and fish. The nomadic tribes of Siberia resisted early collectivization with mass slaughter of reindeer in the early 1930s. Modern breeding and management have made reindeer herding the most valuable husbandry in the north. Workers at a farm coax reindeer to pull a wooden sleigh (above). Here, 15 brigades oversee a herd of 23,500 providers of meat, hides, and hair for mattresses and life preservers. At left, a Khanty woman and child peer from behind a fur-draped tent door. Families no longer follow the herds, and older children spend most of the year in boarding schools far from home.

Fred Mayer, Woodfin Camp

Dean Conger, National Geographic Photographer

L ake Baykal fishermen haul in a netful of omul. Fed by 336 rivers, Baykal's water could fill almost all five Great Lakes. It is the world's oldest and deepest lake, 25 million years old, and supports 1,800 plant and animal species. Most, including the salmonlike omul and a land-locked seal, the nerpa, are unique to its waters. By the late 1960s, overfishing and pollution threatened Baykal's fragile ecosystem. Conservationists protested, and Soviet planners installed an expensive filtration system on a new paper mill and banned omul fishing for several years. Now they plan to develop a 7-million-acre national park and tourist area around the lake. Tourists also travel the Lena, the Soviet Union's third longest river, where sheer cliffs overlook a section (above) near Yakutsk.

THE YANGTZE

T H E   C H A N G E F U L   D R A G O N

By Robert M. Poole / Photographs by Thomas Nebbia

The Yangtze River growled under my feet, its blunt power shuddering up through the hull of *East Wind #6*. At the bow of our ferry, the crewman called Liu braced himself in the chill November wind and swam at the air with his arms, demonstrating how, long ago, he fought this river when it swamped his boat and dumped him in a whirlpool to die.

"It pulled me to the bottom, but I did not think of death," he said. "I did not know *how* to think of death. I fought and fought and fought, finally got to the side of the whirlpool, and it just lifted me out."

Liu fell silent, his story done, and watched the river slog through the mountains of Sichuan, deep in China's interior. Brown waves rose and broke in the wind, one after another slapping our bow, one after another resisting the ferry's progress. Liu, 71, has fought this river all his life, and it shows: He is stooped and gray, his clothing ripped and sun-faded, his old face baked brown, as worn and cracked as a streamside pine. But as Liu watches the river, his eyes still gleam with the old defiance, the defiance that once saved him from the Yangtze, the river that tried to defeat him, the river he defeated instead. Now he makes his living from it, leading passengers across its obstinate current by day, conducting them safely home again by evening.

China, like the boatman Liu, has always faced the river's threat and sought to overcome it. Ancient legend tells of a China beset by monstrous waters that "embraced the mountains and overtopped the hills." An engineer named Kun came forward to battle the rivers. He built dikes and impoundments but could not keep pace with the rising tide. In defeat, he was exiled, executed, and diced up like an onion, a punishment that indicates the importance China attaches to successful flood control.

Kun's successor, a man named Yu, fared better. He deepened the Yangtze to improve drainage. He dug canals north and south of the river to irrigate rice fields and to facilitate boat traffic. He stopped the floods and transformed the Yangtze Valley into a network of silver waterways and green patchwork fields

Wen Feng Pagoda guards the Grand Canal near Yangzhou. A few miles away, the ancient canal meets China's longest river, the Yangtze.

still visible to this day. A grateful China honored Yu with a saying that survived him by 4,000 years: "But for Yu, we should all have been fishes."

The river, the longest in Asia, covers almost the breadth of China, slicing the country in half on its 3,900-mile course to the sea. It begins on a snow-swept peak between Tibet and Qinghai Province, a solitude so distant and forbidding that generations of Chinese assumed the area was inhabited by savages who ate hair and drank blood. Explorers first penetrated that solitude in 1976; they found no savages but did pinpoint the river's source at 21,730 feet. From that lofty birth the river crosses China like a changeful dragon, racing here, loitering there, crashing through limestone mountains and sandstone hills on its way to the sea. On that journey the river feeds on the scale befitting a dragon, swallowing people and tons of earth as it moves across the land.

I planned to spend the autumn following the river eastward, talking to people who lived along its banks and worked upon its waters. I asked to see the river whole, from Tibet to Shanghai, but this was not to be. The source, Chinese authorities said, was then off limits to foreign writers. So my trip began in Chongqing, an ancient city that clings to the mountains of the heartland.

Before dawn one morning, I walked to the river—down a street still wet with rain, past a lighted doorway where a boy in a red neckerchief tugged his knapsack on for school, down a zigzag course of stone steps to the Yangtze. It revealed but a hint of itself in the uncertain morning light: The stream came swirling toward me out of a fog, swept by in a swift curve, and disappeared downstream, merging in clouds that hung low between two mountains.

One by one, stevedores collected on the gray beach. They came to unload a dozen barges, which bobbed on the river like toys on a string. Most of the stevedores bore the sole accoutrement of their trade, the bamboo yoke; others came down empty handed.

A group of 20 women worked without benefit of yoke. Each woman filed up a gangplank and bent over as two colleagues loaded a 50-pound sack of soy flour on her back. I watched one woman. Bent low by the weight of her burden, she labored down the gangplank, stood in line behind a parked truck, and waited for two men in the truck bed to lift the sack clear. Until they acted, she could not raise her head, but advanced in measure without a trace of impatience, her eyes shifting from the ground to the truck and back to the ground as the queue moved slowly forward. Finally the sack was hoisted free. She stood upright and returned to the barge. It was cleared of all cargo in half an hour.

Today, as in the past, China operates on muscle power, the same elemental power that laid the Great Wall across 3,700 miles of mountain and desert, the same power that dug the Grand Canal through 1,100 miles of marsh and rock.

Most of the country's inland cargo travels on the Yangtze, and most of it moves to and from the river on people's backs. I saw Chinese lugging crated

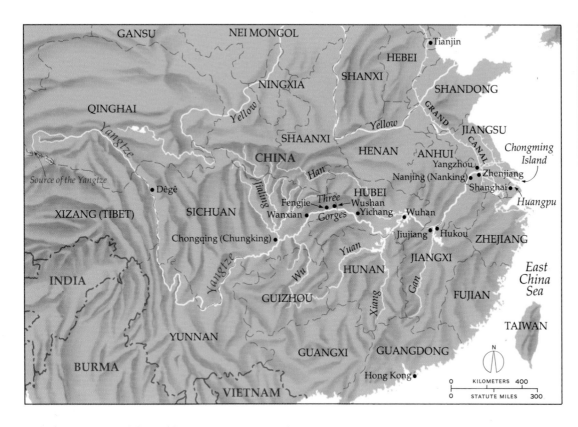

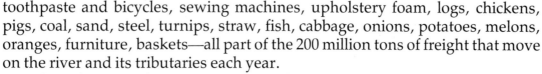

toothpaste and bicycles, sewing machines, upholstery foam, logs, chickens, pigs, coal, sand, steel, turnips, straw, fish, cabbage, onions, potatoes, melons, oranges, furniture, baskets—all part of the 200 million tons of freight that move on the river and its tributaries each year.

Perhaps because the river is a place of work, a thing associated more with drudgery than relaxation, people of the Yangtze tend to view it unromantically, as an American might view Interstate 80. I learned this the hard way, before 20 witnesses in a Chongqing teahouse, where I asked a retired stevedore this question: "If the river were a person, what kind of person would it be?"

There was silence. The old stevedore asked me to repeat the question. I did. He muttered it to himself, then to three others at our table. All shook their heads. Then the stevedore removed his cigar and looked me in the eye: "It is not for me to speak of such things," he said, more in modesty than in admonition. "The river is for the ordinary life of the people, not for poetry."

This no-nonsense view of the Yangtze even extends to the Chinese name for it, which is purely descriptive: They call it Changjiang, or "long river"; or more often and simply, Jiang, or "river," as if there could be no question that more than one exists, any more than there could be but one earth or sky. (Mention the name Yangtze to most Chinese, and they will act as if they never heard of it.

Westerners invented the name, after a ferry crossing named Yangzi Ford or after the ancient fiefdom of Yang—the origins are unclear.)

I left Chongqing by steamer, bound downstream for Wanxian, a market town almost 200 miles away. Thousands took this voyage each day, but there was nothing of the humdrum in it for me. I had just talked to boatmen who recalled 20-hour days at the oars, fighting the river with no thought of sleep. Others had spoken of great floods that swept through Sichuan, smashing houses and drowning thousands. And I had been warned of the lethal waters that had for centuries terrified sailors and destroyed ships on the Yangtze. Now I was going to ride those waters.

Our ship, *East Is Red #39*, blasts its horn three times, swings about, and noses downstream, lumbering past vague forms of tugs and barges hooting in the fog, past green buoy lights that wink on and off in the dark.

The fog melts as the day advances, revealing green mountains that climb down into the river and then out of it again on the far bank, where a fisherman in a straw hat jabs at the rushing current with a long-handled net, the man swaying like a dancer in the effort, retrieving nothing.

As the river lunges eastward, it grows swift and textured, here erupting in water cannons that lob parabolas of spray three feet above the surface, there swirling with whirlpools that could swallow a junk without a burp. We thread through this bedlam of crosscurrents, landing in Wanxian after sunset.

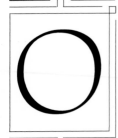

Our steamer brings the town to life. Wanxian exists for river traffic, exporting oranges, tung oil, tea, and goatskins by day, serving passengers by night. The lights snap on and Wanxian fills with people, up from the river and in from the countryside. They slurp noodles at tables in the open air, play cards and Mah-Jongg by the road, and poke through baskets of produce that clutter the sidewalks. Peasants hawk red peppers and potatoes, gingerroot and pig feet, cutting prices in competition, now legal under China's free market economy.

A brown-faced country girl blocks my path. She is built like a fullback—broad shoulders, big hands. She points to her basket of peanuts.

"How much for just one?" I ask.

"The first one is free," she says, handing it over. "You get a bag for just one yuan [about 50 cents], maybe less." I pay the lesser price, about 45 cents, satisfied with myself until I discover cheaper peanuts down the street.

A few days later I am still eating peanuts and thinking of the country girl as I sail for the Three Gorges, a section of the river long celebrated for its beauty and feared for its treachery. At the first gorge the river roars, in the words of the current Chinese tourist literature, "like wild horses stampeding."

I would have welcomed such a sound as we entered the gorges. Instead there was silence, heavy silence, on *East Is Red #42*. On the bridge I watch our captain, Xiong Weimin, direct his helmsman through a channel so narrow that only one ship at a time could pass downstream through it.

The captain holds his right thumb aloft, signaling the helmsman to steer straight. Then the captain signals for a right turn, extending his index finger. Then he signals straight again, avoiding conversation. An osprey escorts us, gliding on the wind, watching for fish. We follow it around a bend, and a tug hies into view, pushing four barges downstream. It is not supposed to be here.

"Reduce speed!" the captain shouts to a mate, who pulls on a lever to signal the engine room. The captain hits his horn, urging the tug to speed up, but there is no answer.

Xiong looks to his first mate, who barks at the tug through a loudspeaker: "Answer! Answer!" he shouts, but there is none, only the sound of the mate's own voice ricocheting off the steep walls of the gorge. Still we gain on the tug. It neither answers nor accelerates, but lolls on the water like a ghost ship. For another 15 minutes we stalk it downstream, our vessel slowed to a crawl, until the river widens. We pass, and for the first time the tug responds: It toots at our backs as we wash by.

"These little boats are such pests," Xiong says later. "They don't know the rules of the river."

We pass a shipwreck, a derelict junk beached on the rocks. The Yangtze laps at it. Xiong shakes his head. "They did not know the river," he says quietly. "You have to know the channels. You have to know the rocks below. You have to know that the bottom of this river is not as flat as any old road."

Xiong crosses the bridge and flips on his depth finder, which flashes digital readouts of the riverbed. The numbers come rapidly: 246 feet, 200, 156, 90, 87, 96, 102, 117, 123, 105, 144, all within three minutes. Here the river runs unforgiving, speeding through the gorges at ten knots and more, dropping on an incline of one foot per mile. It surges over 600-foot pools and flats of 10 feet, so shallow in some parts that Xiong kills the engines and drifts through.

All day the gorges loom above us, dwarfing our ship in walls that rise to a narrow thread of sky, clear blue and inconsequential in the distance. Along one wall a thin, dark scar cuts against the upthrusting limestone of the mountain. The scar, hewn by hand, is a tracker's trail, a gallery where men in harness, sometimes hundreds at a time, once pulled ships upstream through the gorges, fighting the power of the river at every step. Countless people died in that fight, tossed in the river by the slip of a foot or the snagging of a towline.

Zhang Jianming remembers. With some 50 fellow trackers, he was towing a junk upstream in 1948, bound from Yichang to Chongqing with a load of cotton. "It was a summer day, and there was big water," he recalled. The towing cable caught on a boulder along the trail. A man at midline tried to lift the cable clear, but it slipped, and hurled him from the mountain like a pebble from a slingshot. He died on the rocks below.

"Nobody paid any attention," Zhang said. "We kept going. We couldn't stop. The owner wouldn't let us."

Zhang survived by luck. Others, like Xiong the steamer captain, endure by luck and belligerence. "We have to be stronger than the river," Xiong says, punching like a boxer. "Every day I want to struggle against her."

The sun hangs low on the water as Xiong brings our ship through the locks at Yichang, another of his workdays done, another thousand passengers brought safely through the gorges. The Yangtze looks so tame that I hardly recognize it. We have entered its middle reaches.

Here Chinese engineers and workers are building the country's biggest dam, a 1.7-mile wall of concrete stretching from bank to bank northwest of Yichang. The Gezhouba Dam backs the Yangtze up into the gorges, improving navigation there; and it generates electricity for Hubei Province.

"It is a point of pride for us Chinese," a man from Harbin tells me later. We sail east in the moonlight, talking on the fantail of *East Is Red #43*. (All the steamers have the same name; numbers designate individual ships.)

The man from Harbin, who has traveled from the far northeast to sell ball bearings to factories, debates the Gezhouba project with one of his countrymen, a passenger from Sichuan who believes the dam will do no harm.

"But how will we solve the problem of the fish?" asks the Harbin man, referring to the Yangtze River sturgeon, a 20-foot fish that spawns in the river. Scientists worry that the dam could stop the giant sturgeon's spawning runs.

"A project like this makes people very happy," says the Harbin man, "but it makes fish very unhappy." He slams a fist into his open palm—the sound of a fish hitting the wall. "There's no problem," says the Sichuan man. "The sturgeon is being raised by people."

I leave them in the half-light of the stern and go forward. I lean into the wind and watch the banks run by. Stoves and cigarettes flare and fade in the night, marking the places fishermen will sleep until morning. Above them, a billion stars frozen in place; below, the river running black and slick.

Inside our steamer, passengers camp on the lower decks, sprawling on blankets, surrounded by bundles, moving through clouds of cigarette smoke. A farmer makes his annual visit downstream to see his daughter, taking her a gift of melon seeds. Two soldiers play cards, lounging on new wicker chairs they bought upstream, a box serving as table between them. They head home on leave, among the 25 million Chinese who travel on the river each year.

Steamer passengers may choose from four classes of ticket, ranging from fifth class (for floor space among the chickens and cargo on the lower decks) to second class (for a berth in a two-person compartment on the middle decks). There is no first class, at least in name, because the government considers the designation too bourgeois. So second class is first class on the *East Is Red*.

As a second-class customer, I had hot showers, big meals, constant attention, and the use of a forward lounge, where I often gathered with Chinese army officers for tea, reading, chess, river gazing, and the occasional nap in an overstuffed chair. I know of nothing so quieting as to sit in the sun and drift off to sleep, lulled by the rhythm of water and the hum of engines. I napped right past Chibi, scene of the most famous naval battle of ancient China. I woke to see the Yangtze running flat and yellow, a sampan here, a ferry there, but nothing approaching the traffic and noise that must have raged on these waters in A.D. 207, the year in which two generals fought for control of China.

The northern general, Cao Cao, came from the land of Wei to conquer Wu, the kingdom south of the river. He brought 800,000 troops, descending the Yangtze on ships chained together so that his entire army could land at once.

South of the river, General Zhou Yu waited with a force of 30,000. Since he was outnumbered, he relied on cunning: He deployed a fleet of small incendiary ships designed to explode on impact with Cao Cao's fleet. Zhou Yu disguised the fire boats as grain vessels, so the Wei army recognized them too late. The northern ships, still linked by chains, burned quickly, lighting the night sky and southern bank, which was known as Chibi, or "red cliff," ever after.

Through China's long history the Yangtze has figured in the ebb and flow of conquest, a natural political boundary that demarked kingdoms, slowed armies, and sank navies into oblivion, like a Great Wall in motion.

Today China posts sentries along the middle course of the Yangtze to watch both banks, but it is not for fear of the invading horde that they keep this vigil. It is the river they worry about, the river in flood.

"Flood control is the number one mission along the Yangtze River," says Wang Xisheng, an engineer with the Yangtze Valley Planning Commission. To hold back the river, China maintains some 1,900 miles of dikes between Yichang and Hukou. The stream stays within these walls most of the year, behaving itself. But then the summer comes, and the heavy rains of the season, and the Yangtze rises implacably, a force beyond the reach of human contrivance.

When the floods come, the Chinese respond with an age-old genius matched by few other societies—their genius for organizing multitudes to perform public works. In a recent summer when the Yangtze menaced cities in Hubei and Hunan Provinces, the government dispatched ten million citizens to guard the dikes. Word went out to each factory, each army unit, and each commune in the threatened area: Send able-bodied workers to guard the dikes. Night and day for a month or more, one group watched the river and its tributaries as other teams stockpiled gravel, soil, and cement blocks at regular intervals along the earthworks. The dike watchers patrolled the river, looked for signs of weakness in the walls, and summoned special repair crews to fix them.

In Wuhan, a city of 4,000,000 on the middle Yangtze, some 100,000 workers joined the river watch, among them Hu Jianghan. Hu, a 27-year-old stevedore, showed me where he lived on the dikes throughout the emergency.

"Right on this spot," he said, pointing to a grassy place near Cooperation Road. For a month in 1983 he never left those few square feet of land, except to relieve himself. He washed clothes in a basin, ate meals his comrades brought him, and slept in a tent under a steady rain. Party leaders forbade card playing, visitors, conversation, reading, or other diversions for those on duty.

"We trained spotlights on the river," Hu said. "The water was very yellow, and the waves lapped against the dikes." Day by day, Hu watched the water rise. And day by day, provincial officials studied the reports from up and down the Yangtze. Finally, when the government thought the dikes could hold no more, it ordered the release of impounded water on the Han River, an upstream tributary of the Yangtze, to relieve the strain. The waters gushed across the plain, flooding 70,000 homes and 300 factories north of Wuhan.

The northern region suffered, but Wuhan itself survived, the fortunes of the few sacrificed for the benefit of the many. The Yangtze Valley, with 350 million people, is one of the most densely populated places on earth. China tries to reduce inevitable losses, but it is only containment, never victory.

"There's no way in a flood," said an old man, "no way in the world to control the river."

A young woman: "Nothing can change the nature of the river."

An old woman: "It is going to rise whether you like it or not."

From Chongqing to Shanghai I heard such comments from people who accept the Yangtze's seasonal rages, moving in with relatives when the floods come, returning home when the floods go, adjusting their lives to the river.

When I visited Wuhan, the Yangtze had withdrawn to its winter level, exposing sandbars where youths chased soccer balls and wrestled, churning up clouds of dust where the river itself had churned a few months before. For the moment, the floods were forgotten.

I turned from the river and down a side street near the dikes, drawn by the sound of birds, hundreds of them singing in convention, brought here by their owners: There were plump thrushes and yellow finches in cages, green budgerigars posing on pedestals in delicate bamboo prisons, gray pigeons cooing in metal cages strapped on bicycle fenders. Down the street, an escaped thrush hopped across a rooftop, pursued by a man who tried to trap it with his jacket; the thrush, at its leisure, outdistanced him, and took to the trees.

On a Sunday morning the people of Wuhan come here to display their pets, to give them air, to buy supplies. A few years back, such a scene would have been unthinkable: The government considered bird keeping a decadent pastime and a waste of good grain. Those who kept birds kept them in secret. But the pendulum had swung. Birds were in favor again.

But China has its dark side too: The same day I mingled with bird keepers, police executed 15 people on the other side of Wuhan, part of an anticrime campaign that swept China in 1983, claiming an estimated 10,000 human lives.

Crowds gathered in Wuhan to read posters describing the day's executions. Each notice had a huge red check mark through it, and each listed the names of the accused and their crimes (rape, robbery, murder, hooliganism, gangsterism). I joined a group of people who read the posters in silence. Three schoolboys pushed their way to the front for a better look. They pointed and laughed at one notice, then turned their attention to another sheet, faded and tattered. The second poster, on display for several weeks, announced that nine others had been executed here the month before. The children laughed at that one too, until an old man stepped out of the crowd and slapped one youth on the ear. "It is nothing to laugh about," he said, and walked away.

I saw similar posters in Yichang and Chongqing, along with photographs of pinioned criminals being paraded through the streets and shot. And in Wanxian I watched 13 young men who stood bound, heads bowed, in the town square as an officer read their crimes—murder, rape, and even gambling. Several hundred spectators looked on. Then a group of police hustled the accused men down the street and out of sight to an unknown fate.

Even as China pursues such campaigns, it seeks to rebuild from a past excess known as the Cultural Revolution, an era of turmoil in which radicals desecrated temples and exiled intellectuals. It was an attempt to wipe out Western influences and purify the Communist Party—but it also wrecked the country.

In the city of Yangzhou a Buddhist abbot, De Ming, returned in 1980 to find the sacred statues of his temple broken and strewn along the banks of the Yangtze, like victims of some awful shipwreck.

"We brought the pieces back one by one," said De, pointing to a pile of jagged marble arms, legs, and torsos heaped in a mossy corner of Gaoming Temple. Atop the pile was the disembodied head of a Buddha, smiling in serene counterpoint to the sad jumble beneath it. "Most of the heads could not be found," said De.

Today life returns to normal at Gaoming Temple. Many of the old monks have come back. Friends from Japan, Hong Kong, and the United States sent statues to replace the lost ones. And the government even permits youths to train as Buddhists, so there will be new monks to replace people like De, 71.

"Our central government is taking active measures to restore the temple as it should be," De said. In the meantime he spends most days sitting in the meditation hall, quietly chanting the holy Zen phrase "Nian fo shi shei—Who recites the Buddhist scripture," the words that sustained him through his long exile, the 14 years he was banished from the temple and forced to work as a farmer.

"They forbade me to wear my robes, but every time I moved, I would say the words inside myself. Every time I hoed, I would say them inside. There was no way they could hear. Even if I chant them in front of you, you cannot tell."

Then he smiled in such obvious triumph that I laughed out loud, unable to restrain myself at the sight of old De, the tough abbot who refused to be broken. He laughed too, wrung my hand, and sent me on my way downstream.

In its lower reaches the Yangtze sprawls through the delta like an inland sea, more than 25 miles across and more impressive for its size than its power. Chinese consider this Yangtze a generous neighbor, one which nurtures a land that is green to the horizon, winter and summer.

This generosity is helped along by centuries of human encouragement. More than 1,300 years ago, Chinese built the Grand Canal across the river, forming a south-to-north highway that linked the southern grainfields to the northern capital in Changan near modern-day Xian. Farmers attached hundreds of smaller canals to the grand one, and drew the Yangtze's fecund waters into the fields of eastern China. The Yangtze Valley developed as China's major rice-growing region, which now produces 70 percent of the nation's total.

The rich delta attracted merchants from faraway lands, from the 13th century forward. Marco Polo was impressed by the "marvelous great shipping" he saw here. "More dear things, and of greater value, go and come by this river, than go by all the rivers of the Christians together, nor by all their seas."

Other Europeans arrived in the 19th century to cash in on the trade in tea, silk, and porcelain. They transformed the quiet fishing village of Shanghai into one of the world's biggest cities and major ports. By early in the 20th century, French, American, and British colonialists had apportioned the spoils among them, drawing a line through the middle of Shanghai along Yanan Road. South of the road was French, north of it, British. Each side had its own electrical system (110 volts for the French, 220 for the British), and each had its own police, hotels, apartments, churches, banks, and transportation.

Traveling across town was like crossing part of Europe, a Chinese friend told me. "If you wanted to go from the British section to the other side, you had to get off one bus, buy a new ticket at Yanan Road, get on another bus, and proceed to the French part."

All of that changed, of course, when the Communists took power in 1949. The foreigners fled, leaving behind their elegant houses and private drinking clubs. But one still sees the trappings of that era. In the Great Germany Restaurant, for instance, it is impossible to get a cup of tea in this land of tea; all they serve is coffee. At the Peace Hotel one finds plumbing fixtures, in use since the 1920s, imported from Scotland. And along the Huangpu River, a tributary of the Yangtze, the Chinese store cargo in old British warehouses, giving the look of London's Thames to the wharves of Shanghai.

The city developed as China's largest exporter and most modern port, using cranes and forklifts to move 85 million tons of cargo each year. One seldom hears the chant of laborers here. The predominant sound is a roar of diesels and river traffic. From the Huangpu comes the music of commerce—bellowing steamer horns and croaking tugboats, accompanied by barges whose horns honk baritone as they advance and fade on the stream. From the old Bund there is the persistent tingling of bicycle bells and the blaring of automobile horns, all rising in amplitude at sunrise, announcing the passage of time with such precision that I rarely used my clock for morning call.

F or my last day on the Yangtze, I woke in the dark. I walked to the window to see the Huangpu, where the single green eye of a tug moved through the night, rippling the water under barges that still lay sleeping. Over the river, white smoke rolled from a factory and snapped away on the north wind. Autumn had passed. It would be cold and clear for the last leg of my journey, a trip up the Huangpu and out to Chongming Island.

Chongming, a long finger of land about one-third the size of Rhode Island, is the last earth the Yangtze touches before it meets the sea. As the river crosses the continent, it chews at the soil of Tibet and Yunnan, Sichuan and Hubei, Hunan and Jiangsu, dropping a fine mix of the whole at Chongming. The island, made entirely of this alluvium, is a gift of the river.

I toured the island by car, riding down flat roads between willow and bamboo groves that bent and rustled in the wind. On Chongming's south bank, I left the car and approached the river, feeling the squelch of new land underfoot. An old herder tended three water buffalo. The great beasts grazed in their ponderous way, swinging their heads back and forth, back and forth, inching across a green land under a blue sky. The herder walked over to study me.

"What part of China are you from?" he asked.

"America," I said.

"America," he said, mulling over the word. He shook his head as if to say it was a part of China he never heard of. I asked about Chongming. He swept his arms wide, indicating the land around us.

"All new," he said, "new in the last few years."

Along both banks of the island, Chinese have built stone walls that reach out from the shore and into the Yangtze to catch the last few grains of soil, an effort to bring new land under cultivation for a hungry country.

The herder waved goodbye. He returned to his buffalo, I to my river. I followed the jetty out as far as I could. The Yangtze looked like an ocean in fury, all whitecaps and foaming waves, knocking at the jetty again and again.

W alled off by mountains more than two miles high, the Yangtze's source lay sequestered on the Tibetan Plateau for centuries. Then in 1976 a Chinese team found the river's birthplace, a glacier peak named Geladaintong. In the fleet summer of this high country, the river thaws and wanders overland, nourishing pastures where sheep fatten at 15,000 feet. Nomads shear their flock (right) at summer's end, spinning the wool for *bokkus*, the loose blanket coats they wear year round.

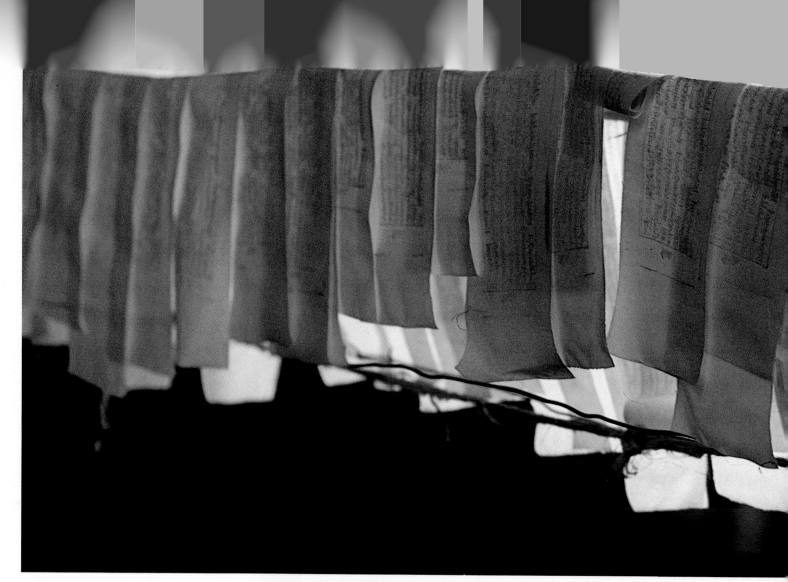

Leong Ka Tai (all)

O n the rugged frontier of Tibet and Sichuan, Buddhists print scriptures for the faithful, keeping a religious tradition that weathers ages of turmoil and war. Workers at a monastery in Dêgê choose texts from more than 200,000 wooden blocks (left), and impress the blocks on insect-resistant paper made from poisonous tree pulp. Ink, concocted from red clay, dries on long text strips in the sun (left, above). Lamas sort the scriptures (above), separating Kanjur, or works of Buddha, from Tanjur, holy commentaries. Leading monasteries keep both works.

In less formal devotion, travelers scribble mantras on bits of cloth and hang them by the roadside (opposite). Buddhists believe the mountain wind blows their prayers to heaven.

257

Wong How-Man (both)

T he Yangtze River sweeps through Tiger Leap Gorge, named for its narrowness. Here, legend says, a tiger could spring from one bank to the other with ease. In Yunnan Province, other riverside travelers inch along a treacherous path (above), the sort of "wild steep road" that terrified a Tang Dynasty poet named Li Bai. Such trails, he wrote, were "more hazardous to take than to try to climb the heavens." These mountains formed a hundred million years ago as continents clashed: India rammed the Asian plate, pushing it skyward.

259

On China's Main Street, boats—not buses—carry most of the traffic. Family-run ferries like the Orange Tree 101 (above) whisk passengers across the Yangtze at Chongqing, a city of six million divided by the great stream. Floating gangplanks (opposite) rise and fall with the river's changing level, which varies by more than a hundred feet from winter to summer. From the countryside, farmers and merchants sail into the city, bearing goods for Chongqing's thriving market. Here shoppers can buy rice cakes, a bowl of fiery noodles, or a goose (left).

Pages 262-263: A farm girl makes her way across the terraced earth of Sichuan, a land enriched by plentiful rainfall and generations of unremitting labor. These slopes bear two or three crops of rice each year.

Opposite: Bruce Dale, National Geographic Photographer

M uscle power contends with water power near Wushan, where the Yangtze boils through a 120-mile corridor of whirlpools and rapids known as the Three Gorges. This harnessed crew (opposite) will haul its junk to Fengjie, a two-day pull upstream—one day if the winds are good. Before the era of steam and diesel, thousands of men pulled ships along these rocky shores, driven by gong and drumbeats, or sometimes by the lash of overseers. Today stone tablets line the riverbank; they mark places where nameless trackers slipped and drowned.

In Jiujiang farmers grow their crops in ponds that support big head carp (right) and many other species. Aquaculture centers throughout China produce tons of inexpensive food. A Jiujiang shopper buys two "snake head" fish in the town market (above).

M onuments to a past and future China emerge in the river cities of Yichang and Nanjing. Carved animals keep vigil on the Spirit Road leading to an emperor's tomb in Nanjing. At midnight the kneeling elephants are said to rise and change place with those that have stood guard all day. Live elephants, once used for imperial ceremonies, fell from grace in 19th-century China—one went berserk and hurled a woman over the rooftops.

Outside of Yichang, Gezhouba Dam takes shape (above and right). In the making for more than a decade, this dam is China's largest, and the first to bridle the Yangtze. Some 180,000 vacationers flock here yearly to admire the hydroelectric project, a symbol, to them, of a nation entering the modern era.

266

Marshalled for a downstream journey, an island of logs crowds the Yangtze near Nanjing. Cut and lashed together in rafts, the timber is shipped in autumn, the best time for steering the ungainly rafts eastward. At Zhenjiang crewmen land the logs with bamboo pikes (above). Such workers live for months in makeshift cabins (background, above) atop their floating cargo.

China began clear-cutting in the 1950s to meet the growing needs of its people. The lumbering worsened flooding on the Yangtze. Officials now encourage tree planting to hold the soil.

Pages 270-271: The Grand Canal, built for imperial grain boats, endures the ages at Yangzhou. Here the Yangtze waters the canal, still a major south-north transportation artery.

L ike bees in a honeycomb of steel, welders shore up a new vessel (right and opposite) at a Shanghai shipyard. Women welders (above) are rare in this company of 10,000, where most skilled jobs still go to men.

Although government policy encourages equal opportunity, women perform most of the stoop labor in the countryside, planting rice, gathering cotton, and picking tea. And city women account for two-thirds of the urban unemployed. But with time the picture improves: Since the 1950s the number of women in urban jobs has increased fivefold. And in Peking some 1,600 women now drive buses, trucks, and taxis, jobs previously reserved for men.

 odern freighter and battered junk call at Shanghai, China's largest city. With the Yangtze at its back and the East China Sea before it, Shanghai developed as the link between China's deep interior and the world beyond. Brothels and opium dens flourished here in the 19th century, but now Shanghai concentrates on commerce of a tamer sort: textiles, chemicals, and ships for export. Shoppers, among the city's 11.9 million residents, crowd Nanjing Road (above), where stores display their Spring Thunder radios and Long March suitcases.

Rafters paddle the Franklin River in Tasmania. By David Hiser.

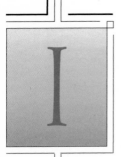

I t was the bitter loss of a dream. From their founding in 1788 of the first white settlement in Australia, on the east coast, English explorers had longed to probe the interior. They imagined mighty rivers lacing green prairies, pouring into an inland sea. Legends say that when the restless adventurers gazed westward from Sydney, aborigines—native hunters and gatherers for more than 40,000 years—would cry out "Never, never!" Never go there, they meant. But the English had found a fertile lowland with large rivers just beyond the mountains. So hopes ran high when a 25-year-old sheep overlander named Edward Eyre led an exploration north from Adelaide in 1840.

No one expected the dust, the blinding sand, the scorching sun, still less the impenetrable salt marshes that turned the expedition back. Eyre returned alive from his trek, but the dream of a lush interior was dying. The veteran explorer Charles Sturt found little more when he pushed farther north in 1844. Drought had turned riverbeds, water holes, and springs dust dry.

Aridity is the stark frame to every portrait of Australia's rivers. Roughly 75 percent of the nearly three million square miles receives too little rain and has too few waterways to be farmed or sown for pasture. Little wonder that most Australians live in the cities that hug the coast. Yet, as the English discovered, a massive web of waterways stems from eastern highlands and spreads across the east-central lowlands. Its principal streams, the Murray and the Darling, bound it. No more fertile land exists in Australia than the 414,000 square miles of the Murray-Darling basin.

To be sure, the Murray-Darling refreshes just one pocket of a largely water-starved continent. It was not always so. Some 150 million years ago, jungle covered much of Australia, with lakes and rivers and inland seas. Then it was part of the great continent of Gondwanaland and lay far south of its present location. By 45 million years ago, Australia had broken off from Gondwanaland and drifted northward. As it drifted, the climate turned colder and drier. But today the face of the land shows scars, evidence of a once great inland delta on the upper Murray. Now Australia sits astride the Tropic of Capricorn under a subtropical high-pressure cell—a hot, dry zone of air.

The Great Dividing Range that spawns the Murray-Darling system wrings from clouds drifting inland the little moisture that is left. Amid lowland basins to the west lies the Channel Country—a parched region that owes its name to a network of streams that drain into inland lakes or fizzle out in sandy soil. Years without rain may be followed by summer deluges. The eight-year-old daughter of one Channel Country settler, shocked by a downpour of rain she had never seen, began shouting, "The water hole is falling down!" During droughts ranchers water livestock by tapping a wealth of artesian basins.

Desert plateau rimmed by stony ridges covers the western two-thirds of Australia. Periodic streams and lakes that are often only salt pans fleck the face of

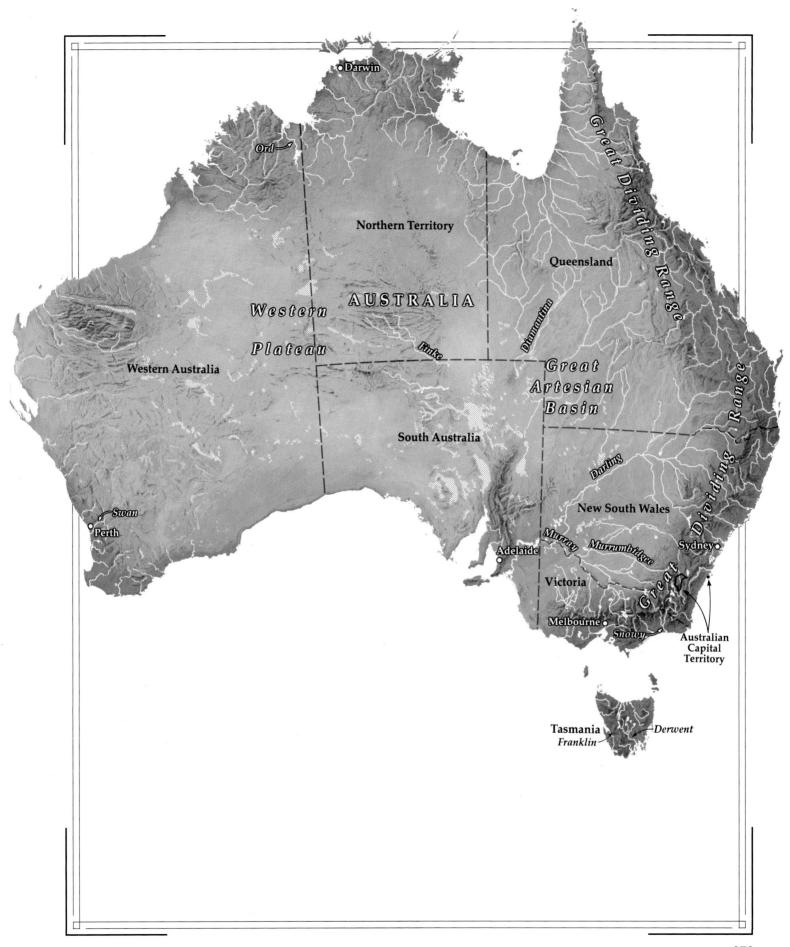

Darwin

Ord

Northern Territory

Queensland

Western

AUSTRALIA

Great Dividing Range

Plateau

Western Australia

Finke

Diamantina

Great

Artesian

South Australia

Basin

Great Dividing Range

Darling

New South Wales

Swan

Perth

Adelaide

Murray

Murrumbidgee

Sydney

Victoria

Melbourne

Snowy

Australian
Capital
Territory

Tasmania

Derwent

Franklin

279

Black swans grace the Swan River as James Stirling and companions bivouac in this 1827 engraving. Near the river's mouth the British explorers chose a townsite. Perth later rose here, the first colonial settlement in Western Australia.

this endless tableland, where a few medium-size rivers occasionally flow.

On the island state of Tasmania, as wet and lush as the mainland is dry, such rivers as the Derwent have carved out fertile valleys, and help to power industries. In 1983 several of Tasmania's beautiful wild rivers, including the lower Franklin, survived a threat to dam them.

In Australia's arid bleakness, the Murray-Darling is a wonder. The Murray itself courses 1,610 miles from the Snowy Mountains to Lake Alexandrina, a lagoon on South Australia's coast. The river slices north through gorges fringed with mountain ash, then west across plains studded with red gum trees. Near Mildura it meets the Darling, on the final leg of its 1,700-mile journey from the coastal highlands of New South Wales. Fed only sporadically by summer monsoons, the Darling usually crawls through dry, red plains. But after those torrential rains, it surges across a land suddenly alive with flowers and grasses.

A haven for wildlife, the Murray-Darling waters have been no less a boon to humans. Long ago the rivers were highways and fishing grounds—teeming with cod—for Australian peoples. An aborigine myth says that the Murray was formed when the ancestral hero, Ngurunderi, rafted west from New South Wales in pursuit of an enormous cod. The darting, weaving fish cleaved the channels and reaches of the river.

The English discovery of the Murray was less dramatic. "Going sou'west we were stopped by a river." So a diary records the moment when explorers Hamilton Hume and William Hovell found the banks of the Murray in 1824. They celebrated by brewing tea with its water. Four years later Hume traveled with Sturt down the Macquarie to see if it might lead to the fabled inland pool. After two months the men broke clear of marsh and gazed on the Darling. Wrote Sturt: ". . . here was a river that promised to reward all our exertions, and which appeared every moment to increase in importance to our imagination."

By the mid-1840s sheep and cattle ranchers had settled along the Murray. By about 1850 they had scattered along the Darling and Murrumbidgee as well. This pastoral migration opened up the continent. After squatters' stations came riverboats; with the riverboats came river towns like Wilcannia and Bourke on the Darling, Echuca and Swan Hill on the Murray. Steamboats thrived until the 1880s, when rail travel strangled the industry.

Spurred by a severe drought in the early 1880s, basin settlers turned to irrigation. In 1915 the River Murray Commission began to build dams along the Murray and its tributaries to funnel water to New South Wales, Victoria, and South Australia. Among other projects, the commission created Hume Lake, the first great source for irrigation water. Today, naturally fertile tracts mingle with irrigated scrubland throughout the Murray-Darling basin. In fact, about two-thirds of the continent's irrigated land lies along the Murray and its tributaries. All told, the system enriches some three million acres that produce Australia's leading exports—wool, beef, and wheat.

In one of the most impressive irrigation schemes, Snowy River water rushes into tunnels bored 30 miles through the Australian Alps and finally empties into the Murray. Along the way, this stream makes a drop of 2,000 feet—the force converted into electricity.

Husbanding of the Darling's waters is vital, for evaporation steals much of the river's flow. Drought can reduce the Darling to a chain of oxbow lakes. The Menindee Lakes Storage Scheme helps meet these challenges with levees that trap Darling floodwaters, to be released as needed to boost the river flow.

North of the basin, beyond the Grey Range, people become more victims than manipulators of the land. Here are the stony desert, braided channels, and truncated hills of the Channel Country. Save for those unpredictable summer downpours, the land blisters from dry heat. In drought, all that remain of its lethargic streams are scattered pools. But these are life-preserving oases for

Cary Wolinsky, Stock, Boston

David Segal

T rees that once lined the banks of the Murray River poke from the shallows of Hume Lake (right) in Victoria. Behind the curve of Hume Dam, the spreading Murray River has drowned the town that once stood on its bank. The dam spares communities downstream from water shortages—a tricky task, since water needed at the far-off fruit-growing center, Mildura, must be released here four weeks beforehand.

Dams exploit the Murray-Darling river system. Croplands and pastures drink from irrigation webs. Swimmers, boaters, and waterskiers frolic on the glassy lakes. Thus Australia confirms the wisdom of Sir Samuel McCaughey in 1906: "The waters of the rivers . . . would be of more value to Australia than the discovery of gold."

Like a peeling sunburn, the Palmer River's bottom (above)

Des and Jen Bartlett

flakes and curls under a rainless sky in Australia's Northern Territory. Absorption by the ground and evaporation drink it dry. Renewed by rain, such rivers may lap at their banks but still dry up downstream as air and ground levy a ceaseless toll: nine gallons of rain for every one that reaches the sea. Yet some rivers may flow on unseen, their waters oozing under the ground even as the sun burns their streambeds. Many scrawl across a parched landscape, only to end in a dotted line of water holes. At one oasis a red kangaroo (above) mirrors the soul of a continent ever thirsting for water.

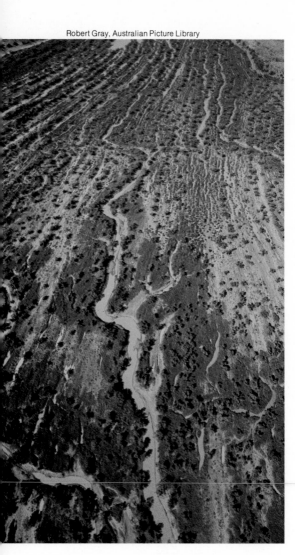

B oaters take a rest in a limestone cave above the Franklin River in Tasmania. The scene paints in fresh colors an ancient tableau, for in caves along the Franklin rest the bones and stone tools of Ice Age hunters who prowled its deep gorge 20,000 years ago. No other sites this far south have yielded human evidence even half as old.

In Queensland the Diamantina River (above) spreads a tattered veil of green where it peters out, to emerge again as the Warburton.

David Segal

struggling sheep and cattle ranchers as well as for flocks of herons, swans, egrets, and ducks. From the aborigines comes a name for the water holes: billabongs. Forever searching them out for survival, these nomads acknowledged in a grisly myth the stranglehold of the billabongs: A river spirit called a bunyip on a whim rises from a water hole to slay people.

In a modern-day ballad with many versions the billabong plays a different role. "Waltzing Matilda" tells the story of a tramp who "camped by a billabong/ Under the shade of a coolabah tree . . ." Seizing a stray sheep, he stuffs the prize in his bag. Along comes a policeman who charges the tramp with theft. To escape prison, the tramp drowns himself in the water hole. "And his ghost may be heard as it sings in the billabong/ You'll come a-waltzing Matilda with me." In its grim way, the billabong gives the tramp what billabongs have given bush peoples for millennia: refuge in a hostile land.

In the Channel Country rain can be a curse when downpours send rivers over the banks. But blessings follow when the waters retreat; billabongs may span 20 miles or more, and reach depths of 30 feet. Pastures suddenly carpet the land, and cattle ranchers from the north scurry in with their herds. In 1865 the Scottish explorer William Landsborough described the territory as "sufficient to supply the whole world with animal food." So-called wet years continued into the 1870s, luring settlers. In the droughts of the 1890s and early 1900s they saw the harsh extremes of the Channel Country. An exodus ensued, leaving—to this day—a mere sprinkling of sheep and cattle stations.

Few soils yield less than the scrubland of the central and western regions. "Not fit for a dog," growled the 17th-century buccaneer William Dampier, who may have been the first Englishman to look out onto this plateau country. Yet here, nature's deceptions can work to human benefit. Weaving southeast from the Macdonnell Ranges is central Australia's longest waterway, the Finke River. Larapinta, the aborigines named it, meaning "permanent water." Most of the year, the Finke is nothing more than a sandy channel. But the aborigines found that a layer of water always lies a few feet beneath the dry bed. Today, this hidden treasure works for ranchers.

East of the Kimberly region, the dammed Ord River irrigates soybeans, sorghum, and rice. Australians must put to work the stronger rivers. On this spread of earth nearly the size of the lower 48 United States, there are no "great" rivers other than the Murray and the Darling. And these pale alongside the world's mightiest. But Australia's waterways perform a precious service: They help people to make a comfortable home on the thirstiest continent.

A stockman and his mob—Australian terms for a cowboy and herd—ford the Murray River near its source in New South Wales. High mountain pastures grow green with irrigation from the Murray and its tributaries.

THE RIVERS OF SOUTH

Peru's Huallaga River cuts off its own loop en route to the Amazon. By Loren McIntyre.

AMERICA

H e went "covered from his head to his feet [in] . . . a second skin of gold," wrote a 16th-century Spanish scribe of a figure in a religious rite performed by Chibcha Indians of the northeast Andes. El Dorado the Spanish called him, The Gilded Man. To the Chibchas, he was the Zipa—their chieftain. Each year, to honor the mother-goddess of the human race, Bachue, the Chibchas gathered at Lake Guatavita, near modern-day Bogotá, in Colombia. Attendants blew gold dust all over the naked body of the Zipa, then rafted him to the middle of the lake. After other worshipers had tossed gold objects into the waters, the Zipa plunged into Guatavita. The gold powder washed off and sank to the depths, the final offering to Bachue.

Word of these rituals led gold-hungry European colonists—Spaniards, Germans, Portuguese, and English—to seek out South America's treasures. Other versions of the El Dorado myth inflamed imaginations further. Guahibo Indians of the llanos, or plains, of modern-day Colombia and Venezuela spoke of an opulent kingdom at the headwaters of the Meta and Guaviare Rivers. Incas claimed that untold riches lay between the Río de la Plata and present-day Peru. So Europeans pushed inland to claim the continent's wealth. There were mineral-rich lands, certainly, but the explorers found no cities paved with gold. They did find a continent endowed with spectacular rivers.

Stretching along the Pacific coast for some 5,000 miles are the colossal ranges of the Andes. The longest of all mountain ranges, the Andes reach almost 23,000 feet high. Raindrops that fall on Andes peaks just 100 miles east of the Pacific shore will drain 4,000 miles eastward to the Atlantic. Although seasonal rains drench much of the land, the narrow coastal plains west of the Andes and semiarid Patagonia receive little moisture. Other dry regions lie along the northeastern shoulder of Brazil and the Caribbean coast from northeastern Colombia to Venezuela.

Andean waterways often meet streams dropping down from the ancient Brazilian and Guiana highlands to the north or east. Rimmed on almost all sides by ranges, streams tend to converge in lowland basins and empty into the sea through a limited number of outlets. The highlands, barriers to rivers, do not prevent northeasterly trade winds from carrying moisture far inland. Dense, humid rain forest adds to the interior's wetness. And so, with highland streams rushing together in the lowlands, fed on their way by tropical downpours, the pattern is complete for a number of titanic rivers.

The Orinoco slices Venezuela in half on its run from the Serra Parima Mountains to the Caribbean; the São Francisco cuts deeply through the Brazilian highlands north, then east, to its Atlantic outlet; the Paraná, joined by the Paraguay and the Uruguay, rushes south from the high plateaus of Brazil to the Río de la Plata gulf between Argentina and Uruguay.

And mightiest of all, the Amazon. From its Apurímac River headwaters in

Orinoco

Magdalena

Negro

Amazon

Amazon

Madeira

Tocantins

Parnaíba

Sao Francisco

SOUTH AMERICA

Paraná

Paraná

Río de la Plata

Colorado

Peru, the Amazon sweeps eastward some 4,000 miles before emptying into the Atlantic. The Amazon counts more than a thousand tributaries. It ranks among the world's most navigable waterways. Its largely forested basin drains an astounding 2,270,000 square miles, so large an area that the northern and southern regions experience opposite rainy seasons.

Perhaps none of the continent's river networks is a more valued highway than that dominated by the Paraná, Paraguay, and Uruguay Rivers. The Paraná bolsters the economy of three countries. Brazil floats forest and farm products down the river to neighboring countries; Paraguay relies on the Paraná to reach overseas ports; Argentina sends out cereals, meat, fruit, wood, and tobacco, and brings in necessities such as petroleum, coal, and iron.

"A place to paddle"—so Orinoco is translated from the tongue of the Warao Indians, who have long lived on its delta. Over much of its 2,200-mile course, the Orinoco slopes gently through rain forests and grasslands of Venezuela. Christopher Columbus, probing the Gulf of Paria in 1498, was the first European to encounter the Orinoco. At its lush shoreline, he was astonished to find its fresh water pushing into the salty Caribbean. Of a nearby landfall he wrote, "I found there some lands, the most lovely in the world and very populous."

In 1531 the Spanish explorer, Diego de Ordaz, sailed miles up the Orinoco to win land for his country and to seek El Dorado. He went as far as the cataracts of Atures above the Orinoco's confluence with the Meta. He found poor Indian villages tucked back from the river, their inhabitants "averse to all friendship and understanding." Hostile Indians and stretches of rugged terrain hindered explorers for centuries afterward.

Beyond the initial impetus to explore the interior lands for riches much of the credit for discovery and settlement along South America's rivers belongs to the Catholic missionaries. In fact, the first book written about the Orinoco was published in 1741 by a Jesuit priest, Father Joseph Gumilla. Exploration, however, was not limited to gold or soul hunters. The exotic vegetation of the New World also attracted many scientists. The German naturalist Alexander von Humboldt mapped much of the river in 1800 but failed to track down its source. Not until 1951 was the Orinoco finally traced to a tiny hillside rivulet.

Strengthened by tributaries, the Orinoco plummets down the Serra Parima slopes to the llanos, then crawls northeasterly to the Atlantic. While countless streams feed into the Orinoco, one steals water away. This unusual channel, the Casiquiare, merges with the Rio Negro, which in turn pours into the Amazon. The result is a linking of two major rivers. The Casiquiare begins its 220-mile trip to the southwest about 220 miles from the Orinoco's headwaters.

A woolly monkey forages for fruit in a caimito tree near a bank of the upper Amazon River. A ravenous appetite for leaves and fruits—and a shape designed to hold it all— earn this jungle dweller the local nickname barrigudo—*potbelly.*

Loren McIntyre (also page 294)

Thousands of years of erosion have breached the low divide that once separated the Orinoco from the Casiquiare. Today floods can send a quarter of the Orinoco's flow to the Amazon through this channel.

The navigable portion of the upper Orinoco ends where it meets the Sipapo. Downstream, churning rapids squeeze between huge granite boulders.

Beyond, the Orinoco meanders eastward bordered by rolling plains and rain forest. Cattle ranching has long been an important industry. At the town of Barrancas, the Orinoco begins to split across its 230-mile-long Atlantic delta. During the rainy season, from May to November, the sluggish stream often turns into a surging torrent. Downpours can bring on flash floods; following these, canoes with outboard motors link fishermen and cattle ranchers in far reaches of the basin. Indians use the Orinoco's annual swelling to advantage. Nomadic farmers they have been called. With the beginning of the dry season in December, they slap up palm huts beside the receding waters. Then they plant corn, beans, and peas on the new silt loam. As the river shrinks more, the plots can grow larger. Harvest comes after seven months, and with the ensuing rains, the Indians pack off to higher ground.

The Warao Indians learned to cope with the waterlogged delta. They put the platforms of their houses and connecting walkways on stilts. They build bark canoes and dugout canoes. Their name means "those who live in canoes," and even young children paddle with skill. These Indians often canoe upriver a day's journey or more to trade. Some Warao are farmers, many are gatherers of larvae and wild vegetable food, but all make their diet chiefly of fish from the labyrinth of waterways in the delta of the Orinoco River.

On the whole, river development has helped the region. The Guri dam provides most of Venezuela's electricity and powers a huge iron ore smelting industry. Much of the ore goes to steel mills in Japan and the eastern United States. As a center for exporting the iron, and also for producing aluminum and steel, in 1961 the government created a new city some 50 miles from the delta. Today, more than a quarter of a million people live in Ciudad Guayana. Farther upstream is the bustling port of Ciudad Bolivar, a trading center for rubber, gold, and diamonds. Within 200

In the Cauca River Valley of Colombia, now extinct Quimbaya Indians crafted a gold and copper poporo *(above). The hand-size container held lime dust from crushed seashells, used to hasten the narcotic effect of chewing coca leaves.*

In a circlet of cloud, Angel Falls thunders 3,212 feet down the crags of Auyán Tepuí, "devil mountain" to Indians of southeastern Venezuela. The world's tallest waterfall starts its run to the Orinoco River as an underground stream gushing from the cliff face.

Bildarchiv Preussischer Kulturbesitz. Page 295: Museo del Oro, Bogotá, Colombia: Loren McIntyre

Bird, beast, and plant surround Alexander von Humboldt (standing) and botanist Aimé Bonpland in a hut by the Orinoco River in Venezuela. Humboldt's explorations in the early 1800s helped shape the sciences of meteorology and physical geography.

miles of this city are enormous reserves of limestone, sulfur, coal, oil, and gas.

The importance of the São Francisco River in the history of Brazil cannot be overestimated. Its pathway linked north and south, seacoast and interior, and united the far-flung regions of the colonial nation. The 1,600-mile-long São Francisco rises in the forested highlands of southeast Brazil. From there it rushes north a thousand miles before angling eastward to the Atlantic. Its upper course cleaves a timbered and grassy valley, where farmers grow cotton, rice, and corn. Frothing cascades break its flow farther downstream as the river pours through coastal ranges to the sea. Here, 150 miles from the Atlantic, thunders the Paulo Afonso Falls, its 260-foot drop among the world's most magnificent. Surrounding the falls zone is the *sertão*, Brazil's thirstiest land, where there is little rainfall, and the salinity of underground water makes it unfit for irrigation. In the sertão, ranchers tend cattle, goats, and sheep. Downstream the São Francisco floodplain, once thickly forested, is now largely cleared for farming.

Iron ore deposits near the headwaters are unmatched anywhere in the world; at Itabira is a wondrous mountain of almost pure ore. There are great stores also of bauxite, platinum, lead, diamonds, and other precious stones.

But it was gold that lured explorers like Amerigo Vespucci up the São Francisco. Former slave catchers, the bandeirantes, roamed Brazil's interior claiming new lands for Portugal, and chipped away at mountain rock to find both gold and gems. Sadly, news of such finds brought renegades up the river, including bands of escaped convicts and many runaway slaves. Less bold citizens, wary of the harsh living conditions, shied away from the region.

And so the blessing of resources ironically wound up stunting the growth of the São Francisco basin. Today, few roads link river villages. People travel by canoe or flatboat. Merchants use shoal-draft riverboats that chug from landing to landing. There is little irrigation. Farmers of the floodplains echo the practice of Orinoco people. Huge cattle spreads, or *fazendas,* thrive both along the river and inland. And great promise for hydroelectric power stems from the Paulo Afonso Falls. Far from fully tapped, Paulo Afonso already provides electricity for nearby cities. South Americans, no longer driven by foreign dreams of gold, understand the treasure of their own land laced with remarkable rivers.

Indians wrestle an alligator under the club of Henry Walter Bates. Arriving from England in 1848, Bates spent 11 years in Amazonia and became its first great entomologist. Some of his work helped support Charles Darwin's theory of evolution.

THE AMAZON

By Jonathan B. Tourtellot / Photographs by David Louis Olson

T-shirts, not beads, adorn most of the Witoto Indian children who run down the muddy riverbank to inspect our floatplane. Their village lies some 20 miles up this small tributary of the upper Amazon, and that's close enough to put them in routine contact with the outside world. The shirt on one boy's scrawny chest proclaims, in English, ROCK 'N' ROLL IS HERE TO STAY.

So it is. I have realized by this point in my trip upstream that the Amazon is not the wilderness river we imagine—a remote, mysterious stream flowing through virgin jungle, where naked Indians hunt jaguars. Bulldozers, tourists, poachers, oil companies, the ever present T-shirt—this is now the Amazon.

Romantic images suited the river better when Francisco de Orellana explored it in 1542. Yet even he fantasized: The name "Amazon" derives from his chronicler's report, now discredited, of Indian women warriors along its banks.

Orellana entered Amazonia by the back door, from the Andes. For the Amazon begins there, gathering river after river as it crosses Peru and Brazil. Where the Rio Negro joins in at Manaus, the flow at times almost doubles.

By almost every measure, the Amazon is Earth's greatest river. It pours more water into the sea than the next seven biggest candidates together. Almost ten times more than the Mississippi. It rivals the Nile in length but carries at least *50 times* the volume. Seven of its tributaries are each over a thousand miles long. It drains the largest watershed—a basin almost the size of Australia. It disgorges 20 percent of all fresh water entering the world's oceans; beyond its mouth this discharge lowers ocean salinity over an area as big as the Mediterranean Sea. Its channel is navigable by boat or barge for almost 3,000 miles. If the Amazon flowed through North America, an ocean freighter could sail from Boston to Denver, and the source would lie 1,700 miles beyond *that*.

My exploration begins where this river of rivers fans out to join the Atlantic. Here about a million people cluster in the port city once known as Our Lady of Bethlehem of Grand Pará—now simply Belém.

Belém has grace. Sedate, weatherworn high rises soar above downtown

Heading for ports scattered along Earth's largest river, an Amazon barco sets forth into the beguiling calm of a land where waters flow slow but change comes fast.

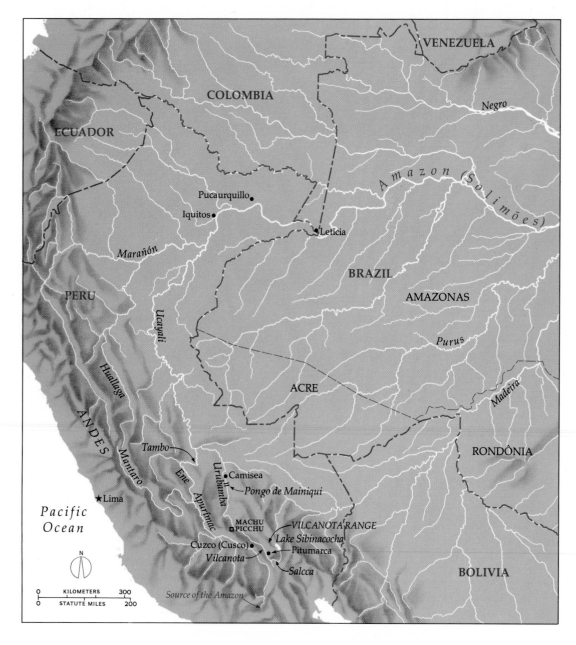

streets lined with mango trees. Elegant, aging mansions lend an Old World flavor, and for good reason; in the late 19th century Belém cashed in on a transatlantic trading bonanza—rubber.

Arlene Kelly, a young American historian working in Belém, tells me why the rubber boom came and went. "One of the first big industrial uses of rubber was for tires, during the bicycle boom in Europe and North America at the end of the 19th century. When Henry Ford began mass-producing cars, rubber was

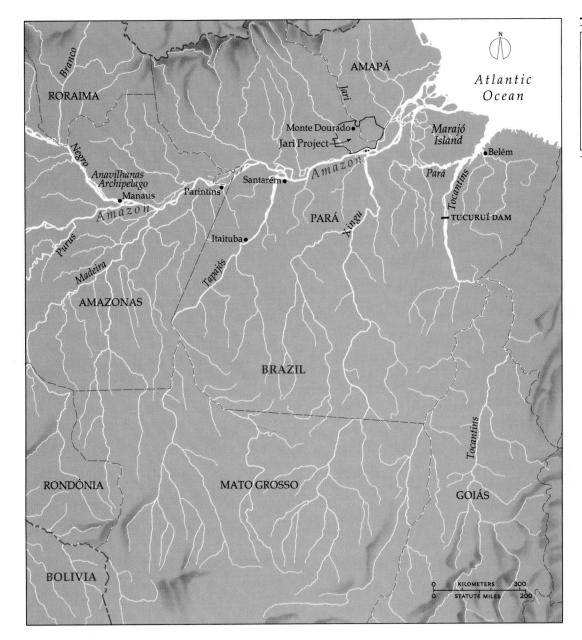

even more needed." Wild rubber trees scattered through the rain forest could supply it, and so the modern world pounced on the Amazon. A rubber *patrão* would stake out a huge claim, sometimes an entire river valley, and virtually enslave his Indian laborers. Many died of disease or maltreatment, but rubber brought prosperity to Belém. The city looked to Europe, not Brazil. "There were people in Belém who used to send their laundry to be done in Portugal."

By 1910 the boom was tapering off; plantations in Britain's Asian colonies had begun selling cheaper rubber, produced by trees grown from Amazonian seeds. For a few decades the Amazon region slept. But by the 1960s Brazilians wanted, as they say, to "occupy" their vast, underpopulated, underexplored Amazon holdings, particularly, went the unofficial thought, before anyone else occupied them. Brazil needed farmland for people from the country's drought-prone northeast. It needed Amazon minerals and timber. It needed room to grow. Settlers and prospectors and developers began moving in.

Ecologists recite a litany of subsequent assaults on the environment: Hydroelectric dams that flood rain forest and disrupt river ecosystems; mining that pollutes the water; overfishing and overhunting, which have decimated such species as river turtles and jaguars. Anthropologists mourn the destruction of Indian tribal identities by forced relocation programs, as well as the loss of Indian lives from disease, infighting, and skirmishes with settlers. But of all these shocks, deforestation ranks highest in ecological impact. Estimates vary greatly on how fast the Amazon's rain forest—the largest in the world—falls to chain saw and torch, but most agree the rate is fast. The cattle ranches and farms that replace the trees are often abandoned within a few years, victims of the Amazon's startlingly poor soils. Yet the clearing continues, and biologists worry about the loss of plant and animal species not even identified yet.

David Oren, an ornithologist in Belém, tells me of biological discoveries just made in a nearby patch of forest, soon to be cleared for resettlement: "Here it looks as if we're on to a new center of endemism—a lot of local species which exist only here—completely unrecognized until now. And we're finding this out at the very last moment, because we've only got about five years to find out what's in this area before it's condemned."

So the scientists race the bulldozers, trying to discover and catalog tens of thousands of species before habitats disappear—with little time to study how individual species behave, and what benefit they might have held for humans.

If development must occur, most ecologists prefer projects designed to use the same land over and over. Such was Jari, where American billionaire Daniel K. Ludwig created a pulpwood plantation on holdings the size of Connecticut along the Jari River. He cleared the land and planted pulp trees that would mature swiftly in the endless growing season. He installed a 17-story-high power plant, towed in one piece from Japan, to run an equally large pulp mill, also towed from Japan. He built a railway to bring harvested trees to the plant. But the billionaire lost his investment, bought out in 1982 by a Brazilian consortium. "Jari, the project that made Ludwig a millionaire," goes one wisecrack.

Jari surprises me; it is pretty. My hotel overlooks a pristine bend in the Jari River. The manager, a rangy woman named Lourdes, keeps two young howler monkeys in a small menagerie out back. As a parrot waddles over and sits companionably on my foot, I ask Lourdes how she got the howlers.

"The young ones cling to the mother very hard, so the men kill the mother to get the little ones," she says matter-of-factly, "and bring them here to sell."

"Just for pets?"

"For pets, yes."

Johan Zweede, the forest manager, was about to leave Jari, last of Ludwig's management to go. "Ludwig is a visionary," Zweede recounts. "He felt the tropics could be used for growing wood fiber." Trial and error taught how to cope with Amazon growing conditions. But shrinking markets and rising strains between an impatient Ludwig and wary Brazilian officialdom proved too much to overcome. Edmundo Barbosa da Silva, president of the consortium that has taken over, must now turn a losing proposition into a winning one. No small visionary himself, he foresees for Jari "Brazilian civilization in the tropics" but admits "we have a challenging effort ahead of us."

Both Oren and Zweede condemned the persistent attempts at Amazon cattle ranching, but praised the appropriateness of water buffalo for the floodplain. Buffalo give richer milk, have fewer diseases, and eat native grasses. So I went to where buffalo are raised in quantity: Marajó Island.

Marajó sticks like a giant cork in the mouth of the Amazon, as big as the southern end of Florida and just as flat and wet. Eduardo de Castro Ribeiro owns the Bonjardim *fazenda*, a ranch two hours up a small Marajó river.

The wooden boat he sends for me, like most of its Amazon kin, is so worn and so often repainted that no sharp edges remain. The boatman offers me a cup of buffalo milk. It is heavy and rich and tastes of buffalo.

On the Bonjardim dock someone has laid out three eight-inch piranhas, still alive. With their powerful jaws and blunt faces they look like J. Edgar Hoover. There is nothing human, though, about the rim of sharp, triangular teeth, weaponry for the notorious mass attacks that can strip a calf to the bone in a minute or two. Blood in the water triggers their feeding frenzies. Otherwise, swimming in "piranha-infested" rivers is reported to be fairly safe, and Amazon residents routinely do so. I push a twig experimentally into one half-open piranha mouth. A convulsive *chomp* shatters it. I decide not to test the reports.

At dinner Senhor Ribeiro tells how he helped launch buffalo ranching on Marajó with a dike system to control water levels in his fields. He says buffalo need watching, though: "I have to have absolute control of the number of buffalo on the land, or excessive trampling will vitrify the soil—turn it glasslike. During droughts buffalo will look for a lake. They will trample and destroy everything in it, even the alligators. They can make oatmeal of snakes."

I have no feel yet for Amazonian distances, so I fly from Belém inland to Manaus, a hop a bit longer than New York to Chicago, to try a boat ride. White riverboats are the buses and trucks of Amazonia, the rivers their highways. The custom is to sleep in hammocks on covered decks. At the Manaus waterfront I pick a boat headed downriver to Santarém, a 34-hour journey—short by Amazon standards. With a deep burbling of the engines, we pull out into the broad river. Astern, a pale red sun sinks through the haze and disappears with equatorial swiftness into the water; the breeze turns cool. After supper I retire to my hammock. In the night beyond the railing another boat churns by; under its deck lights the row of bulging hammocks resembles a cargo of human pupae.

Next morning in the harbor at Parintins freshwater dolphins arc through the silty water. *"Bôtos!"* cries a passenger. "Look, three!" An Irish-Brazilian prospector named O'Reilly tells me of folktales about the dolphins: that at night they come from the water in the shape of men, and seduce unwary women. "In small towns you can still find birth certificates that say the father is a bôto."

On the riverbanks, often miles distant from our boat, second-growth forest alternates with clearings for the vegetable patches and shacks of the *caboclos*, the mixed-blood rural folk. Little virgin jungle survives so near the river.

In Santarém I find sunbathers lazing on a white beach beside the clear Tapajós River. Three types of rivers—"blue," "black," and "white" water—drain the Amazon basin. Blue-water rivers like the Tapajós generally flow from the south, where sandy soil filters the water to a transparency that reflects the sky's blue. Black-water rivers such as the Rio Negro are actually a clear, tealike color. They generally flow from the north and lie entirely within rain forest. Like tea, they owe their tint to leaves: to humic acids leached from the forest litter of their huge watersheds. White-water rivers, like the Amazon itself, flow mainly from the west and are neither white nor necessarily full of rapids; they are a light tan café-au-lait color, from sediment picked up in the distant Andes.

I return to Manaus and check into a room with the moldy-carpet odor of many Amazon hotels. On the TV Spencer Tracy rattles away in Portuguese. The phone book cover shows a satellite image of the nearby confluence of the Amazon and the Rio Negro, each flow larger than any other river in the world.

Manaus houses Brazil's National Institute for Amazonian Studies (INPA). Dr. Herbert Schubart, the vice director, explains that INPA seeks to learn how to use the Amazon's natural resources without destroying them: "We need lots of research, because this tropical ecosystem is so complex, and sometimes so fragile, that we really don't know how to exploit it correctly." One massive, 20-year experiment, aided by the World Wildlife Fund, seeks to find out how large natural rain forest preserves must be for their ecosystems to work properly.

The study areas are on a new ranch being hacked from the jungle a couple of hours' drive north of Manaus. With scientists from INPA I arrive in a brief but blinding rainstorm. Such storms are the Amazon's engines of renewal, fueling the forests and filling the rivers, and rare is the afternoon when you can't see at least a couple on the horizon, like cloud-rigged clippers sailing a jungle sea.

As the rain stops, clouds of mist form among the crowns of the trees. "See that?" says Judy Rankin, one of the ecologists. "That's how the forest manufactures rain." Moisture from leaves—either evaporating from them or released by transpiration—accounts for over two-thirds of the rain that falls in the Amazon basin. This discovery leads scientists to fear the effects on local and world climate if the basin were to lose a lot of its tree cover. Contrary to earlier belief, the Amazon rain forest does not supply much of the world's oxygen; the oceans do. But deforestation does release carbon dioxide, from burn-off and from microbes in the disturbed soil, and that helps warm up the globe.

Before us, a few bony cattle poke through a devastated landscape of felled trunks and graying stumps. Left standing amid the clear-cut wreckage are several virgin forest tracts—study areas of carefully varied sizes. We take a walk through one sample of about 25 acres. Only inches under the root-and-leaf layer is desert—yellow, clayey material low in nutrients. The vegetation lives on its own debris. Tiny roots invade fallen leaves and loot them of nutrients within weeks. It almost seems as if you could walk to the edge of the forest, bend down for a good grip, and pull it up off the land like a rug.

We also visit a floating research station in the Anavilhanas Archipelago, a maze of long, slender islands and channels lacing the black-water Rio Negro. Now, in June, the river is high, and water reaches deep into the forest. On our way upriver the boat leaves a wake of clear brown foam. The Rio Negro's tea-leafy origins give it this rich, organic hue, yet the water is among the purest of any river in the world. It supports little life because it has no nutrient value, no mineral content; hungry forest roots have kept it all. Black-water rivers are relatively mosquito free, because there is little for mosquito larvae to eat. And yet this river is full of fish. The ecological riddle: What do the fish live on?

An American scientist with us, Michael Goulding, hit on the answer in the local fishing lore: that during high water, fish leave the river channels and "go into the woods"—to the inundation forest, called *igapó*, whose trees stand up to their waists in water for months a year. Igapó lines most Amazonian rivers.

Goulding takes us into one, steering the boat through the top branches of some rubber trees. "When these pods burst," he says, "the seeds fly into the water and fish snap them up almost as they hit." He was the first scientist to confirm that rain forest trees support the fish population, findings that raise serious concerns about floodplain deforestation. Put simply: No forest, no fish.

Dusk approaches. We float in a quiet backwater. Two scarlet macaws fly overhead, and in the still water some ducks drift in silhouette on a mirror of sunset. Goulding threads back through the twilit maze of channels, finding his way by reading treetop patterns against the sky. Long before we see the station, we hear the generator's clatter sawing through the night.

A few days later I am in a jet, watching the upper Amazon slide by below. Brazilians call this part of the river, above Manaus, the Solimões. An hour from Manaus by jet, five days by boat, a sliver of Colombia touches the Amazon. Its main town, Leticia, promotes tourism. I decide it is time to sample the tourist's Amazon, and when tourists come to the Amazon they want to see Indians.

I join a day trip to a Yagua village. These Yaguas have lived by the river for 12 years, invited in from deep jungle to be more accessible to tourists—some 3,500 a year, admits our guide. In midday heat we scramble up a mudbank and file down a trail to a sleepy sprinkle of open-walled thatched huts on low stilts. Outside the huts hangs the village's cash crop: necklaces, masks, spears, and other trinkets for sale. Indians stand around idly. The men wear grass skirts, the women wear topless wraparounds, and both wear lifeless expressions. A tribesman gives a desultory demonstration of a blowgun. Fthwit!—the little dart zings into a nearby tree, an incongruously lively act in this place.

"These Yaguas—they wear those grass skirts for tourists, don't they?"

"Oh, no. They wear those all the time."

Inside one hut I notice a clothesline; it is hung with shorts and T-shirts.

Colombia won its corridor to the Amazon from Peru in a 1922 treaty. But Peru still controls almost half the Amazon River, if you measure from the farthest source to the mouth. Iquitos, Peru's "port on the Atlantic," is 2,300 miles from the sea and can still receive small oceangoing freighters. The economy depends on commerce, lumber, oil exploration, tourism, and cocaine smuggling.

I fly in over a hazy enormousness of forest, a gray-green carpet broken only by the looping thread of a lone river. At the airport, hawkers sell more tourist trinkets, including the worst yet in jungle kitsch: dried-piranha pendants.

In town everything seems to be breaking down. Buildings are shabby, blackouts frequent, streets more pothole than pavement. Yet the 175,000 inhabitants go about in a frenzy of activity even as their city disintegrates around them. They throng the market area, where radios blare and shops spill over with clothing, radios, piles of toothpaste tubes, gaudy plastic housewares.

What keeps Iquitos frenzied is motorcycles—cheap to import, deft at dodging potholes. Everyone rides them—merchants and soldiers and bureaucrats; young, dainty women with skirts hiked up over gas tanks; grandmothers with shopping bags dangling from the handlebars; pairs of schoolgirls in gray and white uniforms; even entire families, kids propped between parents' knees.

Photographer David Olson and I decide to visit a real Indian village on a tributary downriver. Our floatplane slips between treetops and a low cloud deck for a hundred miles and lands at Pucaurquillo, where a crowd of Witoto and Bora Indian kids greets us. A little girl in a tattered T-shirt that says MANAUS LOVES ME escorts us to a stilt house. In the kitchen several women are making *masato,* an alcoholic drink, from manioc root. All are in Western clothes.

In the other room a man tinkers with a chain saw. He takes us outside to see some traditional Indian medicinal plants—many of which, botanists suspect, contain drugs unknown to Western medicine. A plant he calls *ishango* looks vaguely like Queen Anne's lace. He says it relieves pain in muscles and joints. David had pulled a shoulder muscle a few days earlier, so our host rubs ishango florets over the area. David's skin breaks out in a painless, bumpy rash. "Watch it," warns our pilot. "I've flown out some cases treated by a faulty witch doctor here. They all died." But minutes later the rash is gone and David announces, "You won't believe this, but my shoulder feels fine." After the single treatment his ache will disappear for three days.

Our honor guard of kids follows us back to the plane. "Good-bye!" calls MA-NAUS LOVES ME, in English. The plane lifts into the drizzle and heads back to Iquitos. Below, a boatman paddles his tiny dugout across the Amazon, a speck in the immensity of sky gray water.

ccording to the theory of plate tectonics, South America is colliding with a piece of Pacific Ocean floor called the Nazca Plate, a process that has raised the Andes to elevations of four miles or so. This high-flung continental wreckage supplies 80 percent of the sediment in the Amazon. The lower basin is too old and too flat to erode very easily, but from the ice fields and high valleys of the Andes young, rambunctious, rapids-filled torrents tear away at the eastern slope in their desperate haste to reach the jungle flatlands, only to be transformed there into lazy, potbellied rivers that wend their middle-aged way toward the distant sea. David and I decide to follow one of the most distant tributaries, the Urubamba, from where it begins back down to its meeting with the jungle.

Where it begins is in the mountains east of Cuzco, among snowpeaks and glaciers and lakes. Our goal is the largest of these lakes, Sibinacocha, at an altitude of 15,500 feet. The packhorse trek there and back will take eight days through Quechua Indian lands. The Quechua, once ruled by Incas, are not so much a single tribe as a language group. They inhabit most of upland Peru.

An Inca footroad leads us through steep-sided valleys and past an occasional village. For more than a thousand years people have farmed and herded here, right up to the snow line, and almost every slope is laced with the grazing trails of sheep and llama. We spend our first night where the little river we are following emerges from a limestone tunnel through a colonnade of colorful deposits formed by mineral springs. Dinner is trout, fresh from the stream.

As the days pass I notice something about the Quechua. In cities their faces show only the stolid, expressionless look of an acculturated people, caught between two worlds. Peter Matthiessen wrote in 1961 of the Quechua shuffling "bent forward, as if forever doomed to walk uphill." But the farther we hike from the highway, and the deeper we penetrate valleys where only Quechua live, the more open and expressive those faces become. Smiles abound, some cheerful, some shy—but almost everyone offers greetings, and many want to chat: Where are we from? Where are we going? Sibinacocha? It's cold up there!

Our third evening we camp by a small lake, Aereacocha (*cocha* is Quechua for "lake"), high in the cold of the open tundra. As I burrow into my sleeping bag I realize that this is the first time on my Amazon journey that I feel truly removed from Western civilization—no radios, no engines, no plastic litter. No T-shirts.

In the frost-etched morning, when the snowpeaks shine brilliant against deep azure, the flamingos come. Eight of them, in airborne single file, long necks stretched ahead, long legs trailing behind, like graceful flying serpents. They reconnoiter the little lake, sweeping in a perfect arc, and the rising sun catches their pink plumage and turns it to flame. And then they are gone.

By afternoon we see Sibinacocha sparkling a deep blue reflection of the high-altitude sky. From one end the long lake drains into the Amazon river system: to the Salcca River, which will join the Vilcanota, which becomes the Urubamba. These headwaters read like a biblical genealogy—the Urubamba will join the Tambo (born the Ene, from the union of the Apurímac and the Mantaro) to beget the Ucayali, which joins the Marañón and so begets the Amazon.

Bundled against wind and cold I walk along the Sibinacocha shore, listening to lapping wavelets. Across the lake a massive glacier looms, and beside it the snow-covered Vilcanota Range. In bright peaks like these, I think, the ultimate source of the Amazon lies—not in water, but in ice.

E very morning what's known as the "tourist train" leaves Cuzco, probes its way into the Inca's fertile Sacred Valley, and follows the Upper Urubamba down to the site of Machu Picchu, that vertiginous Inca city which is one of South America's leading tourist attractions.

We board the train in the Sacred Valley. The cars are noisy with polyglot conversation—English, German, French, a little Spanish, and others. During a short wait at one station, tourists pour out onto the tracks, Instamatics and Yashicas at the ready. They photograph the mountains. They photograph the river, green and white, frothing around the rocks of the chasm. They photograph each other. Several gather to watch a Quechua woman spin llama wool while waiting for another train. They photograph her. A skinny urchin wanders through the crowd, asking without much hope, "Moan-ey? Moan-ey?" After my days among the mountain Indians the tourists look oddly large and white.

From the next station, buses shuttle us up to Machu Picchu, some thousand feet above. The mysterious abandoned city, surely one of the most incredible archaeological finds ever, hangs amid a landscape that is mostly verticals. The uncanny, mortarless stonework, so perfectly fitted, so fluidly shaped, gives credence to the tale that the Incas knew a plant that could soften stone.

At sunset I stand above the city. The valley loops around the ridge like a moat of shadows. Night does not fall here; it rises, dusk chasing sunlight up the mountainsides until the last rays take flight from the highest peak. In evening's quiet the roar of rapids sounds faintly from the darkness below.

Peruvians say that Machu Picchu is at the eyebrow of the jungle. From here the Urubamba splashes on down Andean flanks clad in thickening vegetation. The twisting valley widens and the air grows hazy. The road we follow ends at one of several worn-looking towns strung out along the river. Below this point the Urubamba threads a rapids-filled gorge, the Pongo de Mainiqui, which marks the transition from mountains to jungle flatland, from the realm of the Andes to that of the Amazon. The local guide says that in the village of Camisea, beyond the Pongo, we can find Machiguenga Indians living much as they always have, untouched by the modern world.

In a long, slender launch we head downriver past villages that punctuate the scrubby jungle. Some of the river dwellers are newcomers. The Peruvian government, like Brazil, has been offering land to encourage settlement of the jungle. So the Quechua descend from their cool, open mountains and find themselves in an alien world. They build their huts of the traditional adobe, wrong for the climate, and wear their traditional woolens. The women watch us from the lush foliage, decked in their fedoras, their weathered faces like glacier-worn stones mislaid among the banana trees.

The passage through the Pongo is only mildly exciting; low water has temporarily tamed the famous rapids. But the steep walls of slate drip with vines, trees, and mosses—and waterfalls. Lots of waterfalls, some gushing thickly from between the rocks, some trickling over ledges like beaded curtains, and some that fall in steps, cascade above cascade above cascade. At the end of the gorge two enormous slabs of vegetation-covered slate stand on each side of the river. No one could ask for a more dramatic gateway to Amazonia.

For that is where we are. The river now turns smooth and broad, the terrain flat, the trees typical of low jungle. The altitude is only 1,600 feet, almost three miles lower than Sibinacocha, but we are still 3,400 river miles from the sea.

As we approach Camisea, the "untouched" Machiguenga village, I hear something unmistakably mechanical. We round a bend—and flying right up the river toward us is a bright red helicopter. It lands on a bank across from the village, behind signs that identify Shell Oil's GEOSEISMIC SUB-BASE CAMISEA. Many Machiguengas, it turns out, now work for Shell, exploring for oil.

Do Indians anywhere in Amazonia still live in the old way? Yes, a few, in the forests far up the most remote branches of the tributaries of the tributaries. But not for long. The world is at their door, dressed in T-shirt and hard hat. As the chopper thwak-thwaks away over the jungle, I watch and reflect that for better or for worse, there goes the future of the Amazon. For richer, or for poorer.

A mphibious ranching: A cowboy herds water buffalo on giant Marajó Island, where the Amazon meets the Atlantic. Some ranchers here and on the river's floodplain, the várzea, find that buffalo cope better than cattle with low-grade Amazonian grasses, tropical diseases, and a highwater season that lasts months. In the Amazon basin, known for poor soils, the comparatively fertile várzea offers the best hope for agriculture, especially for water-loving crops like rice.

On a Marajó bayou (top) a lone egret heads for leafy shelter—shelter that is in danger throughout the Amazon. Since the 1960s, deforestation has sparked worldwide controversy: Can humankind occupy the Amazon's rain forest wilderness, home to at least one of every ten plant and animal species on Earth, without destroying it?

311

312

iverside market (top) called Ver-o-Pêso, "Watch the Weight," caters the city of Belém, Atlantic port for the Amazon. Market stalls dispense myriad fruits, vegetables, and jungle remedies, as well as the daily catch (left). Amazonian rivers hold perhaps a third as many fish species as the entire Atlantic, and many are edible: delicious tambaqui, 275-pound pirarucu, even piranha.

Pages 314-315: Centerpiece of a broken dream, the pulp mill at Jari now belongs to a Brazilian consortium. Daniel K. Ludwig, daring American financier, made Jari into a huge pulpwood plantation to exploit Amazonia's ample land and year-round growing season. Project managers learned to cope with plant diseases and difficult soils, but say that economic and political problems kept Ludwig from turning a profit.

313

 hite water meets black off an island at the confluence of the Amazon and the Negro (top). The Negro's discharge outranks all Earth's rivers but the Amazon itself, which wins first place even before arriving here. The two flows—the Amazon opaque with Andean silt, the Negro stained to tea-dark translucency by acids leached from forest debris—can run side by side for dozens of miles before blending.

A third type of river, the bluewater Tapajós (right), mirrors a twilit sky in waters filtered clear by sandy southern uplands.

City at the heart of the Brazilian Amazon, Manaus flourished in the rubber boom at the turn of the century—heady days when rubber barons lit cigars with three-figure bank notes and huge fees drew performers to the Teatro Amazonas opera house, still operating today (above). Boom went bust and decades of neglect followed, but now Manaus seeks new life from Brazil's drive to develop the region. The Teatro's dome has yielded the skyline to a thicket of high rises (right), and the city strives for economic independence as a free port. Duty-free goods like Bohemian crystal (opposite) lure tourists from Brazil's more populated areas far to the southeast. After a thousand-mile trip upstream, a Japanese freighter (top right) unloads in Manaus at a floating dock designed to rise and fall with 30-foot yearly changes in river level.

319

Cultures mix for Amazon Indians; these Witotos of lowland Peru wear Western garb and live in traditional stilt houses walled with pona, a hollow tree that can be split lengthwise and unrolled flat to form an instant panel.

Some Indians, lured by the lucrative and illegal pet trade, strip forests of wildlife to supply dealers. Scarlet macaws (right) can bring $2,000 each in American pet stores, rarer parrots far more.

A lagoon left by the Amazon's wandering channels (above) nurtures water plants, including the green disks of the Victoria regia water lily, up to six feet across. High water may launch "floating meadows," rafts of interwoven vegetation that sail off downriver, spreading seeds and whatever animal life happens to be aboard. In an odd twist, várzea ranchers can round up the meadows to feed cattle trapped by the flood.

M udbank streets one month, canals the next, when high water comes to the sometimes-floating shantytown of Belén (left), a district in Peru's Amazon port of Iquitos. Most Belén houses rest on pontoon logs that lift the flotsam suburb off the mud as the Amazon begins its yearly rise.

Much of the rest of Iquitos travels on two wheels (below). "Iquitos," brags the mayor, "has more motorcycles per capita than any other city in Peru." In this urban island, isolated from the rest of Peru by an ocean of rain forest, motorcycles cost less to import than cars. Before the air age, travel here from Lima, Peru's capital, was easier by sailing around South America and up the Amazon than by crossing the Andes and the jungle beyond. Now the city hopes to see oil riches, and rural immigrants pour into town, seeking jobs.

323

T he sluice of a rainstorm renews life. Scientists have found out that the Amazon forest makes its own rain, recycling into the air some two-thirds of what falls. The forest retains nutrients so well that storm runoff reaching the rivers may contain smaller concentrations of some nutrients than the raindrops themselves.

Perhaps one in five of the world's bird species live in the Amazon basin, and ornithologist Rob Bierregaard studies their behavior by recording them (top). Botanists have tens of thousands of plant species to catalog, such as the molongó (left). Many plants hold practical promise—for anticancer drugs, contraceptives, insecticides—but all need testing. Doctors now use curare, the Indian arrow poison, as an antispasmodic. "Forests of Brazil: pharmacy of the world" says one scientist's T-shirt.

325

P ages 326-327: Peru's Inca city of Machu Picchu perches 8,000 feet above sea level, an altitude midway from lowland jungle to Andean snows. In the gorge below glints the Urubamba River, Amazon bound. The farthest source of the Amazon lies up the next river to the west, the Apurímac.

Harness bells tinkle above a chorus of rapids as a llama packtrain follows the valley of an Urubamba tributary (far right), using an Inca road crafted of stone five centuries ago. An Indian boy (right), probably descended from the road builders, peers from under a llama-wool chullo cap, a guard against the cool climate. His village, Pitumarca (top), is a chilly 11,600 feet high. He speaks Quechua, the lingua franca Incas imposed on their subjects. It has joined Spanish as an official national language.

C old breezes from Andean glaciers slip across the Peruvian alpine lake of Sibinacocha, ten miles long and three miles high. The Amazon, river of eternal summer, rises in these lands of endless winter; Sibinacocha drains into one of the tributaries. Yet a vision of warmer climes survives even here: Flocks of flamingos feed on tiny organisms in the shallows of these Andean lakes. The birds thrive despite freezing temperatures. And here, too, the effects of development threaten; new roads ease the way for flamingo egg collectors, who sell increasing amounts of booty in the markets of the lower valleys. Thus for the Amazon—for its plants, for its animals, for its Indian tribes—the coldest winds of all may be the winds of change.

THE PARANÁ-LA PLATA

By Carol Bittig Lutyk / Photographs by David Louis Olson

They came to the banks of the Paraná by the tens of thousands, peasant farmers and city poor, Brazilian and Paraguayan. Most had never climbed higher than the back of a horse or the seat of a tractor, but here they worked atop structures taller than a 60-story skyscraper. They received free housing, free health care, free schooling for their children, and, all told, 14,000 free meals a day. Laboring day and night for six years, they dug enough earth and rock to cover Manhattan Island $42\frac{1}{2}$ inches deep and poured enough concrete to pave an eight-lane highway from New York to St. Louis. They came to the Paraná to build Itaipu Dam. It will be the mightiest hydroelectric project in the world.

I had come to the Paraná to follow its 2,680-mile run to the Atlantic. Born of the union of two mountain rivers, the Paraná twists southwesterly through deep cleavages in Brazil's ancient highlands, then slips meekly into the great calm lake behind Itaipu Dam. Its waters thunder over the dam's spillway and meander through subtropical forests to Corrientes in Argentina. There the Paraná receives its greatest tributary—the Paraguay River. Turning southward, the Paraná sweeps through the rolling grasslands of the pampas. Then, like the tendrils of a wild vine, the river branches again and again into hundreds of delta channels where it meets the Uruguay River. Together, as the Río de la Plata, they roll sedately past the capitals of Argentina and Uruguay and on to the sea.

For centuries the Paraná, one of South America's most navigable rivers, has moved people, beef, wool, and grain between the continent's interior and the Atlantic. Its muddy waters have carried Indian fishermen, Spanish conquistadores, Jesuit missionaries, gauchos, and the builders of mighty Itaipu.

Doomsayers call Itaipu an "aquatic bomb." They fear that its collapse would inundate Buenos Aires, 870 miles downriver, with five feet of water. Itaipu's

The flood-swollen Iguaçu River sweeps wilderness mud to the Paraná-La Plata, third longest river in the New World and one of the most traveled routes in South America.

concrete megalith did create a tide of destruction, but this tide traveled *backward* 125 miles: The reservoir smothered part of the ancestral lands of the Guaraní Indians. One tribe moved to a new home beside the reservoir and found themselves in a changed world. Their houses still have bamboo walls and thatched roofs; the new wooden pharmacy has glass windows and a metal roof. Their children go to school to learn hygiene and mathematics. Their chief, Fernando, wears T-shirts and jeans. His weatherworn face bespeaks a quiet authority, a wise and friendly spirit. He prefers the old life when his people had room to roam and to hunt. But the Guaraní have borne change stoically over the centuries. Brushing a fly aside, Fernando shrugged and told me: "My people lived along the river before the dam. We will live along the river after the dam."

From Itaipu I drove 25 miles south to Iguazú, the world's widest waterfall. Brown with wilderness mud, water plunges over a sinuous crescent of lava about two miles wide. Above the impact of water on rock hovers a perpetual cloud of mist a hundred feet high, prompting Indians to call this area "the place where clouds are born." Great dusky swifts spiral like windswept leaves above the falls. Vines, palms, bamboos, and orchids grow with exuberance on nearly every ledge and cliff not pounded by water.

As I drove south from sultry Iguazú, charcoal clouds smudged the sky and pelted the earth with a chilling spring downpour. Then a soft wind nudged the storm north. A scent of pine filled the wet air. The land, still cool and sodden from the winter rains, was alive with the coming season—newborn greens, seedlings uncurling to the first warmth. Kiri trees, prized by cabinetmakers for soft and straight-grained wood, sprinkled the dark earth with pale violet petals. The gnarled limbs of yerba maté trees awaited their spring growth.

Maté is a popular drink in the lands of the Paraná. Maté growers dry the bright green leaves over a slow fire of sweet-smelling wood, then age, grind, and blend them before packaging the dried tea. Jesuits from Spain set up the first maté plantations in the early 1600s. The missionaries taught the Indians to raise crops and livestock, weave cloth, make wood carvings of the Savior, and build churches. But the holy fathers did not allow their charges to leave without permission; they even regulated the hours of lovemaking by ringing a bell.

In this disciplined welfare state, the Indians worked communal land as well as their own plots. The missionaries cared for widows and orphans, the sick and the needy. I felt the presence of these long-ago souls, Jesuit and Indian, as I wandered through the ruins of San Ignacio Miní.

Around 1730 some 900 Guaraní families lived at the mission; today it stands empty, a silent testament to the soul-saving fervor of the Jesuits. The roofless buildings, made of soft red sandstone, once housed a well-stocked library, hospital, prison, music school, priests' quarters, workshops, and one-room apartments for the Indians. Centuries ago the mission church, candlelit and sweet

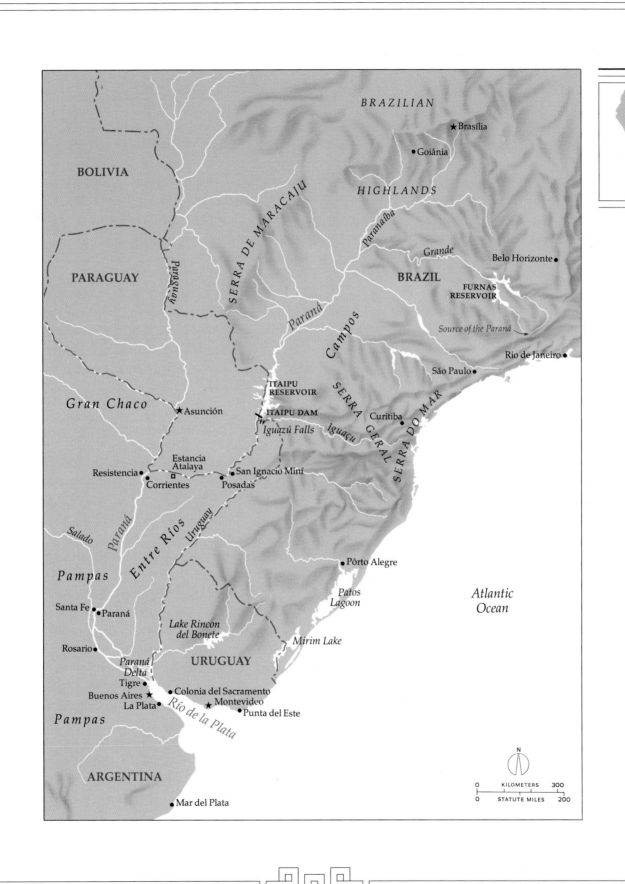

BRAZILIAN

★ Brasília

• Goiânia

HIGHLANDS

BOLIVIA

Paranaíba

Grande

Belo Horizonte •

PARAGUAY

BRAZIL

**FURNAS
RESERVOIR**

SERRA DE MARACAJU

Paraguay

Paraná

Source of the Paraná

Campos

Rio de Janeiro •

Gran Chaco

São Paulo •

**ITAIPU
RESERVOIR**

★ Asunción

ITAIPU DAM

Curitiba •

SERRA GERAL

SERRA DO MAR

Iguazú Falls

Iguacu

Estancia
Atalaya

Resistencia •

• San Ignacio Miní

Corrientes •

Posadas •

Salado

Paraná

Entre Ríos

Uruguay

*Atlantic
Ocean*

• Pôrto Alegre

Pampas

*Patos
Lagoon*

Santa Fe •

• Paraná

*Lake Rincon
del Bonete*

Rosario •

Mirim Lake

*Paraná
Delta*

URUGUAY

Tigre •

• Colonia del Sacramento

Buenos Aires ★

★ Montevideo

La Plata •

• Punta del Este

Pampas

Río de la Plata

ARGENTINA

N

| 0 | KILOMETERS | 300 |
| 0 | STATUTE MILES | 200 |

• Mar del Plata

with incense, held 3,000 worshipers. The ruins emanated so lovely a mood of peace that I lingered awhile, becoming myself a part of the quietness.

Below San Ignacio Miní the land unfolds into the smooth pastures that make Argentina the leading beef exporter in South America. In places, only the backs of the cattle show above the tall grass. Dusty little clouds go puffing over freshly plowed fields (in most places pampas topsoil is at least three feet deep). A horse stands belly deep in a pond of syrupy water, while white egrets high-step through the reeds, cocking a watchful eye. The warm air smells of manure and of charred grass from fires burning off weeds that the cattle find unsavory. Gauchos on short-legged sorrels usher herds of cattle along the Paraná.

The renegade ancestors of these superb horsemen roamed the pampas and fought with Gen. José de San Martín for independence from Spain in the early 1800s. But cattle ranchers have long since fenced the plains, and the descendants of those freedom-loving gauchos are likely to be salaried workers on an estancia. The eight gauchos on Estancia Atalaya, a 25,000-acre ranch near Corrientes, run rice harvesters as well as cattle. I shared a gourd of maté with the estanciero, Marcos Aurelio Moncada, a hard-riding horseman wearing a bright bandanna, baggy gaucho pants, and high leather boots.

Marcos is at peace with his earth and his fields. Yet he has a love-hate relationship with the Paraná, which waters his rice fields but this year has destroyed his irrigation pumps. "The river has flooded my land, so now part of the river is mine, too," Marcos rationalizes. Almost daily he drives 155 miles round trip to Corrientes, where his family lives so his children can go to school.

G rain, beef, wool—the riches of the pampas—funnel into Corrientes and, downriver, into the twin ports of Paraná and Santa Fe. While I was in Paraná, Argentina's two largest labor unions called a 24-hour national strike that shut down stores, restaurants, and gas stations. So I made my way 80 miles south to Rosario on very little: a liter of warm 7-Up, a pack of vanilla cookies, and a few gallons of gasoline obligingly siphoned from a police car by an off-duty patrolman.

Above Rosario the Paraná braids around hundreds, maybe thousands, of islands lying as flat as shadows on the water. A haze of yellow chaff hangs over the harbor. Oceangoing freighters load nearly seven million tons of grain a year, although Rosario no longer ranks as the world's leading grain port.

Near Tigre the Paraná and Uruguay Rivers blend into the silt brown estuary called the Río de la Plata, and the slow water moves darkly toward the sea. The estuary's name, "river of silver," refers not to its color but to the treasure the conquistadores hoped to ship down it. In 1516 Juan Díaz de Solís became the first European to sail into the Río de la Plata. Barely two decades later another Spaniard, Don Pedro de Mendoza, founded Buenos Aires, a crude settlement with a grand name: Our Lady Holy Mary of the Good Air.

Of the Spanish era, little remains in modern Buenos Aires, for developers have rebuilt much of the tightly packed downtown. The only crooked, disorderly streets run through La Boca, the shabby district hard by the old port. There cobbled streets, clogged with soccer-playing children, wind past gaily painted tenements. Hemmed in by half-deserted wharves and meat-packing plants, La Boca stands as a kind of triumph of the spirit, its mournful tangos ringing on the night air, its songs rising through the wayward fog.

Near the old customhouse, which sits with its backside to the oily water, I boarded a sleek hydrofoil and headed for Uruguay's oldest town. In colonial days Spanish Argentina and Portuguese Brazil swapped control of Colonia del Sacramento. Thick-walled houses with barred windows give the old town the look of a living museum—a fragment of the 17th century preserved. At the end of almost every street I could see the river, and I half-expected a Portuguese galleon or Spanish caravel to glide across the dark water.

Between Colonia and Montevideo roadside flowers—a gay profusion of purple verbena and yellow buttercups—are as abundant as the chewing Herefords and Shorthorns. In this land of beef eaters, as in Argentina, gauchos make a fire at lunchtime and grill a steak. (Old-time gauchos would be appalled to know that sheep now outnumber cows more than two to one.)

The Old World still shows on the streets of Montevideo, Uruguay's aging capital. The twin-towered cathedral dominates the Plaza Constitución, as it did before Uruguay won independence from Brazil in 1828. From the plaza I could see the walls and gun emplacements that once protected the city from foreign invaders. The horseshoe-shaped port dripped in a cold mist blowing off the water. I could easily imagine myself at the edge of the sea, for here the Río de la Plata is a hundred miles wide, almost a part of space and the sky.

A nearly unbroken swath of beaches skirts the Río de la Plata from Montevideo to Punta del Este, where the widening estuary mingles with the sea. Into the cold salt water jut great white blocks of condominiums. Sailboats and cabin cruisers rock in the marina, flashing white in the sun. Brown-headed gulls wheel overhead, letting loose their usual hullabaloo. The sea wind carries the smell of fish and of pines that shelter thousands of summer homes, from thatched cottages to elaborate mansions capped with shiny ceramic tiles.

At this playground for the very rich, I felt a newness curiously without past. I thought of the travelers of long ago, boating slowly along the Paraná. The conquistadores, the Jesuits, and most of the Indians are gone. The free-roaming life of the gaucho is almost at an end, though the romanticism has not died. Their legacies survive—in mission walls and town squares, in wood carvings and pampas folklore. In their spiritual and cultural heirs I sensed a rebirth as the Paraná becomes a mighty force in the modernization of South America. The river is a path to the continent's interior—to its future as well as its past.

E lection eve fever 1983: Supporters rally in downtown Buenos Aires for Raúl Alfonsín, winner of the first presidential election held in Argentina in ten years. Thousands crowd the ten-lane-wide Avenida 9 de Julio, acclaimed by city residents as the world's widest street.

The 70-foot obelisk commemorates the founding of Buenos Aires in 1536, when Pedro de Mendoza arrived with 14 ships, 72 horses, and about 2,000 men —one of the largest expeditions ever mounted by a conquistador. But repeated crop failures and Indian attacks forced the settlers to eat rats, snakes, shoes, hides, and even corpses—and finally to abandon their adobe-walled stockade. Not until 1580 did Spaniards resettle the city that is now home to eight million—one out of every three Argentines.

The capital fans inland over 77 square miles from the Río de la Plata, which is so wide it seems a muddy sea. The port ships 80 percent of Argentina's exports and gives the people of Buenos Aires their name, porteños. The "port dwellers" call their city— with its ornate buildings, wide boulevards, and sidewalk cafes— the Paris of South America.

Porteño-style gondolas ferry passengers across La Boca, "the mouth" of the Riachuelo. Where the river winds past the old waterfront of Buenos Aires, draft horses once pulled cargo-laden drays to a traveling crane bridge (above) for transfer to ships.

Near La Boca's aging waterfront the tango was born about 1880, the offspring of African rhythms and the Spanish fandango. The tough and tender, sad and sexy dance swept out of Buenos Aires seven decades ago to shock, then captivate the world.

Dance halls, nightclubs, and cabarets give Buenos Aires its reputation as "the city that never sleeps." After dark, fashionable Calle Lavalle (left) turns into a grand promenade where friends meet for espresso, young people flirt, and couples window-shop. Moviegoers take their pick from 16 cinemas in three blocks.

341

L ike a frayed cord, the Paraná unravels into 1,200 streams and channels at its delta, 20 miles north of Buenos Aires. The muddy water carries the warmth and rich, spongy soil of the tropical north. Hundreds of miles of inland waterways (below) bring citrus fruit, vegetables, and flowers to the markets of Tigre.

In this rural Venice, houses perched on stilts (to withstand flooding) have docks instead of garages, where residents wait for a ferry instead of a bus. As on Venice's canals, much business is conducted by boat. One carries a doctor, nurse, and priest; another is a school bus; a third takes worshipers to church. On sunny weekends, speedboats, kayaks, canoes, sculls, and catamarans jam the network of waterways.

343

S pirited gauchos gallop across a lake on Argentina's flat pampas. Gone are the old-time gauchos, nomadic horsemen who roamed the plains until the late 1800s. Untamed, like the cattle they hunted, they fought a losing battle with the railroads and barbed wire fences that turned the open range into farms and ranches.

Modern gauchos, many belonging to trade unions, ride and rope on huge estancias. These cattle ranches—some sprawling over 100,000 acres—make Argentina the second largest exporter of beef after Australia.

The horsemen of today preserve their predecessors' broad-brimmed hats, baggy pants, and melancholy songs. And the gauchos still drink maté (above). The bitter tea is placed in a cup or hollow gourd, laced with sugar, drenched with boiling water, and sipped through a metal straw.

A s wide as three Niagara Falls, the Iguaçu River roars out of the jungle and over falls between Argentina and Brazil. When the river runs high, an almost unbroken sheet of water cascades over the two-mile-wide horseshoe. The thundering water, which can be heard from several miles away, drenches tourists and causes the ground to shudder (below). Despite the noise, great dusky swifts nest on the shiny black rocks behind the falls.

Pages 346-347: Where Guaraní Indians once netted fish, the muddy Paraná bulges behind Itaipu Dam—longer than 40 city blocks. Everything about the world's mightiest hydroelectric project is big. Cranes hoist concrete in buckets large enough to hold a Volkswagen bus. Even the first construction contract was massive: It weighed 220 pounds.

THE RIVERS OF NORTH

New Jersey docks and Manhattan skyline frame the Hudson River, 1970. By Dewitt Jones.

AMERICA

ature blessed North America with abundant running water, a resource far more precious than the silks and spices sought by the early navigators who searched for a westward passage to the Indies. The coastline of eastern North America welcomed the adventurer and the colonist. Short, broad rivers watered fertile bottomland and opened into the forested piedmont beyond. The Indies seeker, however, found each river route blocked at the fall line of the continental shelf. Beyond these unnavigable cataracts, the Appalachians seemed to raise a formidable barrier. Just north of this mountain range the broad mouth of the St. Lawrence beckons almost arrow straight to the Great Lakes. To the west the headwaters of the Mississippi rise. The Mississippi's two mighty arms, the Missouri and the Ohio, embrace a storehouse of agricultural and mineral treasure.

Much of north-central Canada hardly drains at all but holds its water in uncountable lakes and flat streams, muskeg and tundra. A semicircle of brief rivers etches the mammoth bowl of Hudson Bay, but a long one, the Churchill, has flowed 1,000 miles eastward to reach it. A helter-skelter chain of rivers and lakes forms the Saskatchewan system, almost connecting the bay with the Rockies. This great mountain chain spawns swift rivers that plunge to all points of the compass.

To Spanish explorers, the rivers emptying into the Gulf of Mexico proved a disappointing passageway. Even the river they called Grande, or "great," stretched only to the eastern slopes of the Continental Divide. The Colorado in those days emptied red detritus from the deep-cut rocks of the Grand Canyon into the Gulf of California, called by the Spanish the Vermilion Sea. Long after the last adventurer had given up the vain hope of a Northwest Passage and the myth of the Seven Cities of Gold, the mid-coastal rivers of California would produce the glittering grains sought by so many and found by so few.

The Ohio proved a magnet to the *coureurs de bois* who came from France to trap, fish, and trade for furs. They called the clear, sylvan stream La Belle Rivière, and the pirogues they carved out of tree trunks in emulation of the Indians' smaller dugouts inaugurated the commercial navigation of the interior of North America. English settlers penetrated the Appalachian water gaps to wrest control of the Ohio from the French, but they needed something bigger than pirogues to float their wagons and livestock farther west. The flatboats they hewed out of local timber and pegged and roped together were huge affairs as big as 20 by 60 feet, barely steerable with poles or sweeps. As the boats floated downstream, snags, rocks, rapids, and unpredictable slack and flood waters were the least of the hazards. With rifle and tomahawk Indians resisted the mass invasion, and hid along the shore to ambush boats.

Although river pirates also harassed the boatmen, in 1807 almost 2,000 flatboats and keelboats floated the Ohio to New Orleans, carrying goods worth

NORTH AMERICA

Yukon

Mackenzie

Fraser

Churchill
Nelson

Saskatchewan

La Grande

Columbia

Missouri

St. Lawrence

Hudson

Susquehanna

Colorado

Ohio

Mississippi

Tennessee

Rio Grande

353

more than five million dollars. In 1811 Nicholas J. Roosevelt—T. R.'s great-uncle—brought the Pittsburgh-built steamboat *New Orleans* downriver to inaugurate the age of steam. Just below Louisville, however, a summer drought had exposed the eons-old coral reef that formed the Falls of the Ohio, and the *New Orleans* had to churn back upstream to Cincinnati to await the autumn rains that would float it over the falls to Cairo, Illinois, and into the Mississippi. The 138-foot sky blue craft, propelled by two great paddle wheels, its smokestack belching, impressed the river world mightily.

One outcome of Captain Roosevelt's voyage was the Supreme Court declaration that the navigable waters of the United States would henceforth be the province of the federal government rather than the states. A few years later Kentucky Representative Henry Clay persuaded Congress to help finance a canal to bypass the pesky Falls of the Ohio. It opened in 1830.

When engineer-President Herbert Hoover dedicated the 50-lock canal system in 1929, diesel-powered towboats were pushing barges through the locks. Today all but two of the dams built during the Ohio's fabulous century of development are gone, replaced by higher ones with locks big enough to handle tows of 20 or more barges in a single lift.

In 1933 some visionary Americans set out to manage an entire watershed. The river was the Tennessee. A government agency, the Tennessee Valley Authority, took charge. It aimed to dominate the river's horrendous floods, promote commercial navigation, and generate electricity for farms and industries. In creating dams and reservoirs, it was to reforest slopes bared by decades of overcutting and restore eroded valleys to slow the runoffs that contributed to flash floods. To the forgotten and impoverished descendants of pioneer backwoodsmen, Cherokee Indians, and freed black slaves, it proposed to bring subsidized electrification, demonstration farms, producer cooperatives, bookmobiles, and a blizzard of self-help pamphlets.

Many people called TVA socialistic and unconstitutional. But the Supreme Court ruled otherwise, and where private power companies had brought electricity to only 3 percent of the area's farms in 1933, TVA had electrified more than 85 percent of them 15 years later. The river itself was carrying, by the end of World War II, twice as much cargo as when

Builder of dams, maker of lakes, a beaver gnaws at a branch on this pottery bowl from 13th-century Cahokia. Where the Mississippi, Missouri, and Illinois Rivers meet Indians reared this bustling trade center of some 38,000 inhabitants.

*Canadian Indians "at full sail in a boat made of antelope skin" adorn a journal of about
1700 by a French cartographer. New World Indians owe both sail and firearm to the
Europeans they guided on the rivers of New France.*

the project began. Recreational areas bring a further economic boon.

Few of the families who fought TVA's expropriation of their homes, and who
watched their ancestors' gravesites disappear under dammed-up lakes, would
want to be without TVA's benefits today. But it's not easy to forget: There's the
story of Butler, Tennessee. The TVA flooded this Tennessee River town in
1948. In 1983 the dam needed repair, so engineers drained the reservoir. And
the people came to look at the streets and stores and houses of their childhood.
"It was sad to go back," said Percy Matherly, who was born in Butler. "The
town was all covered in mud, the streets were muddy, and you could even see
the old blacksmith's shop full of mud. It looked like a lost city."

The concrete cliffs that began to rise in the Columbia River Valley dwarfed
TVA dams. In 1933 President Franklin D. Roosevelt advised the allocation of 63
million dollars from the land reclamation budget. The result was the world's

Engraving from *Canyons of the Colorado* by J. W. Powell

biggest concrete dam—almost twice as high as Niagara Falls—and it would back the U. S. portion of the river into a lake 150 miles long. Grand Coulee, as it was called, was only the beginning. Congress quickly authorized another big dam for the Columbia system, and then another, and another.

In 1941 folksinger Woody Guthrie wrote more than 20 songs about the rivers and the work of the great dams. "Roll on, Columbia, roll on," he sang. "Your power is turning our darkness to dawn." Woody said that his music heralded "electricity to milk the cows, kiss the maid, shoe the old mare, light up the saloon, the chili joint window, the schools, and churches along the way, to run the factories turning out manganese, chrome, bauxite, aluminum, and steel."

It hasn't stopped. Now the Columbia is dammed into a series of lock-connected lakes to store water for giant turbines, leaving only one short stretch of the U. S. portion of the river running free. The government of British Columbia has agreed to let power companies build more dams in Canada.

Many western Canadians, however, prefer their rivers wild. Sports fishermen, Indians, and conservationists oppose projects to dam the Fraser, a likely power producer in British Columbia. The Mackenzie drains almost 700,000 square miles—20 percent of Canada—in its 2,640-mile course from Great Slave Lake to an enormous delta on the Arctic Ocean. Canadian writer Hugh MacLennan traveled the Mackenzie in the early 1970s and declared it to be essentially unchanged since its discovery by the Scottish explorer Alexander Mackenzie in 1789. Many scientists believe that the precious balance of life in the Mackenzie Delta is a vital interlocking element in the entire biosphere of Earth. Any upsets in that huge, pristine area could affect our climate as well as the lives of birds, animals, and plants as far away as the Amazon basin.

La Grande River on the eastern shore of James Bay is the focus of nine power dams, which by the year 2000 will light Québec City, Montreal, and many cities in the northeastern U. S. The 15-billion-dollar complex covers an area larger than the state of Illinois and will be the largest hydropower system in the world. But over 22 percent of the surrounding land surface—more than the combined areas of Massachusetts, Connecticut, and Rhode Island—will have been flooded, including Cree and Inuit hunting lands.

Commercial exploitation of North American waterways, which began when the first voyageur broke a beaver dam to set his traps, has done more damage to rivers, lakes, and estuaries in the last 50 years than in the previous 300. The Colorado, drained by cities and farms all along its route, now seldom reaches the Gulf of California but trickles down, salt sickened, in a muddy gulch south

On the job for ten million years, the canyon-carving Colorado River takes geologist John Wesley Powell and crews on a wild ride down the Grand Canyon in 1869. Powell found "sublimity . . . never again to be equaled on the hither side of Paradise."

of the Mexican border. Yet the same river, its upstream reservoirs swollen by heavy rains and snowmelt, in 1983 saw floods from Utah to Mexico.

The lakes that were once the Tennessee River lie under a pall of smoke belched from the coal-fired power plants built by TVA to supplement its hydropower facilities. Shoreside nuclear power plants suck up millions of gallons of water for cooling, then spew it back, heated and faintly radioactive, imperiling the ecology. In the Pacific Northwest, pollution and increased water temperatures in the reservoirs have reduced the salmon catch, now a fraction of its former bounty, and the salmon industry depends on fish hatcheries.

Mark Twain's quip that "whiskey is for drinking, water is for fighting over" still seems valid. All over the United States, Indian groups have gone to court to assert treaty rights to rivers that have little water left in them. Towboat operators want bigger locks through dams so they can push larger strings of barges. Some people argue that commercial users of navigable waters should pay for a portion of the U. S. Army Corps of Engineers' improvements; the controversy blocks scores of projected water control projects.

Environmentalists have advanced legislation like the Wild and Scenic Rivers Act of 1968, which requires that designated rivers be preserved "in their free-flowing condition." But recurrent shortages of energy and of water itself are calling forth ever greater schemes to bend the rivers of North America from their natural courses. From the Colorado alone, the Central Arizona Project will divert every year enough water to cover 2.2 million acres a foot deep, and New Mexico is channeling another flood into the Rio Chama. Upstream, Denver is tapping the river near its source through the Big Thompson tunnel, while Utah will divert its share of the river's water through the Wasatch Mountains to the Salt Lake Valley. This leaves southern California with an increasingly serious water shortage. All over the nation, municipal, industrial, and agricultural pollution has endangered our supply of pure water. Yet, well before the Clean Water Act of 1977 revitalized federal action on the problem, cities and states began getting together to clean up and preserve rivers.

A typical beneficiary of our concern is the New River, protected by the Wild and Scenic Rivers Act. The New flows from North Carolina to West Virginia in one of the greatest and most ancient riverbeds on the planet. It follows part of the course of the Teays, which flowed north and west across North America two million years ago into a bay in what is now the Mississippi Valley. Today as we work to restore the beauty of North America's waterways, we affirm our affinity with the ages.

The Mackenzie River Delta spins silver threads among the pale gold of an Arctic sunburst. Here in northern Canada the river fans out in a waterfowl haven after questing through 1,120 miles of forest and tundra to the Arctic Ocean.

Lowell Georgia

THE MISSISSIPPI-MISSOURI

A M E R I C A ' S   R I V E R

By Amanda Parsons / Photographs by Nathan Benn

The Mississippi's incessant brownness lulled me. I felt as if we were chugging through a stream of hot chocolate. From my pilothouse perch on the towboat *Superior*, I had stared for hours at the young forest of Wisconsin and Minnesota shores. A lone bald eagle—America's bird—glided above me, its wings wide in a grand salute to America's river.

I jerked awake. I caught the muffled curse of Captain Joe French. We were dead aground, the shore eerily steady. The river rushed by. The Mississippi's bottom sands had trapped me and 22,000 tons of grain. "You can channel me, dredge me, dam me, and divert me," the historically ornery waters seemed to taunt, "but I can still whip you."

The deckhands—wrapped against the cold, gullets warmed by bottomless cups of hot coffee from Elsie the cook—hauled the steel lash lines that could slice a body in two, and dismantled the tow. A full rainy day later the river released us. The *Superior* would shove its reassembled load south. And I would learn more of the river's tricks.

The Mississippi-Missouri is a marvel. The system's main stems flow from Montana and Minnesota, meet just above St. Louis, and continue to the Gulf of Mexico. The banks connect 3,870 miles of this country's cultures, climates, and geography. Several thousand tributaries etch these heartlands, draining 40 percent of the United States—all or part of 31 states.

The rivers shaped the nation's frontier. Indians built burial mounds and earth lodges above them more than a thousand years ago. The Indians who followed changed the rivers barely more than the beaver. But after European incursion during the 16th to 18th centuries, pioneers came to exploit and to settle. The Mississippi spawned lumbering, steamboats, and Mark Twain. But by the

The Delta Queen *steams up the Mississippi past St. Louis, Missouri. An authentically restored vessel, the* Delta Queen *is on the National Register of Historic Places.*

1880s iron wheels had replaced paddle wheels. As a commercial route the river fell into disuse. World War I defense needs brought it back.

At the Missouri's headwaters, the Gallatin, Madison, and Jefferson Rivers (fed by the most remote source, the Red Rock) merge in a flat tangle that becomes the sturdy Missouri. It was a quiet beginning for my journey, marked by a dead cottonwood tree tortured by time and mistletoe. I climbed the limestone cliff where Meriwether Lewis drew the first map of the area in 1805.

Down the road stood the weathered ruins of the Gallatin Hotel, where noise from the saloon often kept guests awake at night. Speculators of the 1860s thought Gallatin City would attract steamboat traffic and become the river jump-off for the Rocky Mountains and the Northwest Territories. But the downriver falls stopped navigation at Fort Benton. People moved away.

It is a peaceful, pretty town now. And I understood Marquis Childs's statement that river towns have "none of the blighting respectability of the traditional Main Street." From 1860 to 1880, during the height of the buffalo robe and gold trade, as many as 10,000 people a year passed through a prosperous Fort Benton. So many shady characters lived here that it was a city of aliases. By 1890, the bison were dead, the railroad had reached the city, and an assiduous census taker could find only 624 survivors of the boom.

With guides Don Lundy and Gail Stensland, I put an aluminum outboard into the river below Fort Benton and set out down a dramatically beautiful section of the river. It seemed so isolated that I could have been with Lewis and Clark on their exploration of Thomas Jefferson's Louisiana Purchase. But I knew that people had long struggled over this pristine kingdom, and that its final designation as a National Wild and Scenic River was hard won. We passed the Missouri Breaks, long troughs eroded out of the river bottomlands. We rode by ever more spectacular sandstone formations. No wonder German Prince Maximilian urged his artist Karl Bodmer to sketch constantly during their 1833 journey through this bewitching place.

The only people we saw on our two-day trip were 74-year-old Wilbur Lanning and his family, on their remote riverside ranch. Wilbur's grandparents came from Germany a hundred years ago as squatters. Wilbur raises cattle, and grows wheat and soybeans on his 3,000 acres.

Down the river another homesteading family had not been so lucky. Their deserted stone house, its windy cracks still stuffed with tatters of gunnysacks, was crumbling back into the earth. We inspected the ruins, trying to reconstruct the lives of the former occupants. A log shack could have held supplies. A root cellar probably stored ice cut from the river. A cedar snubbing post stood for tethering horses that would never graze here again.

We pitched our tents across from a steeple-shaped column of rock. Massive bluffs rose behind it in a kaleidoscope of rough and smooth, yellow and

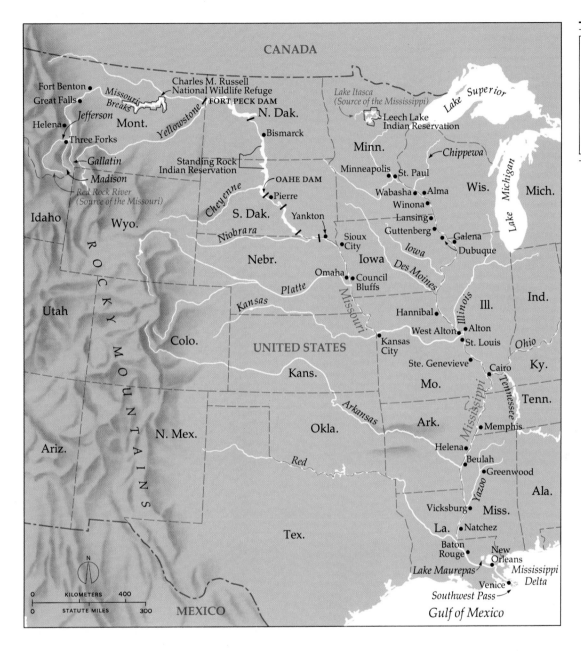

CANADA

Fort Benton • | Missouri | Charles M. Russell National Wildlife Refuge
Great Falls • | Breaks | FORT PECK DAM
Jefferson | Yellowstone | N. Dak.
Helena • | Mont. | • Bismarck
• Three Forks
Gallatin | Standing Rock Indian Reservation | OAHE DAM
Madison | • Pierre
Red Rock River (Source of the Missouri) | Cheyenne | S. Dak.
Idaho | Wyo. | Niobrara | Yankton
| Nebr. | Sioux City
Utah | Colo. | Platte | Omaha | Iowa
| Kansas | Council Bluffs
| | Missouri
Ariz. | UNITED STATES | Hannibal •
| Kans. | West Alton • Alton
| | Kansas City | St. Louis
| | Ste. Genevieve • | Cairo
N. Mex. | | Mo.
| Okla. | Arkansas | Ark. | • Memphis
| | Red | Helena •
| | | • Beulah
| | | • Greenwood
| | Yazoo | Ala.
| | Vicksburg • | Miss.
Tex. | | La. | • Natchez
| | Baton Rouge • | New Orleans
| | Lake Maurepas | Mississippi Delta
| | Venice •
N | | Southwest Pass
KILOMETERS 400 | | Gulf of Mexico
STATUTE MILES 300 | MEXICO

Lake Itasca (Source of the Mississippi) | Lake Superior
Leech Lake Indian Reservation | Chippewa
Minn. | Lake Michigan | Mich.
Minneapolis • | St. Paul • | Wis.
Wabasha • | • Alma
Winona •
Lansing •
Guttenberg • | Galena
Iowa | • Dubuque
Des Moines
Illinois | Ind.
Ill.
Ohio | Ky.
Tennessee | Tenn.
Mississippi

ROCKY MOUNTAINS

mauve. As night fell, the northern lights illuminated the sky, surrounding us with rays of gold and silver. In the arctic glow, my soul merged with this river, its majesty enhanced by the darkened cliff across the waters.

By the time the Missouri reaches North Dakota controversy embroils it. A chain of dams and artificial lakes are part of the Pick-Sloan Plan for power production, irrigation, flood control, and recreation. Fishermen and boaters love them. Local Indians and farmers complain bitterly. *(Continued on page 370)*

B eaver gather branches for their riverbank lodge on the untamed Missouri (below). Trade in their prized pelts drew trappers up the river and opened the West.

Meriwether Lewis gazes out over Black Eagle Falls (bottom), near present-day Great Falls, Montana, during the Lewis and Clark Expedition of 1804-06. By 1845, when artist George Caleb Bingham captured the river's misty grandeur in "Fur Traders Descending the Missouri" (right), beaver had already been trapped to near extinction.

Karl Bodmer, 1833, Mr. and Mrs. Paul Mellon Collection

O. C. Seltzer, Thomas Gilcrease Institute of American History and Art, Tulsa, Oklahoma

Metropolitan Museum of Art

David Hiser. Above: Amanda Parsons

Sam Abell (also below)

Citadel Rock, in the heart of Montana's White Cliffs, looms above the Missouri River (left, top). Today, a traveler to this stretch of the upper Missouri would see much the same landscape as that which awed Lewis and Clark nearly two centuries ago. As Lewis contemplated the soft sandstone bluffs, he saw formations so spectacular that he felt nature tried to "rival the human art of masonry." Above, wind and water have eroded sandstone into what geologists call a washed pattern.

Cliff swallows will return in the spring to rework their gourd-shaped nests (left) on bluffs above the riverbank.

The Missouri was a route into Montana's gold and silver fields during the late 1800s. Now a ghost town (opposite, bottom), Elkhorn boomed when hopeful prospectors passed through.

367

James P. Blair, National Geographic Photographer. Opposite: Dick Durrance II

Bates Littlehales, National Geographic Photographer

T he Missouri pounds over Rainbow Falls (opposite) near Great Falls, Montana. From Fort Benton to the Charles M. Russell National Wildlife Refuge, the Missouri has been declared part of the National Wild and Scenic Rivers System. Backed up by Fort Peck Dam, the river broadens (right) as it wanders through the refuge. Home to bison, mule deer, bobcats, peregrine falcons, and a wide variety of other wildlife, the refuge also leases much of its land for grazing. When young and tender, foxtail barley (above), one of the refuge's many prairie grasses, provides forage for livestock and wildlife.

368

Permanent flooding, according to former Governor Art Link, has lost the state half a million acres and 90 million dollars yearly in farm revenue.

At the annual United Tribes Powwow in Bismarck 10,000 Indians from 17 states had gathered for three days and nights of tribal dancing. The Bismarck powwow was held, according to Indian Center President Dave Gipp, to underscore Indian identity and to air problems. A major concern has been the damming of the Missouri River across Sioux territory. When I drove through the Standing Rock Reservation on the border of the Dakotas, I felt the Sioux's loss. Twisted stalks of dead trees stood belly deep in water, branches bleached to a white meanness by water, ice, and wind.

In Pierre, South Dakota, operator Lowell King showed me the Oahe Dam. As we climbed over and around the mass of pipes, pumps, and generators that can put out 721,000 kilowatts of electricity per hour, Mr. King explained how Oahe, the largest rolled-earth dam in the U. S., stores water for gradual release and keeps the river from flooding.

Farther along the Missouri lie results of fluvial management, such as irrigated farms and, below Yankton, South Dakota, another area with protected wildlife. At Sioux City, Iowa, one of the largest livestock and grain centers in the country, the river becomes a shipping channel. Despite a rare snag, sandbar, or flooded bank, it is no longer said, as it was in 1907: "A steamer that cannot, on occasion, climb a steep clay bank, go across a cornfield, and corner a river that is trying to get away, has little excuse for trying to navigate the Missouri." Barges carry loads of midwestern bounty on to St. Louis, where Missouri River and Mississippi River traffic merges.

I first visited the juncture of the Missouri and the Mississippi in May 1983. Three floods in six months had swollen the land with river water. From the air the confluence looked like a wide, shallow lake dotted with drowning farmhouses. Benedict Venturella, an officer with the U. S. Army Corps of Engineers in St. Louis, explained to me that when the river and land are saturated they are "like a big bowl of Jell-O." Rain has no place to go.

A flash flood broke Helen and Chris Machens's levee a few weeks before I saw them in West Alton, Missouri. Machens family land stretches from Missouri banks to Mississippi banks. "That thing broke and the water just rolled," exclaimed Mrs. Machens. "You could've set a house in the hole it made."

Mr. Machens had built the levee in 1930. The Corps helped rebuild it in 1951 so that its extension along the river guards the town. When waters threaten, townspeople show up with sandbags. The Machens have been flooded before—right up to their windows. According to experts, the entire complex of navigation works sometimes operates at cross purposes with levees.

On my way back to St. Louis, it poured rain. At a dip in the road, I watched in horror as the car in front of me sank to its doors in water. "Flash flood," said a man in a pickup truck next to me, coolly attaching a chain to his bumper to pull out the flooded car. I backed up and rerouted to higher land. The river was having its way again.

The Mississippi's headwaters resemble the Missouri's in their isolation and tranquillity. In the pine woods of northern Minnesota a brook runs out of Lake Itasca. For over 300 miles, from lake to lake the Mississippi is a meandering stream. Recreational canoeists revere it. I drove along the Great River Road which starts here at the source and ends in the bayous below New Orleans.

At Minneapolis, the river becomes a descending staircase of locks and dams ushering barges and other craft down the nation's midsection. The Twin Cities grew between the prairie grasslands and the thick north woods. In 1820, on a gray twist where the Minnesota River meets the Mississippi, the U. S. Army built Fort Snelling. The whiskey allotment at Fort Snelling was a misery-dulling four ounces per day—half of it before breakfast. After a walk through the outpost's stark restored buildings, I understood why. A winter on this icy bluff could have driven any man to drink before breakfast.

I drove south along the River Road, slowly heading for Lock and Dam No. 3 at Red Wing, Minnesota. My towboat awaited. Two deckhands guided me atop the barges. When I reached the towboat's galley Elsie Lockett, grandmother and former cross-country truck driver, sat me at her table. With river hospitality and an Arkansas twang to her banter, she fed me turnips, pork chops, and mounds of mashed potatoes. Properly fed, I was introduced to the 11-man crew. "They're my children," she said with a gleam of cook's pride.

First mate Terry Linck once worked as a hardware salesman. His eyes wandered from wallpaper to the river and he was hooked. Captain Joe French had been in the Coast Guard. Pilot Chuck Simmons caught his first boat at Quincy, Illinois, and worked his way up from deckhand. Each crewman had his favorite river. For rivermen, I learned, the country becomes a series of waterways, of good ships and bad ships. And each river and each ship remains "she."

We pushed down the river, a line of barges out in front of us long and gray like an elephant's trunk. At Lake Pepin, the captain handed me the wheel—actually a bank of levers. In my hands was three million dollars' worth of grain. It was like steering Manhattan Island through jelly. The slightest shift of a lever pulled the load a few degrees off course. I studied the charts and the radar. Soon I handed the behemoth to the pilot.

On the River Road again, I backtracked to Wabasha, Minnesota, and a stay at the Anderson House, a charming inn that has been greeting people since 1856. My riverview room, with Victorian furnishings, evoked snugly memories of my grandmother's house. The inn's cooking—along with the other good food I met along these rivers—convinced me that America's regional cuisines are strong competition for other world fare. With local cheese and farm products plus the worn recipes of Pennsylvania Dutch immigrants, the chefs served up feasts of cheese-and-potato pudding, chicken and dumplings, beef rolls, braised cabbage, red-flannel hash, squash bread, dilly bread, and shoofly pie.

In Winona, Minnesota, Rory Vose, a biologist at Saint Mary's College, explained the river's evolution. The bluffs I had seen were built up half a billion years ago, alternating limestone and sandstone, when ocean waters covered the area. The waters retreated and, during the last ice age, 12,000 years ago, the Glacial River Warren cut through to carve the valley, and the river began to emerge in its present form.

A lover of the river, Rory is also a realist. "That river," he said, eyes flashing, "is biologically fantastic. But," he added sadly, "it is dying. Perhaps my grandchildren will see the beauty of the marshes and wildlife. Perhaps not." Rory partly blames the wild river's decline on the navigation works required to maintain a stable channel for commercial traffic. These include the 29 locks and dams on the upper Mississippi, and water-diverting wing dams that make the river dig a deeper and faster flowing channel. Initially, noted Rory, slackwater pools created by the navigation dams led to some exciting new ecosystems. But now he and other researchers see problems.

Rory discussed the life of the river in the productive backwaters and marshes. Sand from dredging invades these vital reaches in many ways and damages them. Other damage might end if the mouth of the Chippewa River were reshaped. The Chippewa is now a source of much of the Mississippi's natural sand flow. But some environmentalists object to disturbing one habitat in favor of another. For years concerned researchers have studied Weaver Bottoms, an important marsh near Winona that had reached a stage of "early death." Now the Corps of Engineers will help to try and save it. Weaver Bottoms is a major stop for tundra swans on their migration from Alaska to Chesapeake Bay. Rory has spent nights in a canoe tagging the glistening white birds. "If the marsh dies," he asked me, "where will the birds go?"

As I drove south, a succession of towns and small cities reminded me of an earlier time. All had grain elevators, rising like totems. Steamboats used to distribute beer along the waterways. Lumber for beer barrels was floated down the river, and ice cut and stored during the winters kept the brew cool through hot summers. In Prairie du Chien, named for an Indian chief called Dog, I visited Villa Louis. In this riverside mansion lived the family of Hercules Dousman, an agent of John Jacob Astor's American Fur Company. Dousman's furs traveled downriver to New Orleans by keelboats and steamboats that returned bearing elaborate furnishings for his home.

Crisscrossing downriver between Iowa and Illinois, I drove through rolling farmland and rocky woods. Over my head flew the wedge-shaped flocks of mallards and Canada geese, migrating along the Mississippi Flyway.

In Hannibal, Missouri, Robert Clayton, a lawyer and river buff, led me through the hometown that inspired Samuel Clemens to write—as Mark Twain—*Life on the Mississippi, The Adventures of Huckleberry Finn,* and *The Adventures of Tom Sawyer.* We walked to the museum honoring that quintessential American writer. The managed tidiness of Sam Clemens's boyhood bedroom belied, I thought, the unruliness of the characters he brought to life.

Helen Knighton remembers Samuel Clemens in his Mark Twain white suit. The spry Mrs. Knighton was just ten years old in 1902 when her parents threw a party on the author's last trip to his hometown. Laura Hawkins, the childhood sweetheart whom Twain immortalized as Becky Thatcher, had aged, and a bored Clemens, Mrs. Knighton remembered, toyed with his pocket watch.

J ust above St. Louis the Missouri joins the Mississippi. On my second trip there were no floods, but the zone I entered seemed in constant battle with fickle river waters. Perpetually sandbagged Sainte Genevieve, Missouri, became one of my favorite river towns, with its architecture displaced from somewhere in France. Geologists say that the delta begins at Cairo, Illinois, where the blue waters of the Ohio muddy at their churning merge with the Mississippi. The river coils like a snake, depositing silt on the banks as it flows to the Gulf. New Madrid, Missouri, is literally shaky. In 1811 and 1812 earthquakes shifted the river's course, creating a lake and causing the Mississippi to flow backward for three days—so the terrified people said. The town still feels tremors.

In Helena, Arkansas, I pondered the many devastating floods that led engineers and politicians to seek greater control of the river. The 1927 deluge left more than 600,000 people homeless. Some victims believed that the Great Lakes had burst and were sweeping over the South. David Solomon remembered his Boy Scout troop packing sandbags and watching the sand boils tunnel under the levee. The '37 flood all but repeated the performance. Mrs. Johnnie Stephens Schatz said she woke up one morning and "all of down there was up here"—people, cattle, and tents all in her plantation home yard.

"Miss" Johnnie's daughter Katherine Hill invited me to Estevan Hall for breakfast. Eight generations of the family have observed the river since Fleetwood Hanks built the house in 1826. Land grants, slave-documents, and family diaries line one wall. Katherine showed me Uncle Millander Hanks' notation of the 1870 race between the steamboats *Natchez* and the *Robert E. Lee.* Despite nearly 160 years living by the river, few Hanks family members ventured out onto it. "There are too many obstacles," I was told, "too many fickle currents, too many unknowns."

In Vicksburg, Mississippi, I found people who quantify the unknowns. The Corps of Engineers' Waterways Experiment Station began work in the aftermath of the '27 flood. The station has hydraulic models of Corps projects all over the country. The Mississippi's Locks and Dam No. 26 at Alton, Illinois, for instance, have been modeled twice—most recently as a new proposal now under construction. Engineers run water through the model and monitor changes to the shoreline and shipping channels. To simulate disasters, they turn to a complete model of the Mississippi basin in Jackson, Mississippi.

The stretch from Natchez, Mississippi, to New Orleans, Louisiana, was the languid romance of my river trip. When I climbed aboard the 1926 steamboat *Delta Queen*, I was riding a noble and friendly ghost. The teak railings, brass appointments, and sweeping staircase enchanted me. "Steamboat Tommie," his gold and diamond-studded teeth flashing a nonstop smile, served four sumptuous meals a day. A dixieland band played on the deck where passengers congregated for sightseeing. Calliope concerts gave melodic accompaniment to the steady rhythm of the paddle wheel.

We tied up at Baton Rouge, and from the top of the State Capitol, I looked north to the river's petrochemical corridor and south to this garden city. Later, as we went under the Sunshine Bridge, we sang "You are My Sunshine," written by former Governor Jimmy Davis, who built the span. We passed Lutcher, in the rich delta land where farmers grow perique, a spicy, fragrant tobacco.

Captain Harold DeMarrero, with white wavy hair parted in the middle and a handlebar mustache, is a fifth generation river pilot. His son will be the sixth. "I never learned the profession," said Captain DeMarrero, "I grew up in it."

He took me to the pilothouse, where we found 79-year-old Oren Russell. As Pilot Russell deftly maneuvered the boat, I sensed a gentle inner fortitude that must have served him well in his 54 years on the nation's waterways. He reached up and pulled a worn wooden handle—one long blast and two short ones, the "Hello" signal of the *Delta Queen*.

This veteran has seen myriad changes on the river, but he is more impressed by its willfulness. "In high water," he said, as if talking about a stubborn animal, "the river will move just about anything she wants to." When the Corps cut off bends to straighten the river's navigation channel, Pilot Russell had to tackle a new river with different quirks. In most ways, he thinks, it is tamer today. But as we approached an eroding patch of sand and mud, he noted that 35 years ago the mound had been a good-size island. "When we return from New Orleans," he prophesied, "there won't be nothin' left."

New Orleans arrived, with its French Quarter, noisy narrow streets, wrought iron balconies, a city mostly below sea level, preserved only by levees and pumps. Although 75 miles of Mississippi flow south of here, this is where river commerce meets Gulf commerce. From here, by ship, the whole world is accessible.

The city's fortune once was at the mercy of invasion both by foreign powers and the elements. There are still floods and hurricanes, but now an all but inevitable turning away of the Mississippi to the Atchafalaya channel threatens to bring to the city backed-up salt water from the Gulf.

Seven flags have flown over the port and left behind a rich culture. New Orleans jazz roots reach to French opera, quadrilles and other dances, the music of slave gatherings at Congo Square, music halls, and the entertainment of the gamy "social aid" and "pleasure" clubs. And the food—oh, the food! It is a racy union of the culinary traditions that have passed through the city's kitchens in the past 250 years. Coming down the river, I had eaten chili, barbecue, wild rice soup, and giant cinnamon rolls puffed and hot from the oven. In New Orleans, jambalaya, gumbo, and crawfish rule. "How could you listen to jazz," someone asked as Ellis Marsalis teased his sounds from the piano keyboard, "without an oyster sliding down the back of your throat?"

The drive to Venice and the end of the Great River Road is a lonely one. Venice is a world of oil riggers and fishermen. I walked into a restaurant and patrons stared. I was the only woman eating in the place.

Coast Guardsman Gordon Haughey joined me in a 17-foot skiff to travel the last 30 miles to the end of the river. The skies were gray and wet. The misty shore looked menacing. Foghorns blew, seeming to intensify the chill.

Downriver to the Head of Passes and on out to the Gulf of Mexico is a maze of waterways. Along them mingle freighters, fishing boats, Corps dredges, oil company helicopters, herds of cattle, and Plaquemines Parish orange groves. At the Head of Passes, arms of the river knot, then stretch to the ocean.

We stopped at Pilottown for a lunch of boiled shrimp, stuffed crab, and a hearty gumbo. Two groups of pilots work out of this isolated spot. The river pilots take the ships from here up to New Orleans. The bar pilots maneuver them from here down to the Gulf. These men are legends up and down the river—"a breed apart," Gordon told me. "You have to be born in or marry in," one of the pilots confirmed.

"How do you decide which kind of pilot to be?" I asked. "It depends upon what your father is," came the quick grin of an answer.

At the end of Southwest Pass, the river's main navigation channel, we found Coast Guard Petty Officer Rick Schneider, the last lighthouse keeper who will serve here. He does little now but monitor the automated system that will take over lighting duties and let him go to a new assignment. We climbed the spiral staircase to the light and the reflecting disc that signals the juncture of river and ocean. I looked out at the oil rig drills pumping black energy and the freighters awaiting pilots. The river behind me was quiet. Below the lighthouse the brackish waters were brown. Ahead was the green of the Gulf of Mexico. Back in the skiff, a salt spray caught my face.

Barges and cargo ships travel the Mississippi in this view upriver at New Orleans. A bend in the river here, as it flows eastward toward the Gulf of Mexico, conferred upon New Orleans the name Crescent City.

In total tonnage, New Orleans leads all United States ports, handling an annual average of 177 million tons of freight in recent years. In 1982 the port exported eight billion dollars' worth of corn, soybeans, wheat, coal, crude oil, chemicals, and food products; some 4,300 vessels called at New Orleans docks.

The river is the city's greatest source of wealth, but the Father of Waters can also be a threat. Although New Orleans is 75 miles from the Gulf of Mexico, parts of the city lie as much as five feet below sea level. A 120-mile-long harness of levees, some as high as 25 feet, holds the Mississippi and tidal waters from the Gulf in check. Pumps keep low-lying areas dry through the 60 or so inches of rain that fall every year.

igh-stepping, singing loud and proud, Ellyna Tatum leads the Andrew Hall Society Brass Band (left) through the New Orleans French Quarter. The performers in this parade are celebrating the 35th anniversary of the New Orleans Jazz Club. Dixieland jazz was born in New Orleans, and it syncopates through the streets to celebrate births, weddings, holidays, and funerals. The masks in a shop window (below) embody the festive, exotic, masquerading spirit of the French Quarter.

ald cypresses draped in Spanish moss rise from southern Louisiana's Blind River (opposite), where it empties into Lake Maurepas. The delta land of southern Louisiana is a network of small rivers and bayous that weave through lowland swamp and marsh. The Blind is protected as a natural and scenic stream.

A resident of tiny Beulah, Mississippi, chops wood (above) in river-bordering Bolivar County. Rich delta soil here produces bumper crops of winter wheat, soybeans, rice, and cotton.

Along the Yalobusha River (left)—a tributary of the Yazoo, which is a tributary of the Mississippi—a fisherman brings yellow catfish from a flooded field.

G rand reincarnation of the Old South, a house under restoration (left, top) defies the floods of the Yazoo River.

In Natchez, Mississippi, eight Daughters of the American Revolution pose at Rosalie (opposite), a mansion that served in 1863 as the headquarters of Union Army Gen. Walter Gresham, during the occupation of the city.

Every day Thomas Bennett of Natchez (left) raises the flag on his front porch to honor American servicemen.

In Vicksburg a citizen (above) represents a private of the 23d Alabama Infantry in a memorial re-creation of the lives of ordinary soldiers during the 47-day siege in 1863. The emblem on his hat, a Union Corps badge, is worn upside down in the manner of Confederate soldiers who flaunted captured insignia.

erformers like Little Bobby Tilson and his wife Debbie (opposite) keep the Memphis blues alive today. In the early 1900s the musician called the "father of the blues," W. C. Handy, was a Memphis bandleader who began collecting, polishing, and harmonizing the melodies that gave birth to contemporary blues.

The Heartbreak Hotel Restaurant (left) commemorates the 1956 song that launched Elvis Presley on his career as "king of rock and roll." Elvis began recording in Memphis in 1953.

At a cotton-processing plant in Memphis, Tennessee (above), women mix cotton in a hopper. It next travels by conveyor belt to be ginned. Memphis is the largest cotton marketing center in the U. S., but its heyday as the royal city of King Cotton is over.

385

ans of the St. Louis Cardinals baseball team fill Busch Memorial Stadium (right), a pool of white light on a summer evening. Along its outer edge the cantilevered canopy of the stadium echoes the motif of the Gateway Arch, which rises 630 feet between the stadium and the Mississippi River. Constructed of 16,000 tons of steel and concrete and covered with nearly 900 tons of stainless steel plates, the gleaming arch is located here to commemorate St. Louis's position as gateway to the West for American pioneers.

A young Cardinals fan roots for her team (below)—evidence of the philosopher's statement that "whoever wants to know the heart and mind of America had better learn baseball."

eaded upstream to take on another load, a towboat and its collection of empty barges ruffle the reflection of a Mississippi River sunset. The barges have just passed through Locks and Dam No. 26, at Alton, Illinois, a bottleneck for commercial traffic. In 1980 the U. S. Army Corps of Engineers began building a new, larger lock (above) two miles below the original. The cylindrical barriers, called a cofferdam, hold back the river while the new dam and lock are under construction.

Pages 390-391: The fields of an Iowa farm hug the mile-and-a-half-wide Mississippi near Guttenburg. Iowa lies at the heart of the corn belt, the most productive farmland on the planet. These fields are part of the 98 percent of Iowa soil under cultivation.

ike gold in a giant coffer, the wealth of the Midwest piles up in an Illinois corncrib (left). Iowa and Illinois perennially lead the U. S. in the production of corn. Much of this corn fattens hogs, and every year 23 million of them end their lives as bacon, chops, roasts, and spareribs at meat packers in Iowa and Illinois. At FDL Foods, Inc., in Dubuque, Iowa (right), processors belong to the 36 percent of Iowa workers who are in farming or agriculture-related jobs.

Hamburgers, cake, and ice cream draw residents of Lansing, Iowa, to an ice cream social to benefit the Methodist church (above). Lansing lies in northeastern Iowa, the state's most productive dairy farming region.

T he low black clouds of a summer storm swirl over a grain elevator (above) at Savage, Minnesota, on the banks of the Minnesota River. Opposite, corn pours from an elevator chute into the gaping hopper of a river barge, as an inspector from the Minnesota Department of Agriculture uses a "pelican sampler" to catch a few kernels for testing and grading. In hot pursuit of profit, traders gamble on harvests of the future in the pit of the Minneapolis Grain Exchange (right).

Pages 396-397: An eight-man scull from the Minnesota Boat Club races past downtown St. Paul. Though they must dodge boats and barges, members of the club have been skimming the river for pleasure since 1870.

O n Leech Lake, near the Mississippi's Lake Itasca headwaters in northern Minnesota, a Chippewa Indian poles a canoe through a tangle of wild rice stalks (above). His partner sits in the bow, holding a tapered stick in each hand. She bends the plants down with one stick and flails them with the other, knocking grains to the bottom of the canoe. Only ripe rice falls; the rest remains on the stalk. It will ripen at its own speed and fall into the water, reseeding the lake.

Two Chippewa boys lose themselves in the dance at the annual powwow on the Leech Lake Reservation (right). The powwow gives Chippewa from all over the state a chance to meet and celebrate their heritage.

THE YUKON

By Bill Thomas / Photographs by George F. Mobley

The warm winds of August blew through the valley, but fresh snow covered the bald-faced mountains of the Big Salmon Range. During the night winter had begun along the upper Yukon River. I thought about the fortune seekers and explorers who had approached the Yukon before me. It yielded to them reluctantly, viciously, as if to secure the secrets of its wealth and beauty. Many had to pass two fierce tests—Miles Canyon and Whitehorse Rapids. Once past those obstacles, travelers faced the possibility of starvation, drowning, insanity, freezing, scurvy, and, if nothing else, a voracious breed of mosquito, which, according to legend, could pierce bedrock with a single jab.

"Couldn't vouch for it," wrote Jack London, "but Jim watched them and said they rushed the netting in a body, one gang holding up the edge, while a second gang crawled under. . . . I have seen them with their proboscis bent and twisted after an attack on [a] sheet iron stove."

But mosquitoes were a later reward for the persistent traveler. First, one had to survive Miles Canyon, where the Yukon River rolls northward from British Columbia. The river breaks Alaska in two parts: North of the Yukon the land sprawls flat to the horizon, an arctic terrain barren of trees, punctuated only by the gray hulk of the Brooks Range; south of the river, green forests and the snow-dusted Alaska Range dominate the view.

Near its source, the river cuts through Miles Canyon, where thousands of gold seekers lost their meager fortunes before they ever entered the land that promised true wealth. Crowded by black basalt walls for a mile, the river crested more than three feet at midstream, boiled into whirlpools, then tumbled down Whitehorse Rapids.

In 1896, William B. Haskell and Joseph Meeker watched helplessly as the Yukon swallowed their raft, food, and prospecting equipment—800 dollars worth of irreplaceable goods. "All we had left," Haskell wrote later, "was the sack of sugar and a few beans; nothing to cook them in. We had no tent to sleep in . . . 250 miles from Juneau and 500 miles from the nearest trading post. . . . I

A midnight mist crawls through the forest in Canada's wilderness,
where the Stewart River joins the Yukon.

sat down on a rock on the bank and felt very blue."

Haskell and his partner were lucky. They survived their induction into the harsh realities of Yukon life. Hundreds of others did not; they drowned at the gateway, lost in the emerald waters of Miles Canyon.

I followed the Yukon through Canada, across Alaska, and to the sea, a journey of 1,979 miles. At the start I wondered if those old adventurers would recognize Miles Canyon if they could see it now. Through it the Yukon still runs swiftly—7 m.p.h. at midstream—but no longer threatens travelers. A dam downstream near the town of Whitehorse raises the water to safe levels, covering the rapids, smoothing out the once dangerous canyon run. Where bodies and splintered boats rushed on the current, tourists now sail *upstream* against the river, an enterprise unthinkable in the days of Haskell and Meeker.

This part of the Yukon is one of the few places that shows the permanent effect of human tampering. (There is only one other small dam on the river.) People swarmed here in the gold stampedes, but when they died or left, the wilderness moved in again, covering their tracks, rotting their cabins, rusting the pickaxes and shovels they left behind.

Flying over the land, I watched the river meander northward, edged by stunted spruce and poplar. The Alaska Highway, interrupted here and there by spur roads leading to rustic cabins, sweeps alongside the Yukon, which makes many abrupt turns, banking against high clay cliffs that divide the river from a subarctic forest.

The largest river city, Whitehorse, has a population of just 16,500. Settlement is sparse, and the Yukon runs unhampered by civilization, much as it has for thousands of years. One of the true wilderness rivers of North America, the Yukon rises from its fjord-like source near the Pacific, pushes northwest through Canada, and meanders into Alaska, where it meets the Arctic Circle. There, as if the river has hit a wall, it swings abruptly southwest, and wanders to the Bering Sea.

As I moved north with the river, I watched its waters turn from clear green to opaque white, a measure of the silt and meltwater it takes on from one of its tributaries, the White River. I drove through rain showers along the Klondike Highway to Dawson, once a gold-mining boomtown of 30,000. Only 838 people live there now. No paved sidewalks or roads grace the town, so visitors and residents slog through a sea of summer slush as the land thaws, just as they did in 1898. In Gold Rush days, merchants trod these same muddy lanes, offering fresh produce to sourdoughs who had passed the winter on a diet of flapjacks, beans, and bacon. Customers were willing—and able—to pay $30 for a gallon of milk and $1 for an apple. The town's first watermelon, imported in that giddy spring of 1898, must have been an object of rare beauty. Someone willingly paid $25 for it.

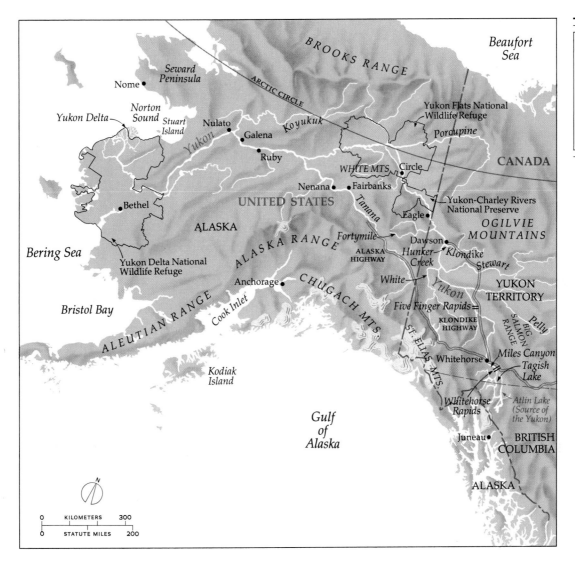

Corporations with bulldozers and large crews dominate the mining around Dawson these days, but a few descendants of the Klondikers still search for gold the old way. John and Bob Gould learned gold mining from their father, who staked a claim on a Yukon tributary, Hunker Creek, in 1903. I found the Gould brothers, now in their 60s, coupling two lengths of ten-inch pipe on the hillside their father once worked. To one end of the pipe the brothers attached a nozzle; the other end connected with a reservoir uphill. Bob climbed the hill, turned a valve, and released the water, which gushed from the pipe, melting the dirt on the hillside and pushing mud into sluice boxes at the bottom of the hill; there the sludge would separate from the heavy gold flakes that sank to the bottom of the containers.

John lives year-round in Dawson. His brother drives up from British Columbia every spring, and they live out of a trailer, working the family mine site. They find a few ounces of gold and sell it to Dawson's Bank of Commerce.

"This is a way of life with us," said John. "If we mined it all out, we wouldn't have anything to do the rest of our lives. . . . We want the gold to last."

Part-time residents like Bob Gould flood Dawson during summer, along with tourists who arrive to try panning gold. Earlier in the year, usually in May, the town faces floods of a more menacing sort—from the river itself. With the thaws of early spring, ice swirls down the river in huge chunks, gashing the banks, shaving trees off islands. The ice also piles up and wedges in the narrow twists and turns of the Yukon. The rising water builds higher and higher behind these ice dams, threatening the countryside. The United States government was so concerned when such a dam threatened the town of Galena in 1945 that a squadron of B-17s was dispatched to bomb the obstruction; it took 168,000 pounds of bombs to break it and clear the river.

S ome 75 miles downstream from Dawson, the river crosses into Alaska and sweeps by the village of Eagle. The evening I arrived in Eagle, I stood watching a young man and woman aboard a homemade raft that was careening down the current. It was nearly dark, and both of them paddled furiously, trying to bring the raft to shore. But the river would not let go, and as I watched, they shot past tall rock bluffs and out of sight.

The next morning I met Jess Knight, who took me downstream to the Yukon-Charley Rivers National Preserve, a 2.5-million-acre wilderness section of the valley. Here peregrine falcons and caribou outnumber the people. Jess guided his 14-foot johnboat past a fish wheel, an Indian contraption that looks something like a Ferris wheel with baskets instead of seats. It faced downstream so that the current turned it round and round, catching salmon as they swam against the stream. From either shore, poplar and spruce forests climbed the slope where moose, bears, and Dall's sheep often search for food.

"You seldom see anyone on the river," Jess said. "There's only an occasional barge, perhaps two or three a year." The engines throbbed against the current as we headed back upstream. Jess pulled close to the bank and cut the engines so we could listen to the boiling water and hissing silt. We started up again as storm clouds swept in, tier upon tier. The rains came. Then they left and came again, pelting the river as we ran against the current, in and out of sunlight. A rainbow shimmered, leading us back to Eagle.

My next stop was Circle, a town of 81 souls, a place named for its proximity to the Arctic Circle. (Actually the founders miscalculated; later surveys fixed the real location of *the* Circle some 50 miles northwest of the town.) When I arrived, I was met by the forlorn call of sandhill cranes, the same sound I had heard many times in the Midwest. A dozen of the great gray birds rose from a patch of cattails and flew slowly across the river. As I stood watching them in the twilight, a voice behind me broke the silence.

"Pretty sight, ain't they?" I turned to see a rotund fellow who resembled Santa Claus. He was Carl Desch, 87 years old and for 45 years a trapper in the Yukon backcountry. I promised to meet him the next day, pitched my tent by the river, and let the music of flowing water lull me to sleep.

Next day Carl took me to his cabin in town to show me where the river was eating at his yard. "The river," he said, "has come close to getting me a number of times. It piles slabs of ice on my roof during breakup, and I've had to leave because the ice choked off the river. Each year the river comes a little closer to my house. Another 25 feet, and it'll have it. By that time," he added, "I'll be finished with it. If I had it to do over again, I'd not build a cabin on the Yukon. I'd build over on the Porcupine. It runs clear and is a good trout stream. It's hard to catch a fish in this silt water."

After Circle I left the river and my car and flew toward the sea. I watched the Yukon, broad now, loop back and forth across the flat land, leaving false channels here, sloughs and oxbows there.

I toured the delta with Mike Rearden, assistant manager of the Yukon Delta National Wildlife Refuge. More than 130 species of birds nest and raise their young here, taking advantage of the incredible wealth of plant and insect life that thrives in the brief arctic summer. It was September in the delta. The marsh and bogs had already changed into the muted yellows, rusts, and reds of autumn. Flying over the Yukon's mouth, I began to see dark specks on the Bering Sea, the specks strewn on the water as far as I could see. "Pintails," Mike said. Behind each duck ran an unmistakable furrow on the shallow river bottom, showing where each bird had fed that morning, fattening for its long trip south. Mike estimated that more than 100,000 ducks swam below us that morning. Scattered among them were smaller flocks of whistling swans and an occasional gaggle of Canada geese, bobbing on the water.

Mike suggested that we fly away for a bag lunch—on Nanvaranak Lake near the Yukon's mouth. "There's a wonderful shell beach there," he said.

We splashed down lightly on the lake, left the plane approximately a hundred feet from shore, and waded in hip boots to the beach. How old were these weathered shells? They may have washed ashore only a year or two before. But Mike said they were much older—perhaps 10,000 years old. "Sometimes after severe summer storms, you find mammoth bones and tusks of ivory protruding from the bank in back of the beach."

We sat and ate quietly, listening as the water clattered through the shells as it had done for eons. From the distance I heard the faint drone of a passing airplane, then silence returned again, the silence of true wilderness.

ages 406-407: A setting sun tints the Yukon as the river wanders below Five Finger Rapids.

P

At Dawson the restored Palace Grand Theater (opposite) stands as a reminder of Gold Rush days on the Klondike River. The gold-bearing gravel of the minor Yukon tributary lured thousands to this boomtown. By 1899, the population of Dawson reached 30,000—including seven clergymen, eight members of the Salvation Army, and a troop of Belgian prostitutes. Dredges later replaced prospectors, spitting out tailings that still twist along the Klondike's banks (left). In recent years high gold prices sparked a second rush to places like White Channel (above). Here a machine eats away at bedrock to lay bare its hidden wealth.

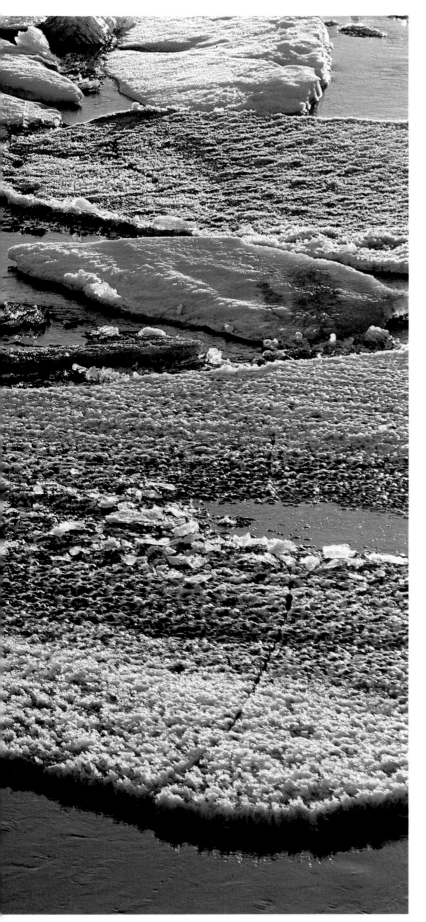

Stephen J. Krasemann, DRK Photo

A t spring breakup, river-borne ice rolls along a Yukon tributary. Alaskans mark the event each year with an ice lottery at Nenana, betting more than 100,000 dollars on the exact moment of breakup. Spring officially begins when the first stirrings of the ice set off a clock on the frozen Tanana River, a Yukon tributary. For the next two or three weeks, ice chunks, some as large as automobiles, hurtle downstream. Warm weather also brings moose to the ice-free waters of the Charley River, where this cow (upper) shakes dry after nibbling underwater plants. Moose can dive as deep as 18 feet to feed and can submerge for half a minute at a time. In alpine meadows in the Ogilvie Mountains, flowers like the mountain avens (lower) announce the arrival of spring.

411

W here prospectors once stampeded for gold, villagers trudge through a quiet street in Ruby (right). Only a handful of Indians and prospectors remain in this Yukon River town. Seclusion helps preserve the traditions of Nulato, a river village where Athapaskan Indians (above) hold a ritual stick dance. Men and women take special roles in the week-long ceremony honoring a dead villager: The women may dance for 20 hours at a stretch, accompanied by men who sing and clap sticks together to make music. The spruce pole represents the link between living and dead. Villagers carry it through the streets for luck, then break it and toss it in the river—a ritual once banned by missionaries who lived here in the 1930s.

THE ST. LAWRENCE

A RIVER OF BOUNDARIES

By William Howarth / Photographs by Nathan Benn

It's late May, and spring has just come to the St. Lawrence River. Apple trees are blooming, tulips and lilacs are putting on a bright show. At Alexandria Bay, New York, I board the first boat of the year for a tour of the Thousand Islands.

The actual count is closer to two thousand, for an island here is any land above water that supports at least two trees. Some crags barely meet those terms, such as Tom Thumb Island—almost too small for Tom to lie down—or Just Room Enough, where a modest cottage covers most of the land. Other "cottages" boast ballrooms, sculpture on the lawns, and yachts in the river, for the Thousand Islands have been a millionaires' retreat since the 1860s.

At Heart Island I disembark to wander over the grounds of Boldt Castle. Its soaring turrets and broad, echoing rooms remind me of a grand hotel. George Boldt made his fortune from the Waldorf-Astoria. One day his chef improvised a salad dressing; Boldt called it Thousand Islands.

The castle was to be a gift to his wife, but she died before its completion. Boldt sent the workmen home, closed Heart Island, and never returned. On the walls of his empty, unfinished castle, lovers have scrawled their names in lipstick, hearts entwined. Outside, the day has turned gray and cold. Spring comes late to the river's southern reaches, and never for long.

The St. Lawrence flows 750 miles from Great Lakes to Atlantic Ocean, from fresh water to salt. Its current runs smooth and steady all year, rarely flooding. The river is very young to behave in such a stately manner. Geologists date its birth at a mere 6,000 years ago, when a deep fault opened in the Canadian Shield, the great sweep of tundra, lake, and forest surrounding Hudson Bay.

On its way to the sea the St. Lawrence creates and crosses many boundaries. It divides Canada from the United States, then passes from English-speaking Ontario to French-speaking Québec. Along this course I can follow our continental history back into its aboriginal past.

Crossing the international bridge into Ontario, I drive north beside a modern engineering feat: the St. Lawrence Seaway. Before 1959 large ships could not

Emerald islets scattered on a field of blue lend enchantment to the Thousand Islands of the St. Lawrence River. Here, unfinished Boldt Castle recalls a tycoon's tragic romance.

navigate the rapids between Lake Ontario and Montréal. But construction of the seaway's locks and dams opened the Great Lakes to oceangoing vessels. Toronto, Detroit, and other inland cities turned into prosperous seaports.

Deepening the seaway channel, engineers constructed the 3,300-foot-long Moses-Saunders Power Dam. The impounded water flooded eight communities and 225 farms. Officials of Ontario Hydro designed new towns and helped 6,500 people move. Historical buildings went to Upper Canada Village, a museum near Morrisburg that re-creates pioneer life of the early 1800s.

Fran Laflamme, a school librarian in the new town of Ingleside, still mourns the lost villages, settled 200 years ago by United Empire Loyalists who fled America after the Revolution. "Most of the old houses were leveled because they couldn't be moved," she told me. "I saw my father's house burn down. I should never have watched it go. We are Hydro victims."

But Ontario Hydro has its defenders. Fran admits that the new Long Sault Parkway affords a pleasant drive on a sunny afternoon. Bridges cross from island to island, several the resting place of a vanished village. On Dickinson Island we pause. A road enters the river, emerges to cross a small island, then falls away into the water again. Fran points out old landmarks. She was born nearby in Wales, a village now submerged.

Driving into Québec Province, I notice that all road signs are in French only—the effect of recent legislation. Since 1976 Québec has pressed for political sovereignty, yet the habits of a bilingual culture die slowly. No wonder. Just as the Ottawa and St. Lawrence Rivers meet near Montréal, so do languages merge and flow. In Montréal a sign at a jewelry shop reads: *"Les Doo-Dads."*

Two of every ten Montrealers speak English as a first language in this dappled city. A stroll along Avenue Laurier takes me through Portuguese, Italian, and Vietnamese neighborhoods. Hasidic Jews from the Ukraine move in pairs to a Sabbath meeting. They speak Yiddish, punctuated with "Okay, okay."

Next morning I climb Mount Royal. Breton seafarer Jacques Cartier dubbed this low mountain Mont Réal in 1535, claiming its environs for Old France. Four and a half centuries later, joggers and bikers rest here after an uphill run. A turbaned Sikh adjusts his stereo headphones, then coasts downhill.

Below lie the narrow streets of Old Montréal. Its blackened stone buildings give way to a modern port, 109 berths open year round. Ships from 50 countries dock here, mostly with petroleum and grain. A Japanese freighter takes on grain—in exchange for headphones, perhaps.

Beyond Montréal the river begins to broaden toward the estuary, subject to daily tides. On both shores French villages nestle below church steeples. The great towers, spires of prayer, soar above treetops.

Downriver, church steeples punctuate the skyline of Québec City, an old fortress piled high on a rock. The city rests upon layers of history. Three hundred

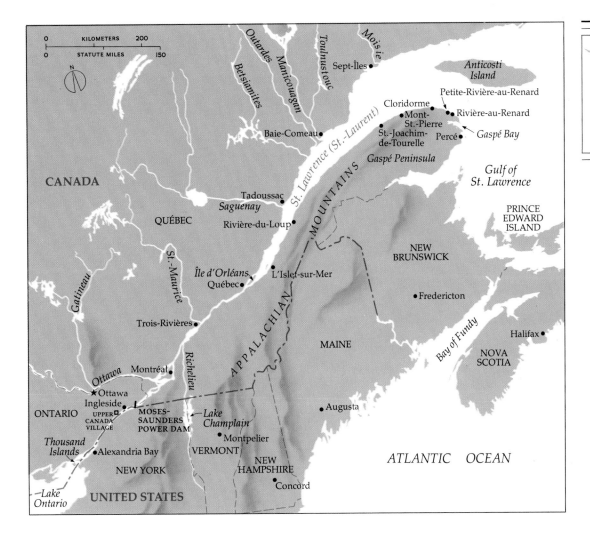

feet above the river, I walk across the Plains of Abraham, the battlefield where Britain won control of Canada from France in 1759. I look down on the walled Upper Town, once the administrative heart of New France. At the base, old shops and docks in Lower Town cover the site of a Huron Indian village.

I have come to Québec City on July 17, the last night of Summer Festival. Music is everywhere: In the streets I hear classical duets and country trios, marvel at a man playing syncopated spoons. But the best entertainer is perfectly silent. A human mannequin, he moves in pantomime, fixing his eyes on the crowd. He never blinks, until a tall blonde girl begins to mimic him. They lock hands, dance silently, and finally kiss. The crowd applauds. July 17 is a night of high summer romance, when no one dreams of winter.

The weather has been hot and dry for weeks. On Île d'Orléans, within sight of Québec City, local crops are ripening too fast for market. Billboards picture bright red strawberries and beg *"Cueillez vous-mêmes—Pick your own,"* so I stop to oblige. Farmers fence their land long and narrow, with each homestead fronting the river. The houses have swooped eaves to fend off rain and snow.

All signs now point to the coming sea. Above the fields, ring-billed gulls glide and dive, hunting for lunch. Lighthouses on the shores wait for night and fog. The river is dark and cold, now partly salt water.

In winter the bitter cold freezes even salt water, so icebreakers work to keep the channel open as far as Montréal. At the Bernier Maritime Museum in L'Islet-sur-Mer, I board a retired icebreaker, the *Ernest-Lapointe*. In its cramped quarters the crew slept in coffinlike bunks. Many sailors passed the long hours of winter duty by carving wooden ship models and weather vanes.

From April until January a ferry from Rivière-du-Loup to the north shore carries a hundred cars and up to 450 passengers—with time on their hands. Life turns to a slow throb at 12 knots. People stretch. Some sleep in the sun, others scan the horizon for milky white belugas. Downstream, other whales—inquisitive minkes, the prodigious finbacks, and rare blue and humpback whales—congregate in this broad estuary, where the mix of fresh and salt water, warm and cold, sustains a rich array of marine life.

No whales today. Instead, the river is crowded with boats, barges—and tourists looking in vain for whales. For four centuries, whalers hunted here—Basques from France and Spain, then French and English crews. Most hunting stopped in 1972, but the belugas declined to a few hundred because they were not fully protected. Now their numbers may be increasing.

Along the north shore, wild and sparsely settled, stretch miles of forest. Frequently I cross streams flowing to the St. Lawrence, where they have cut deep bays that make good coves for fishermen. Commercial boats take shrimp, crab, cod, and halibut from the St. Lawrence, while up the Saguenay and rivers to the east lie the salmon runs of Québec.

Atlantic salmon hatch and spend their earliest years in fresh water, dwell in the sea until maturity, then return upriver to spawn. Many perish before completing the ritual. At Tadoussac a hatchery tries to increase their numbers. In long tanks and pens, salmon of all ages swirl and grow, safe from hazards.

A soft, cool rain is falling—just a hint of next autumn. In the brief Canadian summer, work proceeds apace. Every town has oval eel weirs on the water, stacks of cordwood in its yards. At Baie-Comeau, a big town with a short history, the evening sky turns yellow with sulfurous smoke. This could be Detroit or Pittsburgh a century ago. Founded in 1937, the port grew quickly by reaching into Québec's interior and plucking forth wood and water. These raw materials flow to local industrial plants and leave as paper and electricity.

Crossing by ferry to the south shore, I look downriver into the Gulf of St. Lawrence. White-capped and wave-lapped, the water rolls to a far horizon—a truly oceanic scene. Where the gulf begins, there also lies the Gaspé Peninsula, a high ridge of northern Appalachians that spills into the sea.

Morning brings heavy fog to the coast. I can make out only simple forms: a boat, a fishing shack, a cliff of layered shale. The road curls away from me, running with confidence into the fog.

Along the shore every village backs into a headland cape, high cliffs that drop sharply into the water. I drive through small towns with long names: St.-Joachim-de-Tourelle, Petite-Rivière-au-Renard. Out here French is the only language spoken, even at some tourist bureaus. But tourism prevails. At Mont-St.-Pierre visitors hang-glide from the cliffs and windsurf on the bay.

Far out on the Gaspé juts Forillon National Park, a finger of land pointing to Nova Scotia. Overhead wheel gannets and kittiwakes, diving to find meals. Rocky headlands shelter basking seals. Whales surface offshore, spouting mist and raising the tourist cry: *"Baleine! Une grande baleine, fantastique!"*

In the park several miles of marked trails lead through meadows dense with wildflowers. Rambling with the sun, I traverse coves where families once farmed and fished. Beside the garden of one homestead lean racks for drying cod. Open to the public, this old house has bright interior colors: orange walls with red trim, pink ceilings above yellow floors. Perhaps this touch of warmth cheered the long dark winters.

At Grand-Grève a small fishing fleet still calls at the wharf with loads of cod, herring, flounder, and mackerel. Gaspé Bay abounds with marine food. Two park naturalists put on wet suits and scuba tanks to demonstrate. They swim out to a depth of 60 feet and disappear. Soon they return with baskets of plants, sea urchins, starfish, and other specimens. Visitors play tug-of-war with the kelp and taste the sea lettuce—"Wet cardboard!"

My journey began at the Thousand Islands; it ends on one. Bonaventure Island lies off Percé, beyond the mouth of the St. Lawrence. Lichens flourish in this pure air. More than 40,000 gannets nest on the eastern shore. I sit only inches from these colonists, nearly deafened by their clamor.

Beyond this cliff I see no land, only the broad Gulf of St. Lawrence, open here to all the Atlantic provinces—New Brunswick, Prince Edward Island, Nova Scotia, Newfoundland. Not long ago they were all newfound lands, for mankind has been in this region just a few thousand years. After the glaciers came Indians; after them, the Europeans: Viking warriors, Portuguese and Breton fishermen, French voyageurs and priests, then the French and English settlers.

In late August a touch of autumn is in the air. Soon the gannets will leave, then snow geese and ducks move south along the St. Lawrence Valley. Frost will disband the tourists, and snow and ice again cover the land and the river. Beneath the ice, the river flows on.

Bruce Dale, National Geographic Photographer

P leasure and commerce furrow the waters of the Thousand Islands, where the St. Lawrence River spills from Lake Ontario on its 750-mile run to the sea. Here, an oceangoing freighter plows past Just Room Enough, one of the 1,700 or so islands that make up the archipelago. Vacationing islanders (above) enjoy an outing in a motor launch built by a local boat company in the early 1900s.

The St. Lawrence, a key waterway linking the Great Lakes and the Atlantic, each year handles some 50 million metric tons of cargo, mostly grain, coal, and iron ore. Since 1959, canals, locks, and dams along previously unnavigable stretches of the river have provided direct access by ocean vessels to inland cities, such as Detroit and Duluth.

ew dimensions for an old city: Montréal, a Huron Indian village named Hochelaga when Jacques Cartier explored the St. Lawrence in 1535, soars tall—and plunges deep—on the wings of a building boom that began in the 1950s.

Place Desjardins (opposite) is part of a self-contained mini-city above and below ground level. Metro tunnels and sheltered walkways link it with other downtown developments known collectively as The City Below. On the main concourse, shoppers and strollers gather to enjoy and participate in a popular variety show televised on location.

Stepped and angled towers of a high-rise office building (right) catch light and provide breathtaking views of the city. The building helps symbolize the rebirth of downtown Montréal after years of decay and attests to the city's thriving commercial life—despite economic uncertainties brought about by the attempts to separate largely French-speaking Québec Province from the rest of Canada.

On a busy Saturday near old Québec City, buyers and sellers at a farmers' market carry on their ancient commerce.

Pages 424-425: Heart and soul of French-speaking Canada, old Québec City nestles along the St. Lawrence waterfront, guarded by the fog-shrouded turrets of Château Frontenac. The 92-year-old grand dowager hotel commands this split-level capital of Québec Province.

R ivière-au-Renard, a fishing hamlet at the mouth of the St. Lawrence, stands crisply mirrored in the aftermath of a summer storm. Some of its inhabitants trace their ancestry to Irish immigrants cast ashore and taken in by French-Canadian families when their ship foundered on the rocks of the Gaspé Peninsula.

At nearby Cloridorme (right) cleaned and gutted cod are spread to dry on a flake, an airy platform made of poles and chicken wire. Painstakingly dried and salted over a period of several weeks—in a process called the Gaspé cure—most of the fish will be baled in bulk or packed into casks for shipment overseas.

428

THE RIO GRANDE

A L L   V I G O R   S P E N T

by Edward Abbey

Why not begin at the end? I stand on the hot sand of the beach and watch the Rio Grande merge its thick, sluggish, algae-green water with the bright blue of the Gulf of Mexico. This is Boca Chica (Little Mouth) and here, near Brownsville, Texas, one of the great American rivers finally completes its journey to the sea. Barely makes it. The water seems not to move at all, as if worn out, exhausted by its 1,885-mile descent from the San Juan Mountains of Colorado, through the canyons of New Mexico and Texas, over and through dozens of dams, diverted, processed, recycled, all vigor spent, until at the end the river is little more than a warm, slow catfish creek, 20 feet wide and only waist deep.

The river is not as dead as it looks. Dozens of fishermen wade in and out of the gentle surf on either side of the Rio Grande's little mouth. With long poles and heavy lines baited with *camarónes*—shrimp—they are seeking their supper. One man opens his ice box to show me his catch: three whiting and two five-pound red snappers.

Why are the fishermen clustered here at the mouth of the river? Because the effluents from upstream, the sewage and fertilizers and garbage from towns and farms attract the hierarchies of small organisms, including shrimp, that attract in turn the large game fish that attract human predators.

Although this is a weekday afternoon, whole families are here. Wives and mothers sit in the shade of battered automobiles and sea-rusted pickup trucks, watching their men. Children play in the firm sand at the water's edge and in the high dunes behind the beach. All but myself appear to be Mexicans, or Mexican-Americans. Here on the international boundary, in this neutral zone, one's actual citizenship makes little difference. The uniformed police of the U. S. Border Patrol are nowhere in sight.

The air is soft, warm, humid, semitropical. It feels to me like potential hurricane weather, but today the sky is clear except for a few small clouds out over the rim of the sea. Sandpipers scurry along the edge of the surf; a few terns fly

Twisting and turning, the Rio Grande veers around the Chisos Mountains of Texas, carving deep canyons through ancient deposits of limestone. Big Bend National Park preserves this spectacular scenery.

above, occasionally diving straight down into the water to emerge, a moment later, with or without their prey. Like the men, the terns are fishing.

An old lighthouse stands on the Mexican side of the river's mouth. Hard to believe now, but only a few decades ago the Rio Grande was navigable for almost 200 miles upstream. In the other direction, northeast, I can see huge resort hotels and condominium towers under construction on the south tip of Padre Island. Boca Chica, however, is still uninhabited—at least for now.

I drive a mile up the hard, damp beach and go for a swim, wading a hundred yards from shore (thinking about stingrays and sharks) before the tepid water becomes chest deep. I float on my back under the hot sun, letting the waves roll over me, and think about the other end of the Rio Grande, the beginning.

Only two weeks earlier my wife and I had been camping at Stony Pass, nearly 13,000 feet above sea level, under green-gold aspen and shaggy spruce, deep in the San Juan Mountains above the mining town of Creede, Colorado. We intended to find the origins of the Rio Grande, the source. *La Source:* I envisioned a mythological maiden in a flowing, diaphanous gown, pouring crystal clear Rocky Mountain springwater from a jug on her shoulder. What we really found was something much finer. But I'll get back to that in a minute.

After my swim I drive back to Brownsville and walk across the international bridge over the Rio Grande to the Mexican town of Matamoros. Unmuffled tanker trucks (hauling drinking water, I am told) thunder across the bridge from Texas into Mexico. The Mexicans, it seems, are having problems with their water supply again. Matamoros, far off the main travel routes, is a fairly presentable place, unlike most border towns. I notice a few leaking sewer lines, a few shoeshine boys and little girls selling chewing gum. The general appearance of homes and public buildings is one of genteel decay, shaded by date palms and brightened by the red flowers of bougainvillea.

The worst sleaze is on the American side of the border in downtown Brownsville, among the bars, go-go joints, and block after block of little clothing stores. Here I see one of the saddest things I've ever seen, anywhere. Inside a shop labeled *Ropas Usadas* (Used Clothes), a dozen weary little Mexican women, all pregnant, sit among mountains of old clothing, each woman patiently sorting through these trash piles in search of children's garments and stacking her selection in a small heap at her feet. Both temperature and humidity are in the 90s. The air in the place is stifling, swarming with flies, and dense with the unmistakable, unforgettable smell of poverty. The manager of this dump, the only male in view, waits in the corner for the women to finish their sorting and hand over their faded paper pesos. Hordes of children play outside on the slime and broken glass of the street.

Watching this intolerable, unacceptable scene, which nevertheless we tolerate and accept, I think again of Stony Pass in the San Juans, the clear, cold

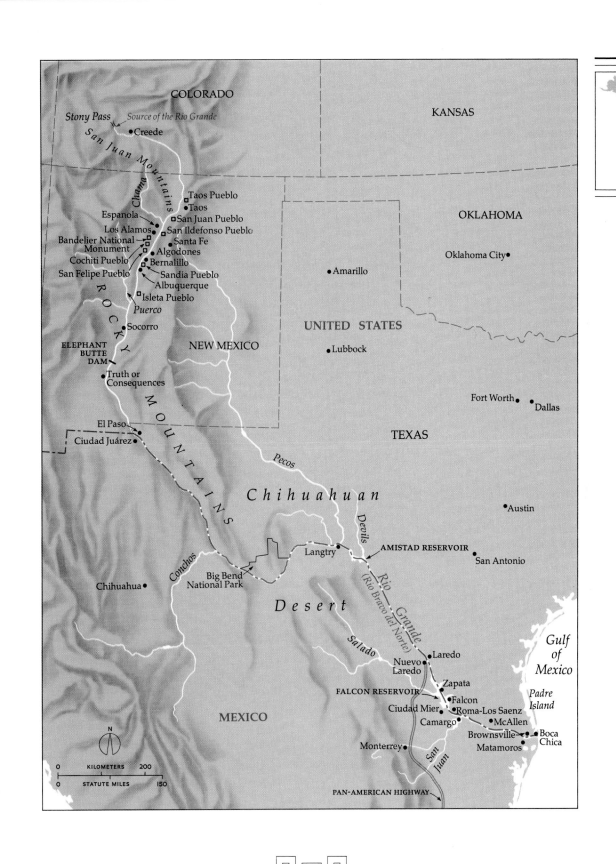

COLORADO

KANSAS

Stony Pass   *Source of the Rio Grande*
●Creede

San Juan Mountains

OKLAHOMA

Taos Pueblo
Taos
Espanola   San Juan Pueblo
Los Alamos   San Ildefonso Pueblo
Bandelier National   Santa Fe
Monument   Algodones
Cochiti Pueblo   Bernalillo
San Felipe Pueblo   Sandia Pueblo
Albuquerque
Isleta Pueblo
Puerco

Oklahoma City●

●Amarillo

●Socorro

NEW MEXICO

UNITED STATES

ELEPHANT
BUTTE
DAM

●Lubbock

●Truth or
Consequences

Fort Worth●   ●Dallas

El Paso
●Ciudad Juárez

Pecos

TEXAS

Chihuahuan

Devils

●Austin

AMISTAD RESERVOIR
Langtry●

Conchos

Big Bend
National Park

San Antonio●

Chihuahua●

Desert

Rio Grande
(Rio Bravo del Norte)

*Gulf
of
Mexico*

Salado

*Padre
Island*

●Laredo
Nuevo
Laredo●

MEXICO

Zapata●
FALCON RESERVOIR
●Falcon
Ciudad Mier●   Roma-Los Saenz●
Camargo●   ●McAllen
Brownsville   ●Boca
Chica
Monterrey●   Matamoros

*San
Juan*

N

KILOMETERS   200

STATUTE MILES   150

PAN-AMERICAN HIGHWAY

431

mountain air, the peaks covered with fresh snow, and the bright virgin waters of the Rio Grande trickling from their multitude of secret beginnings under the rocks and the tundra and the alpine flowers. The elk were on the move, through the pines and aspen; in the evenings we'd hear the bull elk bugle forth his challenge to the world. That is another world, a sort of paradise compared to this. It is a world that these women and probably most of their children will never see.

Leaving this town behind, I drive for 30 miles northwestward along what is left of the river—the same sluggish green creek I saw at the shore of the Gulf—through cotton fields, citrus groves, and seedy plantation towns. Cotton and poverty, like coal and poverty, are often found together. But the roads are lined with palms, and the old Rio Grande, unfenced and unguarded, meanders with tolerant indifference past poverty and wealth alike. The many horses in the many lush pastures on either side of the river look content. Like the marsh hawks overhead and the dark green wild ebony trees in the fencerows, life in its various forms goes on, continues despite our human efforts to overcomplicate it and oversimplify nature.

Think about something pleasant. Think about the river, the Rio Bravo del Norte, as the Mexicans style it, the Great River, as writer Paul Horgan called it in his prizewinning book of the same name. The Rio Grande descends from the glorious mountains of Colorado and rolls into the high plains of New Mexico, carving a deep and narrow gorge through the black basaltic rock laid down over the eons by the old volcanoes of the region. Already diminished in volume and quality by irrigation farming upstream, the river nevertheless runs cold, clear, and deep enough to support a thriving population of native brown trout and hatchery rainbow trout, making it a favorite stream of Southwest anglers.

We camped here, too, for a couple of days, on the rim of the gorge a thousand feet above the river, near Taos. The water was low in mid-September. We could hear the murmur of the riffles, the cries of pinyon jays and Clark's nutcrackers. We saw a kingfisher and a mountain bluebird, flashes of color against the dark rock and olive drab sagebrush, and flocks of cliff swallows. A few local fly-fishermen stood on the gravel bars at the side of the river, near the dirt road and the antique structure known as John Dunn Bridge. Resolutely, over and over, they cast their lines; we saw no strikes.

On the other side of the river, the west side, some middle-aged flower children from the hip-boutique city of Taos were bathing in one of the several natural hot springs at the river's edge. A few years earlier the native Chicano folk and the newly arrived Anglo hippies had been bitter enemies, but now, at the moment, things seemed peaceful enough. My wife and I cooked our supper over a fire of juniper coals and enjoyed the splendor of the evening.

Below Taos the Rio Grande emerges from its dark gorge and enters the broad valleys of north-central New Mexico. Here it passes some of the most colorful, picturesque, and richly historic towns and cities of the United States: Santa Fe, of course, the most famous of them all; and then the ancient agrarian villages of the Pueblo Indians: San Gabriel, San Juan, Santa Clara, Puye, San Ildefonso, Cochiti, Santo Domingo, San Felipe, Zia, Santa Ana, Sandia, and Isleta. Between San Ildefonso and Cochiti the river cuts into the mesas of the city of Los Alamos, home of the first atomic bomb and today, more than ever, an active center for nuclear research and weaponry. Intermingled with the Indian villages are the towns first settled by the Spanish some 400 years ago—not only Taos, Albuquerque, and Santa Fe, but also Espanola, Algodones, Bernalillo, and many other little farming villages now gradually congealing into a continuous suburban mass from Albuquerque to the charming, handsome town of Socorro. Albuquerque is the major city of the state, a huge, dusty, windblown center of commerce and industry with a population, including its not-yet-annexed suburbs, of almost half a million souls, and growing daily.

Somehow in the midst of all this Spanish and Anglo-American pressure, the Pueblo Indians have managed to preserve a great deal, perhaps the best, of the outward forms of their centuries-old culture. But the agrarian and self-sufficient economy on which that culture was based, which formed the heart of its religion, ceremony, and customs, has been largely outmoded or absorbed. Its future seems problematic at best. When the children and grandchildren of corn farmers, deer hunters, and pastoralists study auto mechanics and computer programming, it seems unlikely that the roots and essence of an earth-based culture can survive.

But the river flows on, more or less, though drained of much of its volume by the countless development projects along its banks. At Albuquerque the Rio Grande is a broad, shallow stream, muddy gold, hemmed in by the enormous city on either side but still capable of sustaining cottonwood groves and a few farms along its shores.

South of Albuquerque, the Rio Grande enters the northern outreach of what geographers call the Chihuahuan Desert, a vast region of sand hills, gravel mesas, and isolated desert mountains. Here the juniper and pinyon of the high range are seen no more; the typical plants are mesquite and the hardy creosote shrub, spreading from Socorro far south into Old Mexico. The dredged and diked river glides along through barren and largely uninhabited terrain, much like that of the Nile in southern Egypt.

Near the town of Truth or Consequences, New Mexico, the river is stoppered by Elephant Butte Dam, creating a 40-mile-long reservoir that is slowly filling up with silt and sediment washed down from the outlying drainage basins. From here to the Gulf of Mexico, the Rio Grande, like so many other American rivers, becomes more like a canal than a river, completely dedicated to the needs of industrial agriculture and expanding municipalities. Cotton, alfalfa, pecans, peppers, and citrus serve a useful purpose for the ever growing populations of the United States and Mexico, but the river itself, under such intensive management, offers little to other human needs—the need for natural beauty, for example, and the need for physical and moral adventure.

With one great exception. About two hundred miles southeast of the city of El Paso, the Rio Grande, reinforced by its tributary the Rio Conchos from Mexico, has cut several magnificent canyons through the limestone plateau of Big Bend National Park. Two of them, Santa Elena Canyon and Mariscal Canyon, reach depths of more than 1,500 feet, with sheer vertical cliffs on either side; Boquillas Canyon is almost as deep.

Beyond Boquillas Canyon, at the eastern edge of the park, the river runs for another hundred miles through farther, if lesser, canyons, in a remote and largely roadless region inhabited only by a few cattle ranchers and a transient population of smugglers, illegal aliens, stray cattle, mountain lions, and wild horses. Friends and I have made several boat trips through these canyons, where the river alternates between stretches of lazy indolence and violent, white-water rapids worthy of respect. This is the most primitive country to be found along the Rio Grande, a harsh and lonely land of spectacular beauty.

Commercial raft trips are available in the upper canyons when the water flow is high enough, and Big Bend National Park is easily accessible to motorized tourism. Some of the best descriptions of the land and people of the Big Bend area can be found in Tom Lea's fine novel, *The Wonderful Country*, published 30 years ago but not forgotten.

At the old frontier town of Langtry, Texas, made famous a century ago by Judge Roy Bean, "the law west of the Pecos," the river leaves the desert mountains and begins its long, placid journey through the low hills and then the flatlands of southern Texas and northeastern Mexico. En route it bisects the twin cities of Laredo and Nuevo Laredo, roadhead of the Pan-American Highway and one of the major gateways between the two nations.

For its final hundred miles, rapidly diminishing in volume, the Rio Grande again becomes the servant of humankind, nourishing another belt of cotton plantations, oil fields, citrus groves, and many towns and cities—Zapata, Falcon, Ciudad Mier, Roma-Los Saenz, Camargo, McAllen, Brownsville, Matamoros. Finally it twists and turns across a broad delta, no longer a river but only a little stream, to rejoin the ultimate source of all rivers, the open sea. There, under the power plant of the sun, the clouds are forming, day and night, to carry the precious water vapor back to the mountains once again.

Every river returns to its source.

P age 435: Rafters meet rapids in the upper Rio Grande's awesome gorge. Some 52 miles of the river in northern New Mexico are protected as a National Wild and Scenic River.

Prehistoric cliff dwellings (opposite) notch the steep canyons of New Mexico's Bandelier National Monument, where mountain streams flow to the Rio Grande. Later Indians abandoned these canyons and built a string of pueblos—towns—along the Rio Grande itself. At Taos Pueblo (above), modern Indians strive to retain their centuries-old way of life. Downstream, the city of Santa Fe celebrates its Spanish heritage with an annual fiesta (right). The city was founded by the Spanish in 1610 as the northern outpost of their new empire.

W orkers from both sides of the border harvest peppers in farmlands
near El Paso, Texas. The federal
Rio Grande Project, begun in
1905, transformed the desertlike
valley into richly productive agricultural land. Elephant Butte
Dam, near the town of Truth or
Consequences, New Mexico, begins a series of dams, reservoirs,
and canals that irrigates 196,000
acres in the United States and,
by treaty, guarantees water to
52,000 acres in Mexico. The
project also provides flood control, hydroelectric power, and
recreational fishing, swimming,
and boating.

Though the Rio Grande again
runs free through its gorges in
Big Bend National Park, most of
the river's flow from central New
Mexico to the Gulf is tightly con-
trolled in service to humankind.

438

T he city of El Paso (opposite) arose where the Rio Grande cuts a low pass through the southern Rockies. Spanish explorers chose this route—El Paso del Norte—for their highway from Mexico City to Santa Fe. In 1659 Franciscans built a mission here on the southern banks of the Rio Grande. The city that eventually grew on both sides of the river was split in two in 1848, when the Treaty of Guadalupe Hidalgo established the Rio Grande as the boundary between Mexico and the U.S. The Mexicans renamed their city Ciudad Juárez.

Thousands of Mexican workers cross the bridge daily to jobs in El Paso's fields and factories. A shantytown (above) near Juárez shelters people waiting to enter the U.S., legally or otherwise. Where the Rio Grande is shallow, enterprising men earn a living carrying Mexicans across.

441

George F. Mobley, National Geographic Photographer

Danny Lehman

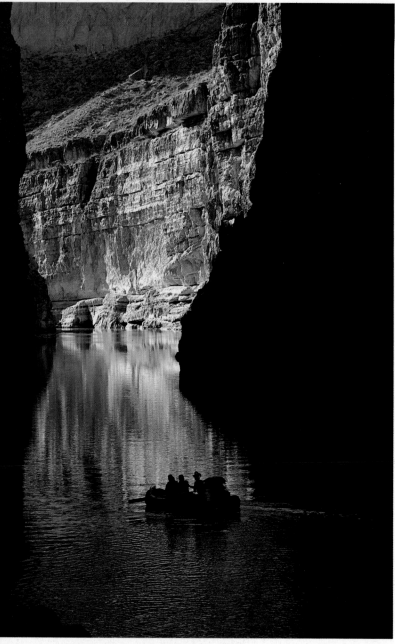

reat-tailed grackles roost beside Falcon Dam's 60-mile-long reservoir in the lower Rio Grande Valley (right). A joint project of the U. S. and Mexico, the dam ended disastrous floods. But as the valley's woods and brushland are cleared for farms and homes, vital bird habitat is destroyed.

At Big Bend National Park, Texas, the Rio Grande swings in a wide bend around the Chisos Mountains, carving three major gorges. In Santa Elena Canyon (above), rafters float in silence and solitude.

EARTH'S LONGEST RIVERS

Rank by Length	Length (miles)	Drainage Area (square miles)	Average Flow at Mouth (cubic feet per second)	Source	Mouth
1 Nile	4,160	1,170,000	100,000	Burundi and Rwanda	Mediterranean Sea
2 Amazon	3,920	2,270,000	6,100,000	Andes Mts. (Peru)	Atlantic Ocean
3 Yangtze	3,900	698,000	1,030,000	Tanggula Range (China)	East China Sea (Pacific Ocean)
4 Mississippi-Missouri	3,870	1,247,000	640,000	Minnesota/Montana (U. S.)	Gulf of Mexico
5 Yenisey-Angara	3,440	996,000	692,000	Sayan Mts./Lake Baykal (U.S.S.R.)	Kara Sea (Arctic Ocean)
6 Yellow (Huang)	3,400	290,000	53,000	Qinghai Province (China)	Yellow Sea (Pacific Ocean)
7 Ob-Irtysh	3,360	1,154,000	441,000	Altay Mts. (China)	Kara Sea (Arctic Ocean)
8 Zaire (Congo)	2,900	1,440,000	1,400,000	Katanga Plateau (Zaire)	Atlantic Ocean
9 Amur	2,800	730,000	441,000	Siberia (U.S.S.R.) and Heilongjiang Province (China)	Sea of Okhotsk (Pacific Ocean)
10 Lena	2,700	961,000	579,000	Baykal Range (U.S.S.R.)	Laptev Sea (Arctic Ocean)
11 Mekong	2,700	303,000	530,000	Tanggula Range (China)	South China Sea (Pacific Ocean)
12 Paraná-Río de la Plata	2,680	1,197,000	809,000	Brazilian Highlands (Brazil)	Atlantic Ocean
13 Mackenzie	2,640	697,000	343,000	Northwest Territories (Canada)	Beaufort Sea (Arctic Ocean)
14 Niger	2,600	850,000	215,000	Loma Mts. (Guinea)	Gulf of Guinea (Atlantic Ocean)
15 Volga	2,300	533,000	280,000	Valdai Hills (U.S.S.R.)	Caspian Sea
16 Murray-Darling	2,300	410,000	25,000	Great Dividing Range (Australia)	Encounter Bay (Indian Ocean)
17 Zambezi	2,200	548,000	250,000	Katanga Plateau (Zambia)	Indian Ocean
18 Orinoco	2,200	373,000	600,000	Serra Parima (Venezuela)	Atlantic Ocean
19 Madeira	2,010	463,000	770,000	Bolivia	Amazon River
20 Yukon	1,980	295,000	240,000	British Columbia (Canada)	Bering Sea (Pacific Ocean)

Source: John C. Kammerer, U. S. Geological Survey; and others

ACKNOWLEDGMENTS

We thank the individuals, groups, and institutions who gave us generous help in the preparation of this book. Special thanks go to John C. Kammerer, hydrologist, U. S. Geological Survey. In addition, we gratefully acknowledge: Carl G. Osborne, Chesapeake Bay Foundation; Bob Hume and Bob Seedlock, U. S. Army Corps of Engineers; Marion Marts, University of Washington; Nico Scheepers, Rand Afrikaans University; David Lampis, University of California; Thomas Q. Reefe, University of North Carolina; C. Michael Bailey, National Aquarium; Thomas T. Helde, Georgetown University; Helmuth K. Kohrer, Linz; Heinrich Eder and Angela Frohn, Vienna; Imre Mailáth, Szentendre; Ferenc Eross and Eva Kovács, Budapest; Predrag Djordjevic and Marina Zivanovic, Belgrade; Nicolae Păduraru, Bucharest; Robert Casile, Service Navigation Rhône-Saône; Diane Creedon and Mary Lyons, Food and Wines from France; Jacques de Place, Lyon; Michel Durand-Roger and Isabelle Carsol, Avignon; Pierre Gilibert, Compagnie Nationale du Rhône; George Hern, French Government Tourist Office; Jean-Louis Horn, Port Autonome de Marseille; Jacques and Suzanne Pic, Valence; André Senglet, Geneva; Igor G. Kozak, East-West Features Service; Louisa Ozhogina and Tom Yanin, Volgograd Intourist; Ludmilla Volodina, Ul'yanovsk Intourist; D. K. Burman, Varanasi; Sanjeev Saith, New Delhi; John Seidensticker, National Zoological Park; Sonja Lindblad and William Bikales, Lindblad Travel, Inc.; Huan Wenchan, China International Travel Service; Huang Yuanjun, Yangtze Valley Planning Office; Franklin Ayala Flores, Universidad Nacional de la Amazonia Peruana; Thomas E. Lovejoy, World Wildlife Fund; Loren McIntyre, Arlington, Virginia; Robert Randall, Ollantaytambo, Peru; Herbert Schubart, National Institute for Amazonian Studies; Violeta Marien Almeida, Itaipu Binacional; Marcos Aurelio Moncada, Estancia Atalaya; Edward A. Greene and Harry A. Dolphin, U. S. Army Corps of Engineers; Jeffrey A. Smith, American Waterways Operators, Inc.; Rory N. Vose, Saint Mary's College; Louis B. Parent, Québec Government Office of Tourism; Maxime St-Amour, Forillon National Park; David E. Sergeant, Department of Fisheries and Oceans of Canada; Jerry E. Mueller, New Mexico State University.

We extend thanks also to the embassies of the many nations where we traveled; the U. S. Department of State; the World Bank; and the U. S. Geological Survey. We are also indebted to Barry C. Bishop, Dean Conger, John G. Morris, and Jennifer Moseley of the National Geographic Society, and to the National Geographic Library and Travel Office for their special efforts on our behalf.

Defender of wilderness and occasional park ranger and fire lookout, *Edward Abbey* has been "floating rivers . . . downstream, the easy, natural way" for 25 years. His home in the desert Southwest provides the setting for much of his writing, including *Desert Solitaire, Down the River,* and many other books and articles.

Nathan Benn, a contract photographer with the National Geographic since he graduated from the University of Miami in 1972, has worked on subjects ranging from medicinal plants in Asia and Africa to biblical archaeology in the Middle East.

Ross S. Bennett, associate director of Book Service and a veteran of more than 25 years' service with National Geographic, first wet his feet on the subject of rivers in 1966 as editor of the Society's perennial best-seller, *America's Wonderlands, Our National Parks.*

Geographer *Ronald Reed Boyce* serves as Dean of the School of Social and Behavioral Sciences at Seattle Pacific University. He has written and edited textbooks and numerous articles on a range of geographical subjects.

Free-lance photographer *Robert Caputo* has traveled extensively in Africa. He filmed wildlife in Tanzania for television and drove the length of the Nile. He has taught at the American Museum of Natural History in New York. His works appear in children's books and many national magazines, including the NATIONAL GEOGRAPHIC.

Born in London, *Mary B. Dickinson* studied French language and culture at the Sorbonne and Oxford University. A writer and editor at National Geographic, she was assistant editor of *Journey Into China.*

Ernest B. "Pat" Furgurson, a national columnist and chief of the *Baltimore Sun*'s Washington Bureau, spent three years in the Soviet Union and has traveled as a journalist in 65 countries. His magazine essays reflect an enduring interest in the land and local lore.

Free-lance writer and photographer *Georg Gerster* lives and works in his native Switzerland. His travels in pursuit of his specialty, science, take him from Alaska to Antarctica and have resulted in articles and photo essays in many popular journals and magazines, including the GEOGRAPHIC.

A painter and sculptor before launching into photography in 1953, free lance *Farrell Grehan* produces work which appears regularly in the NATIONAL GEOGRAPHIC magazine, as well as in Geographic books and other national and international publications.

William Howarth is a professor of English at Princeton University. His interest in the life and works of Henry David Thoreau has led to studies of the 19th-century writer and to articles in the NATIONAL GEOGRAPHIC and other magazines.

John M. Kauffmann, a conservationist and author of *Flow East: A Look at North American Rivers,* has been a park planner with the National Park Service. His writings have been published by the U. S. Department of the Interior and by National Geographic.

Carol Bittig Lutyk, a National Geographic writer and editor, has traveled extensively. An anthropologist by training, she was assistant editor of the National Geographic book *Lost Empires, Living Tribes.*

George F. Mobley has rambled the world several times since he became a National Geographic staff photographer in 1961. His pictures of China, France, India, Norway, Canada, Mexico, Africa, and the Arctic illustrate numerous books and magazine articles.

Geoffrey Moorhouse lives in Yorkshire, England. His books, which have been translated into several languages, cover a range of topics, including monasticism, the history of India, cricket, and his 2,000-mile camel trek across the Sahara. He is a Fellow of the Royal Society of Literature and a Fellow of the Royal Geographical Society.

A combat photographer during the Korean War, *Thomas Nebbia* joined the National Geographic staff in 1958 and worked on assignments in many parts of the world before turning to free-lance work. His pictures have appeared in many major publications and museum exhibits.

Free-lance photographer *David Louis Olson* graduated from the University of Minnesota with a degree in Latin American studies and served with the Peace Corps in Brazil. He has traveled throughout South America and lives in São Paulo, Brazil.

Amanda Parsons, an anthropologist and free-lance journalist, has served as a consultant to the National Geographic Society. She has studied American folklife and lived among Indians of Mexico. In 1982 she contributed a chapter to the National Geographic book *Lost Empires, Living Tribes.*

Robert M. Poole was a newspaper reporter in North Carolina, Boston, and Washington, D. C. before joining National Geographic. He traveled through China by barge in 1981 and wrote about the trip for *Journey Into China.*

A former teacher of writing and literature, *Margaret Sedeen* has been a National Geographic writer and editor for ten years. Her Volga trip capitalized on a lifelong interest in Russian language and life.

A free-lance photojournalist, *Bill Thomas* began his career as a newspaper reporter in Kentucky in 1955. He is the author of several books, including many travel guides, and has written magazine articles.

Cameron Thomas, a writer now living in British Columbia, grew up along the Thames River. He remembers well the guards at Tower Bridge who spent their summer days "chasing a bunch of scruffy kids determined to swim there." Thomas is retired from a career in Canadian television.

A free-lance travel and science writer before joining National Geographic, *Jonathan B. Tourtellot* has followed his interest in "human ecology" to places as diverse as England, Brazil, Australia, Iceland, and Africa.

Cary Wolinsky, a National Geographic contract photographer, worked for *The Boston Globe.* He has done free-lance work since 1972. His photographs illustrate articles on many parts of the world in *Smithsonian,* NATIONAL GEOGRAPHIC, and other national magazines.

Adam Woolfitt is a free-lance travel photographer and a regular contributor to magazines that cover the world. His most recent NATIONAL GEOGRAPHIC story, on Washington, D. C., was one of many award winners. At home in London, Woolfitt is a city person, but he enjoys working in country settings.

INDEX

Illustrations appear in **boldface** type, picture captions in *italic*, and text references in lightface.

A bu Simbel, Egypt 39, 40, **62-63**
Agriculture 11; Amu Dar'ya **190;** Danube 98, 103, *106,* **122-123, 124, 125;** Ganges 188, 198, 200, 201, **208-209, 224-225;** Indus 188, 189; Irrawaddy 188; Mississippi 374, *381,* **390-391, 392, 393;** Missouri 362, 370; Niger 24; Nile 34, 38, 40, 41-42, 43, **48-49,** *55, 57;* Orinoco 295; Rhône *173, 174, 178;* Rio Grande 432, 434, **438-439;** São Francisco 296, 297; Volga 136, 137, **144-145,** *145;* Yangtze 243, 252, **262-263**
Alaknanda, Asia 201, *222;* map 197
Albert Nile, Africa 34; map 35
Allahabad, India 200-201, 203, *216,* **218, 219**
Altmühl, Europe 99; map 96
Amazon, South America 299-331; color 304, *316,* **316;** delta *see* Marajó Island; fish 303, **312,** *313,* **313;** history *297,* 299, 300-301, 306; length 292, 299; maps *291,* 300, 301; navigation 292, 299, 306, *318;* ports 306, **318-319,** *323;* source 290, *328*
Amazon Basin, South America 307; cattle ranches 302, 303, water buffalo 303, **310-311;** deforestation 302, 305, *311;* development 299, 302, 309, *313, 318;* inundation forests 305; medicinal plants 307, *325;* rain forests 301, 302, 304-305, *311,* **324, 325;** soil 305, *311;* wildlife **293,** 302, 305, **311, 321**
Amu Dar'ya, Asia 192, 193; canal **190-191,** 193; irrigation *190, 191,* 193; map 185
Amur, Asia 189, 192, 231; map 185
Anchovies: Chesapeake Bay 20
Andes Mountains, South America 290, 304, 307, *316,* **326-327, 330-331**
Angara, Asia 231, 232, 235; dams 232, 234, **237;** maps 185, 233; source 231, 232
Angel Falls, Venezuela **294**
Apurímac, South America 290, 308, *328;* map 300
Aswân, Egypt 40-41, 42; tourism 41
Aswân High Dam, Egypt 39, 40, *62*

B anana Point, Zaire 74, **82**
Bandelier National Monument, N. Mex. **436**
Bansi ki Pahi (village), India 200, 203
Baykal, Lake, U.S.S.R. 231, 232; fish 232, **240-241;** pollution 233, *240,* cleanup 233, *240*
Belém, Brazil 299-302; market **312-313**
Beluga whales: St. Lawrence 418
Benue, Africa 24, 30; map 25
Bhagirathi, Asia **222, 226, 227;** Ganges distributary 195; Ganges source stream 201, 202, 203, *228;* map 197; source 202, 203, **228**
Bhakra Dam and Canal System, India 188
Big Bend National Park, Texas **428,** 434, *438;* gorges **442**
Billabongs: Australia 287
Black Eagle Falls, Mont.: painting **364**
Blackwater Natl. Wildlife Refuge, Md. **18-19**
Blau, Europe **108**
Blind, North America **380**
Blue crabs: Chesapeake Bay 20
Blue Nile, Africa 33, 34, 36, 37, **49,** *58;* maps 25, 35; source 33, *45, 46;* waterfall **44-45**
Blue whales: St. Lawrence 418
Bluefish: Chesapeake Bay 7, 20
Boyoma Falls, Zaire 70; fishermen 70, **75**
Brahmaputra, Asia 195; maps 185, 197
Bratsk, U.S.S.R.: dam 234, **237**
Breg, Europe 96; map 96
Brigach, Europe 96; map 96
Budapest, Hungary 102; baths **118;** May Day rally **119;** museum **116-117**
Buddhism: China 251-252, **256-257**
Buenos Aires, Argentina 333, 336, 337; election rally **338-339;** port 337, *338,* **341**

C abora Bassa dam, Mozambique 31
Cacapon, North America 11; map 9
Cairo, Egypt 41, 42-43, **66-67**
Calcutta, India 195, 196, 197-198, *206;* Hindu festival **204-205, 207**
Camargue (region), France 167; ranching *180*
Canals 7; Amu Dar'ya **190-191,** 193; Europe 89, 91-92; Ganges 201, *220;* Indus 188; Irrawaddy 188; lock **88;** Nile 34, 36, 43, *57,* excavation **57;** Ohio 354; Rhône 167, 168; Tigris 193; Volga *150,* **150;** Yangtze 243, 252 *see also* Grand Canal
Carp, big head: Yangtze **265**
Casiquiare, South America 292, 295
Cataracts: Nile 38, 41, **44-45;** Orinoco 292; Zaire 70, 73, **81;** *see also* Waterfalls
Catfish: Danube **126-127;** Yalobusha *381*
Chama, North America 358; map 431
Chambeshi, Africa 69; map 71
Channel Country, Australia 278, 281, 287
Charles M. Russell National Wildlife Refuge, Mont. *368*
Charley, North America: wildlife **411**
Châteauneuf-du-Pape (wine region), France 168, **176-177,** *179*
Chemung, North America 10; map 9
Chesapeake Bay (estuary), North America: area 20; drainage 7, 10; fish 7, 20-21; geologic history 7, 8; history 6, 7; map 9; pollution 21; wildlife *18,* **19,** 20, 21
Chippewa, North America 372; map 363
Chongming Island, China 253
Chongqing, China 244, 245, **260, 261**
Chub: Thames 161
Churchill, North America: length 352; map 353
Ciudad Juárez, Mexico *441;* shantytown *441*
Clams: Chesapeake Bay 20
Cockles: Thames **164**
Cod: St. Lawrence 418, 419, *426*
Colorado, North America 352, 357, *357,* 358; color 352; floods 357-358; map 353
Columbia, North America 355, 357; map 353
Conchos, North America 434; map 431
Congo, Africa *see* Zaire
Cowpasture, North America 21; map 9
Crabs: Chesapeake Bay 20; St. Lawrence 418
Crayfish: Volga canal 145
Cunene, Africa 26, 31; map 25

D ams: Amazon Basin 302; Angara 232, 234, **237;** Columbia 355, 357; Danube 103, *121;* Ganges 197, 201; Guri 295; Huang 187; Irrawaddy 188; La Grande 357;
Mississippi 371, 372, 374, *389;* Missouri 363, *368,* 370; Murray 281, **282-283;** Niger 30; Nile 39, 40, *62;* Ohio 354; Paraná 333-334, **346-347;** Rio Grande 429, 433, *438,* 442; St. Lawrence 416, *420;* Susquehanna 11; Tennessee 354, 355; Tigris 193; Volga 132, 137; Yangtze 248, **266;** Yenisey 235; Yukon 402; Zaire 74, **81,** *82;* Zambezi 31
Danube, Europe 95-129; agriculture 98, 103, *106,* **122-125;** fishing 104, 105, *126,* **126-127, 129;** maps 87, 96, 97; source 95, 96-97
Danube Delta, Romania 105, **126, 127, 128-129**
Darling, Australia 278, 280, 281; map 279
Dawson, Canada 402-404; restored theater **408**
Deltas: Amazon *see* Marajó Island; Danube 105, **126, 127, 128-129;** formation 8; Ganges *see* Sundarbans; Irrawaddy 188; Mississippi 373, 374, **380,** *381;* Mackenzie 357, **359;** Niger 30; Nile 43, *66;* Orinoco 292, 295; Paraná **342-343;** Volga 132; word origin 43; Yangtze 252; Yenisey 235; Yukon 405
Derwent, Australia 280; map 279
Devil's Cauldron (whirlpool), Zaire 74
Diamantina, Australia **284;** map 279
Dnieper, Europe: dams 92; map 87
Dolphins, freshwater: Amazon 304
Donaueschingen, West Germany 96-97
Donauquelle (pool), West Germany 97
Donzère-Mondragon (canal), France 168

E els: St. Lawrence 418; Thames 154, *164*
Edfu, Egypt 42, **62**
Elephant Butte Dam, N. Mex. 433, *438*
El Mahmûdîya Canal, Egypt 43
El Paso, Texas 434, **440;** agriculture **438-439**
Estuaries 8, 20; Amur 192; Chesapeake Bay 6, 8, 20; Río de la Plata 336; St. Lawrence 418; Yenisey 235; Zaire 69, 74, *82*
Ethiopian Orthodoxy: church **47;** monastery **46**
Euphrates, Asia *186,* 193; map 184

F alcon Dam, Mexico-U. S. 442
Falls of the Ohio, Ky. 354
Festivals: Hindu 196, 200-201, **204-205, 207, 212-213,** *216,* 220, **220-221;** Québec City, Canada 417; Santa Fe, N. Mex. **437**
Finback whales: St. Lawrence 418
Finke, Australia 287; map 279
Fish: Amazon Basin 303, 305, **312,** *313,* **313;** Lake Baykal 232, **240-241;** Nile 36, 40, **55;** Rio Negro 305; St. Lawrence 418, 419; Volga 135, *143;* Yalobusha **381;** Yangtze 248, **265;** Yenisey 235; Zaire 73, 74; *see also* species
Fishermen: Ganges 196; Kolyma **236;** Lake Baykal **240-241;** Nile 36, **55;** Rio Grande 429, 432; St. Lawrence 418; Saône *175;* Thames 154, **161;** Volga **149;** Zaire **68,** 70, 71, **75**
Flood control: Amur 192; Huang 184, 187; Mississippi-Missouri system 370; Rio Grande *438,* 442; Thames 158, **164-165;** Yangtze 249-250
Floods 8; Colorado 357-358; Huang 184; Mississippi-Missouri system 370-371, 373; Orinoco 295; Paraná 336; Salween 187; Yangtze 246, 249-250, *269;* Yukon 404
Flounder: St. Lawrence 419
Fort Peck Dam, Mont. *368*

Franklin, Australia 280, **284-285**
Fraser, North America 357; map 353

G allatin, North America 362; map 363
Gambia, Africa 24, 26; map 25
Gandak, Asia: map 197; ritual bathing **215**
Ganges, Asia 195-229; agriculture 188, 198, 200, 201, **208-209, 224-225;** canal 201, *220;* delta *see* Sundarbans; distributaries 195, 196, 197, 198, *206;* ghats (steps) 199, **214, 220-221;** length 203; maps 185, 197; mythical tributary 201, *216;* myths *195;* sacred to Hindus 188, *195, 195,* 199, 203, *215;* source **194,** 195, 202; tributaries 201, *212, 216;* waterfall **227**
Gangotri Falls, India **227**
Gangotri Glacier, India **194,** 202, 203, **228**
Gaspé Peninsula, Canada 419, *426*
Gates of Hell (cataracts), Zaire 70
Geneva, Lake of, Europe 167, 170-171
Gezhouba Dam, China: construction 248, **266**
Gorges: Danube 95, 103, **120-121;** Pine Creek 8, **15;** Potomac 10; Rio Grande **428,** 432, *437, 438,* **442;** Urubamba 309; West Branch Susquehanna 8, **14-15;** Yangtze 246-248, **258-259, 264**
Grand Canal, China **242,** 244, 252, **270-271**
Grand Canyon, Ariz. 352, **356**
"Grand Canyon," Pa. 8, **15**
Grand Coulee Dam, Wash. 357
Grand-Grève, Canada 419
Guri dam, Venezuela 295

H alibut: St. Lawrence 418
Han, Asia: flood 250; map 245
Hardwar, India 201, 203, *220;* ghat **220-221;** New Year celebration **220-221**
Harrisburg, Pa. 10-11, **16**
Head of Passes, La. 375
Henley on Thames, England: regatta 156, *161*
Herring: St. Lawrence 419
Hinduism: festivals 196, 200-201, **204-205, 207, 212-213,** *216, 220,* **220-221;** funerals 195, 199, **214;** holy men 199, 202, 203, **216, 226;** ritual bathing 188, 195, 199, 203, **215,** *216,* 220; temples 196, **222, 223, 226**
Hooghly, Asia 195, 196, 198; map 197
Howrah Bridge, Calcutta, India 198, **206-207**
Huang, Asia 184-187; maps 185, 245
Huangpu, Asia 252, 253; map 245
Hume Lake, Australia **282-283;** creation 281
Humpback whales: St. Lawrence 418

I guaçu, South America **332,** *348,* **348-349;** map 335
Iguazú Falls, Argentina-Brazil 334
Incas 290, 307, *328;* ruins 308-309, **326-327**
Indre, Europe: château *90*
Indus, Asia *186,* 188-189; map 185
Inga, Zaire: dams 74, **81,** *82*
Iquitos, Peru 306; shantytown **322-323**
Irkutsk, U.S.S.R. 231-232, 234
Iron Gate Gorge, Yugoslavia 95, 103, **120-121**
Irrawaddy, Asia 188; map 185
Irrigation: Amu Dar'ya *190, 191,* 193; Ganges 188, 201, 203; Huang 187; Indus 188, 189; Irrawaddy 188; Mekong 187; Missouri 363, 370; Murray *282;* Niger 30; Nile 40, 41, 42, **56-57, 65;** Ord 287; Rio Grande 432, *438;* Tigris 193; Yangtze 243, 252
Itaipu Dam, Brazil-Paraguay 333-334, **346-347**
Itasca, Lake, Minn. 371, *398*

J ames, North America 6, 10, 11, 21; map 9
Jari, South America 302; map 301; pulp-wood plantation 302, 303, *313;* pulp mill **314-315**

Jonglei Canal, Sudan: excavation 34, 36, **57**
Juárez, Mexico *see* Ciudad Juárez

K abalega Falls, Uganda: wildlife **50-51**
Kainji Dam, Nigeria 30
kambas (fish): Zaire 73
Kara Kum Canal, U.S.S.R **190-191,** 193
Kenana (region), Sudan: irrigation **56-57**
Khartoum, Sudan 33, 36, 37, **58;** prohibition 38
Khartoum North, Sudan 36, 37, **58**
kharyus (fish): Lake Baykal 232
Kinshasa, Zaire 73, **80;** population 73, *80*
Kisale, Lake, Zaire 70; papyrus island **68**
Kisangani, Zaire 70-72, 73
Klondike, North America: gold mining **409;** Gold Rush 402, 403, *409;* map 403
Kolyma, Asia 231; ice fishermen **236;** map 185
Kotorosl', Europe 131; map 133
Krasnoyarsk, U.S.S.R. 235; dam 235

L ackawanna, North America 10; map 9
La Grande, North America 357; map 353
Leech Lake Reservation, Minn. **398, 399**
Lena, Asia 231, *236,* **240;** exiles 234, 235; maps 185, 233
Linz, Austria 99, *110;* dock **110;** industry **111**
Livingstone Falls, Zaire 73-74, **81**
Lock and Dam No. 3, Red Wing, Minn. 371
Locks and Dam No. 26, Alton, Ill. *389,* **389**
Loire, Europe 91; bridges 91; map 86
Loire Valley, France: canals 91-92; château *90*
London, England 157-158; history 88, 153; pubs 157, 158, *162,* **162**
Lost, North America 11; map 9
Lualaba, Africa 69-70; map 71
Lungfish: Zaire 74
Luxor, Egypt 41, 42
Lyon, France 170, **174, 175**

M achu Picchu, Peru 308-309, **326-327**
Mackenzie, North America 357, **359;** map 353
Mackerel: St. Lawrence 419
Malebo, Pool, Zaire 73, **78-79**
Manaus, Brazil 299, 303, 304, **318-319**
Maps: Africa 25; Amazon 300, 301; Asia 184-185; Australia 279; Chesapeake Bay drainage basin 9; Danube 96, 97; Europe 86-87; Ganges 197; Mississippi-Missouri 363; Nile 35; North America 353; Paraná-Río de la Plata 335; Rhône 169; Rio Grande 431; St. Lawrence 417; Siberia 233; South America 291; Susquehanna system 9; Thames 155; Volga 133; Yangtze 245; Yukon 403; Zaire 71
Marajó Island, Brazil 303; bayou **311;** water buffalo ranch 303, **310-311**
Maurepas, Lake, La. **380**
mbotos (fish): Zaire 73
Mekong, Asia 187, *189;* map 185
Melk, Austria 99; abbey 99, **112, 113**
Memphis, Tenn. **384, 385**
Menhaden: Chesapeake Bay 20
Menindee Lakes Storage Scheme 281
Miles Canyon, Canada 401, 402
Minke whales: St. Lawrence 418
Minnesota, North America 371, **394**
Mississippi, North America 361-399; agriculture 352, 374, *381,* **390-391, 392, 393;** delta 8, 373, 374, **380,** *381;* maps 353, 363; model 374; river pilots 375; shipping 361, 371, 372, 374, 375, **376-377, 388-389;** source 352, 371; tributaries 371, 373, *381*
Mississippi-Missouri system, North America 361; flood control 370; flooding 370-371, 373; length 361; levees 370, *376*
Missouri, North America 352, **368;** dams 363,
368, 370; fur trade **364, 364-365;** map 353, 363; source 362; waterfalls **364, 369**
Missouri Breaks 362
Montréal, Canada 416, **423;** shoppers **422**
Moses-Saunders Power Dam, Canada-U. S. 416
Mudfish: Nile 36
Murray, Australia 278, 280-281; cattle raising **286;** dam 281, **282-283;** map 279
Murrumbidgee, Australia 281; map 279

N anjing, China: elephant statues **267;** timber rafts **268-269**
Nanvaranak Lake, Alaska 405
Nasser, Lake, Egypt-Sudan 39-40, *62*
Natchez, Miss. 374, **383;** mansion **382**
National Wild and Scenic Rivers System: Missouri 362, *368;* Rio Grande *437*
Negro, Río, South America 299; color 304, 305, *316,* **316;** fed by Orinoco 292, 295; inundation forest 305; maps 291, 300, 301
nerpa (seal): Lake Baykal *240*
New Madrid, Mo.: earthquakes 373
New Orleans, La. 352, 371, 374-375, **376-379**
Niger, Africa 24, 30; history 26-27, 30; inland delta 24; map 25; metalwork from **31**
Nile, Africa 33-67; agriculture 34, 38, 40, 41-42, 43, **48-49,** *55,* 57; delta 8, 43, *66;* fish 36, 40, **55;** history 33-34, 36, 37, *58;* irrigation 40, 41, 42, **56-57, 65;** length 24, 43; maps 25, 35; sources 33-34; waterfall **44-45;** wildlife *45,* **50-51**
Nile perch: Nile 36, **55**
Novo Selo, Bulgaria 103-104

O ahe Dam, S. Dak. 370
Ob, Asia 231, 235; maps 185, 233; port **230**
Ohio, North America 352, 373; dams 354; maps 353, 363
Omdurman, Sudan 36, 37-38, **58-59**
omul (fish): Lake Baykal 232, **240-241**
Ord, Australia: agriculture 287; map 279
Orinoco, South America 290, 292, 295; history 292, *296;* map 291; tributaries 290, 292, 295
Otsego Lake, N. Y. 7, 10, *13*
Ottawa, North America 416; map 417
Oxus, Asia *see* Amu Dar'ya
Oysters: Chesapeake Bay 20

P adma, Asia 195; map 197
Palmer, Australia: bed **282**
Paraguay, South America 290, 292, 333; map 335
Paraná, South America 290, 292, 333-349; dam 333-334, **346-347;** delta **342-343;** estuary *see* Plata, Río de la; length 333; maps 291, 335; tributaries **332,** 333, **348-349**
Patapsco, North America 7, 21; map 9
Paulo Afonso Falls, Brazil 296, 297
Perch, Nile: Nile 36, **55**
Pine Creek, North America: gorge 8, **15;** map 9
Piranhas (fish): Amazon 303, *313*
Pirarucu (fish): Amazon *313*
Plata, Río de la (estuary), South America 290, 333, 336, 337; maps 291, 335; tributaries *see* Paraná; Uruguay
Po, Europe 92; canal lock **88;** map 87
Pollution *16;* Amazon 302; Chesapeake Bay 21; Europe 92; Lake Baykal 233, *240;* Potomac **16,** 21; Susquehanna 21; Thames 153, 154
Potomac, North America 6-7, 10, 11, **18;** map 9; pollution **16,** cleanup 21; source **17;** waterfall **13**
Pucaurquillo, Peru: Indians 306-307
Pyramids: Burundi 33, 34, 43; Gîza, Egypt 42; Meroë, Sudan **60-61**

Q uébec City, Canada 416-417; farmers market **423;** waterfront **424-425**

R ainbow Falls, Mont. **369**
Rapids: Rio Grande 434, **435;** Urubamba 309; Yukon 401, *409;* Zaire 73, 74
Red snappers: Rio Grande 429
Regen, Europe 99; map 96
Rhine, Europe 86, 89, 92, 98; maps 87, 96
Rhône, Europe 86, 167-181; agriculture **173,** *174;* maps 87, 169; source 167, 171, **172-173;** vineyards 167, 168, **176-177**
Rhône Glacier, Switzerland 171, **172-173**
Rio Grande, North America 352, 429-443; agriculture 432, 434, **438-439;** canyons **428,** 429, 434, **442;** maps 353, 431; rapids 434, **435;** wildlife 429-430, 432, 434, **442-443**
Rivers, physical characteristics of: cataracts 38; channels 8; colors 37, 184, 304, *316,* **316-317,** 402; deltas 8; drainage 7, 10; drainage patterns 8; erosion 8, *15;* estuaries 6, 8, 20; floodplains 8; floods 8; gorges 8, 10, **14-15;** headwaters 7; loops 8; meanders 8; oxbow lakes 8; pollution *16,* **16,** 21; rills 7-8; sediment 8, *18,* 20; silt 8

S agar Island, India 196, 203
St. Lawrence, North America 352, 415-427; geologic history 415; history 415, 416, 417, 418, *423;* maps 353, 417
St. Lawrence Seaway, Canada-U. S. 415-416
St. Louis, Mo. 370, 373, **386-387**
Salekhard, U.S.S.R. **238, 239;** harbor **230**
Salmon: hatchery 418; Saguenay 418; St. Lawrence 418; Thames 154; Yukon 404
Salween, Asia 187-188; map 185
Samarkand, U.S.S.R.: market **191;** mosque **191**
San Ignacio Miní (ruins), Argentina 334, 336
San-men Gorge Dam, China 187
Santa Fe, N. Mex. 433; fiesta **437**
São Francisco, South America 290, 296-297; map 291
Saône, Europe 91, **175;** map 169
Saraswati (mythical river) 201, *216*
Saskatchewan, North America 352; map 353
Sea urchins: St. Lawrence 419
Seals: Lake Baykal *240;* St. Lawrence 419
Seine, Europe 86, 88; history 86; map 87
Sélénga, Asia 233; map 233; source 231
Senegal, Africa 24, 26; map 25
Shad: Chesapeake Bay 7, 20
Shanghai, China 252-253, **274;** port 252-253, **274-275;** shipyard **272-273**
Shannon, Europe 88; map 87
Shrimp: Rio Grande 429; St. Lawrence 418
Siberia (region), U.S.S.R. 184, 231-241; map 233
Sibinacocha (lake), Peru 307, 308, **330-331**
Silversides: Chesapeake Bay 20
Simbirsk, U.S.S.R.: history 134, 135, 141
"snake head" (fish): Yangtze **265**
Snowy, Australia 281; map 279
Solimões, South America 306; maps 300, 301
Sonpur, India: elephants **210-211,** *212;* fair **212-213**
South Branch Potomac, North America: map 9; source **12**
Stanley Falls, Zaire *see* Boyoma Falls
Starfish: St. Lawrence 419
Stewart, North America **400;** map 403
Striped bass: Chesapeake Bay 20
Sturgeon: Danube *126;* Volga 137, *143,* **149,** *150;* Yangtze 248; Yenisey 235
Sudd (swamp), Sudan 34, 36; agriculture *55;* fish *55,* **55;** herdsman **54**

Sundarbans (Ganges delta), Bangladesh-India 196; wildlife 195, 196, 203, conservation 196
Susquehanna, North America 6-21; estuary *see* Chesapeake Bay; geologic history 7, 10; maps *9,* 353; source 7, 10, *13*
Swan, Australia: map 279; painting **280**

T ambaqui (fish): Amazon *313*
T'ana, Lake, Ethiopia: monastery **46;** reed boat **48;** source of Blue Nile 33, 45, 46
Tanana, North America: map 403; spring breakup **410-411**
Taos Pueblo, N. Mex. **437**
Tapajós, South America 304; color 304, *316,* **316-317;** map 301
Tennessee, North America 354, 355; map 353
Thames, Europe 6, 153-165; flood control 158, **164-165;** maps 87, 155; pollution 153, 154, *164;* source 153-154
Thames and Severn Canal, England 154
Thames Barrier 158, **164-165**
Thames Head, England 153, 154
Thousand Islands, Canada-U. S. **414,** 415, 419, **420-421;** history 415
Three Gorges, China 246-248, **264**
Tiber, Europe 88; map 87; pollution 92
Tiger Leap Gorge, China **258-259**
Tigerfish: Zaire 73
Tigre, Argentina 336, *343;* waterways **343**
Tigris, Asia *186,* 193; map 184
Timbuktu, Mali 26, 27, 30
T'ïs Ābay (waterfall), Ethiopia **44-45**
Transylvanian Alps, Europe **120-121,** *125*
Trout: Otsego Lake 7; Rio Grande 432
Tsaritsa Gorge, Volgograd, U.S.S.R. 136
Twickenham, England 156-157

U lm, West Germany 97-98, *109;* cathedral 98, **109;** market **109**
Ul'yanovsk, U.S.S.R. 134-135, **140;** church **139**
U. S. Army Corps of Engineers 358, 370, 372, 373-374; construction **389**
Upper Ganges Canal, India 201, *220*
Urubamba, South America 307, 309, **327;** map 300; source 307, 308, *330;* tributary **328-329**
Uruguay, South America 290, 292, 333; estuary *see* Plata, Río de la; map 335
Uttarkashi, India 201; terraces **224-225**

V aranasi, India 199, 203, **214,** *215*
Victoria Falls, Africa 26, **28-29;** painting of **30**
Victoria Nile, Africa 34, *49;* map 35
Vienna, Austria 100-101, **114, 115;** history 100
Volga, Europe 88, 131-151; agriculture 136, 137, **144-145,** *145;* length 132; maps 87, 133; sturgeon 137, *143,* **149,** *150*
Volga-Don canal, U.S.S.R. 137, *150*
Volga-Kama Cascade, U.S.S.R. 132
Volgograd, U.S.S.R. 135-136; docks **130;** history 136-137, *146;* industry **149;** monuments *146,* **147**
Volgograd dam, U.S.S.R. 137; canal 150

W achau Valley, Austria **94,** 99-100
Wanxian, China 246, 251
Waterfalls: Andes Mountains 309; Ganges 227; Iguaçu 334, **348-349;** Missouri **364, 369;** Potomac *13;* St. Lawrence 418, 419; São Francisco 296, 297; tallest **294;** widest 334, **348-349;** Zambezi 26, **28-29,** painting of **30;** *see also* Cataracts
Waterholes: Australia 281, **283,** 287
Weaver Bottoms marsh, Minn. 372
West Branch Susquehanna, North America 8,

10, **14-15;** map 9; tributary 8
White, North America 402; map 403
White Cliffs, Mont. **366-367**
White Nile, Africa 34, 36, 37, *58;* color 37; maps 25, 35; riverboat **52, 53;** sources 34
Whitehorse Rapids, Canada 401
Whiting: Rio Grande 429
Willendorf, Austria 99-100
Wuhan, China 250-251

Y akutsk, U.S.S.R. **237**
Yalobusha, North America: fishing **381**
Yamuna, Asia 201, *216;* map 197
Yangtze, Asia 243-275; canals 243, 252 *see also* Grand Canal; dams 248, **266;** floods 246, 249-250, *269;* gorges 246-248, **258-259, 264;** length 184, 244; maps 185, 245; transportation 243, 248, *260*
Yangtze Valley, China: agriculture 243, 252, **262-263;** population 250
Yangzhou, China 251; canal **242, 270-271**
Yaroslavl', U.S.S.R. 131, 132; churches 132, **138, 139;** monastery 131; port **138-139**
Yazoo, North America *381,* **382-383;** map 363
Yellow, Asia *see* Huang
Yenisey, Asia 231, 235; maps 185, 233; tributaries 231, 232, 234, 235
York, North America 6; history 7; map 9
Yukon, North America 401-413; history 401-402; maps 353, 403; tributaries **400,** 403, 405, *409,* **409, 410-411;** wildlife 404, 405
Yukon-Charley Rivers National Preserve, Alaska 404
Yukon Delta National Wildlife Refuge, Alaska 405

Z aire, Africa 24, 26, 69-83; cataracts 70, 73, **81;** fishermen **68,** 70, 71, **75;** hydroelectricity 74, **81,** *82;* maps 25, 71; source 69
Zambezi, Africa 26, 31; map 25; waterfalls 26, **28-29,** painting of 30

Type composition by National Geographic's Photographic Services. Color separations by Beck Engraving Co., Inc., Langhorn, Pennsylvania; Chanticleer Co., Inc., New York, New York; Graphic Color Plate, Inc., Stamford, Connecticut; The Lanman Progressive Companies, Washington, D. C. Printed and bound by R. R. Donnelley & Sons Co., Chicago, Illinois. Paper by Mead Paper Co., New York, New York.

Library of Congress CIP Data

Great rivers of the world.

Includes index.
1. Rivers. 2. River life. 3. Stream ecology.
I. National Geographic Society (U. S.)
GB1203.2.G74 1984   910'.02'1693   84-1163
ISBN 0-87044-537-5
ISBN 0-87044-539-1 (deluxe)

GREAT

RIVERS

GREAT

RIVERS

GREAT

RIVERS

GREAT

RIVERS

GREAT

RIVERS

GREAT

RIVERS

GREAT

RIVERS

GREAT

RIVERS